Atlas of the Pacific Northwest

Ninth Edition

Edited by Philip L. Jackson and A. Jon Kimerling

Oregon State University Press

Corvallis

The paper in this book meets the guidelines for permanence and durability of the Committee on Production Guidelines for Book Longevity of the Council on Library Resources and the minimum requirements of the American National Standard for Permanence of Paper for Printed Library Materials Z39.48-1984.

Ninth Edition © 2003 Oregon State University Press
All rights reserved.

Library of Congress card catalog number: Map 62-50.
CIP data available on request
ISBN 0-87071-562-3 (cloth)
ISBN 0-87071-560-7 (paper)
Printed in the United States of America

Oregon State University Press
101 Waldo Hall
Corvallis OR 97331-6407
541-737-3166
fax 541-737-3170
http://oregonstate.edu/dept/press

OREGON STATE
UNIVERSITY

Contents

Maps, Figures, and Tables

Chapter 1

The Region

Philip L. Jackson

From a geographer's perspective the Pacific Northwest is a region unified by several important locational attributes. Among these are: the far northwest geographic position shared by the states of Oregon, Washington and Idaho, the cooperative regional use of the Columbia River system, and a westward focus of trade and transport to the Pacific Rim. This is also a region of shared history, of immense scenic beauty, wilderness and wild lands, and a region exceptionally rich in agricultural, forest and fishery resources. Together, the states of Oregon, Washington and Idaho occupy the far northwest corner of the contiguous United States, facing the Pacific Ocean, and separated from large Midwest population centers by the Rocky Mountains and vast prairies. To the south, the rugged Klamath-Siskiyou and Trinity Mountains of rural northern California separate the Pacific Northwest from major population centers in the Sacramento Valley and the San Francisco Bay Area.

While geographic location and considerable distances still separate the Pacific Northwest from the rest of the United States and the world (see maps 1-1 and 1-2), the region has evolved from a position of geographic isolation to a region of expanding opportunity through investment in high technology industries and electronic communication, and by improving the advantages inherent in the use of the Columbia River system for recreation, power, irrigation and transportation. Pacific Rim international trade has been expanded through port development, international air transportation, and technological improvements in intra-regional rail, barge and highway transportation. This is a region

THE PACIFIC NORTHWEST IN THE WORLD

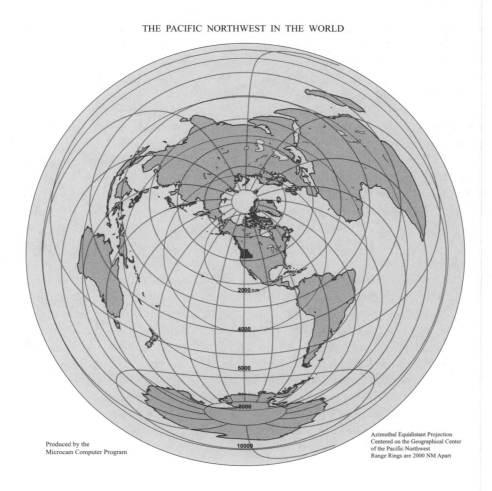

2000 n m

4000

6000

8000

10000

Produced by the
Microcam Computer Program

Azimuthal Equidistant Projection
Centered on the Geographical Center
of the Pacific Northwest
Range Rings are 2000 NM Apart

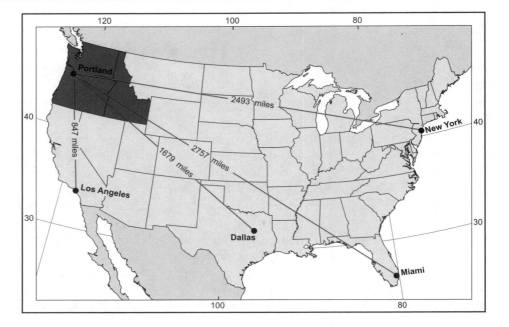

Map 1-2. Position of the Pacific Northwest in the Conterminous United States

with pride in its natural environment, and concern for quality of life—it is also a region seeking to manage and accommodate the effects of rapid population growth in some areas, while stabilizing and increasing employment to stem the loss of economic opportunities in others.

This is a large and complex region, and one way to simplify this complexity is to provide an introductory sketch of the Pacific Northwest in terms of some the basic features of its sub-regions. The description will provide a brief regional overview, and it will focus on similarities in local landform regions, and the basic land uses and population distributions in these areas.

Perhaps the most distinctive feature of the region's overall population distribution is its urban-rural character. Over 80 percent of the 10.6 million people of the Pacific Northwest live in metropolitan areas, and more than half live in the Puget Sound and Willamette Valley sub-regions (see map 1-3). The Seattle-Tacoma-Bellingham area, alone, is home to over 3.3 million people. Consequently, there are strong urban-rural differences that often translate into west- and east-of-the-Cascade contrasts. But in reality, small towns, rural landscapes, and low population densities characterize much of the western portion of the region as well as the eastern. Politics in the region, however, are often dominated by the concerns of the much larger population centers. On some issues, such as environmental preservation or land use planning, Seattle, Portland, and Boise may have more in common with each other than they do with their rural state counterparts.

The voters in Idaho's rural northern panhandle often see state issues somewhat differently from their neighbors in the more populated Boise Valley and the Snake River Plain.

Land ownership plays a part in these regional differences. Nearly all of the Willamette Valley and Puget Lowland is privately owned, but vast tracts of land in the Oregon Coast Range and the Cascades are managed by the federal government as national forests, national parks, national monuments, and wilderness. In the eastern portion of the region, federal management dominates land ownership patterns, with the largest privately owned tracts of rural lands found in Idaho's Snake River Plain, the Spokane-Coeur d'Alene valleys and in the Palouse Hills of the eastern Columbia Basin. Rural land use patterns and low population densities characterize a landscape dominated by federal lands and a traditional resource-based economy. However, the earlier urban centers are rapidly expanding to accommodate a diversifying economy, and some smaller communities are emerging that cater to new residents interested in retirement, and to the recreation and tourism industry.

The Pacific Northwest is composed of a remarkable variety of sub-regional landscapes. Since in the chapter discussions that follow, physical landform regions are commonly named, these areas of the Pacific Northwest are briefly discussed here and illustrated in map 1-5, to provide a basic geographic reference.

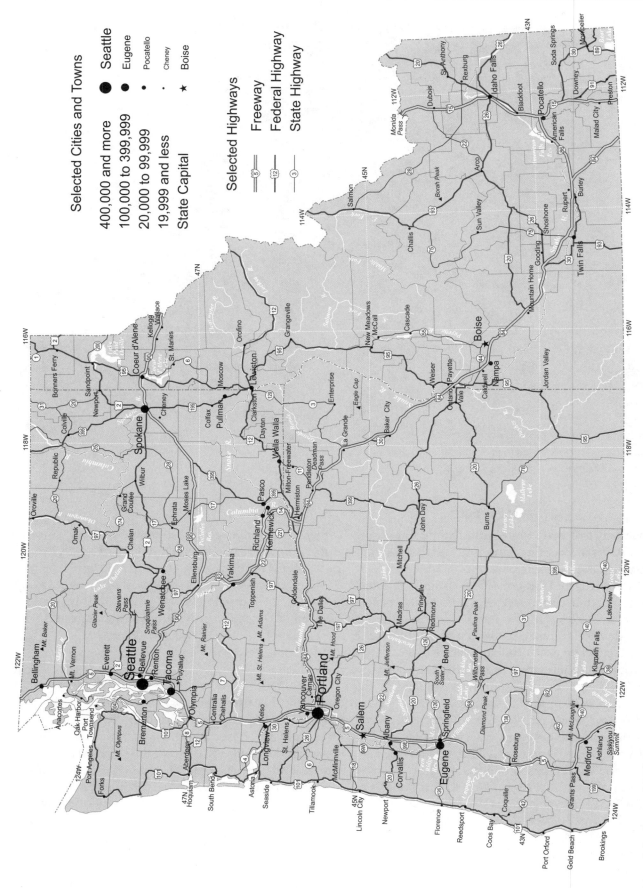

Map 1-3. General Reference

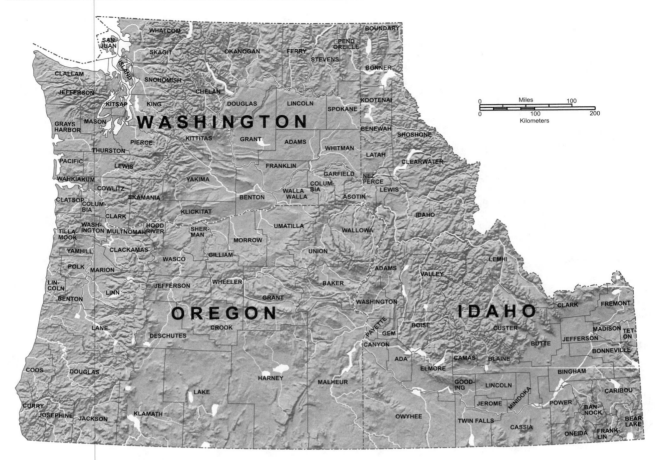

Map 1-4. Pacific Northwest Counties

Southwest Oregon

In the far southwest, the Klamath and Siskiyou Mountains of Oregon form a unique topographic, geologic, and ecological transition zone between the California and Oregon Coast Ranges. Situated at the northern terminus of California's coastal range, and between the Pacific Ocean and the Cascade Mountains, is an extremely rugged and wild landscape, with forested slopes, and deep, narrow river valleys carved by the tributaries of many rivers, including the Klamath, Smith, Chetco, and Rogue. The natural beauty of the southwest seacoast is enhanced by wave-cut headlands and magnificent groves of coastal redwoods. Small towns and harbors characterize settlement in the coastal area; larger population centers include Brookings, Bandon and Coos Bay-North Bend. Together, Coos Bay-North Bend form the largest contiguous population center on the southwest Oregon Coast, with slightly over twenty-five thousand people. Inland, the narrow Rogue River Valley, at the eastern edge of the Siskiyou Range, contains southern Oregon's

largest and fastest growing towns. Jackson County's population of 181,269 has created a particularly strong demand for residential and commercial land use in the Ashland-Medford I-5 corridor, and housing developments now compete for a limited amount of land traditionally used to grow some of the highest quality orchard crops in the Pacific Northwest.

The Coastal Lowlands and Mountains

The Pacific Ocean shorelands of Oregon and Washington extend for over five hundred miles from California to the Canadian border. A narrow littoral zone is wedged between the Pacific Ocean and the steeply rising Coast Range and the Olympic Mountains. Rocky, forested headlands extend to sea, forming capes and points that enclose narrow sandy beaches. The numerous bays and estuaries found at river mouths along the Oregon and Washington coasts support many small communities with economies based largely on tourism and recreation, but also on high-value specialty crops such as cranberries and flower bulbs, and the industries of

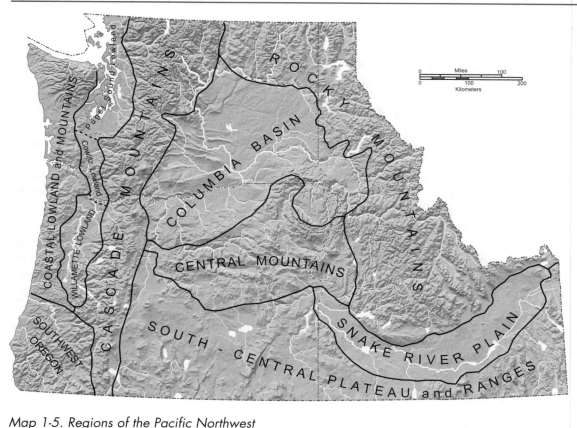

Map 1-5. Regions of the Pacific Northwest

The Columbia Gorge divides Oregon from Washington. (Photo by Philip L. Jackson)

dairying, forest processing, commercial fishing, and port facilities.

The Columbia River estuary, shared by Oregon and Washington, forms the entry to the region's inland waterway system that provides continuous water transport from Astoria, Oregon to Lewiston, Idaho. Astoria is the major commercial center for Oregon's north coast, providing rail and sea transport services at the Columbia River gateway. From the mouth of the Columbia River northward, the coastline transitions to broad sandy beaches with large embayments and forested meadows characterizing the southern Washington coast. Aberdeen and Hoquiam at Grays Harbor, remain major timber processing towns, with a combined population of more than thirty-five thousand. The Olympic Mountains in northwest Washington rise dramatically from a rugged rocky coastline to snow-capped, cloud-shrouded peaks. With more than 200 inches of rainfall annually, these slopes support a lush coniferous forest known locally as the "Olympic Rainforest." By comparison, the Coastal Mountains of Oregon and Washington to the south are relatively low in elevation, but they too are favored with copious winter rainfall and cool, frequently foggy summers. The West's great conifer forests of fir, hemlock, spruce and cedar are found here.

The Willamette, Cowlitz, and Puget Lowlands

The Willamette Valley and the Puget Sound Lowland are the most densely settled areas of the Pacific Northwest. Favorable topography, soils, climate and accessibility assisted in the historical development of agriculture, forestry and commerce. The Willamette Valley, between the Coast Range and the Cascades, is over 130 miles long and 25-35 miles wide. Stretching from the Portland Metro Area on the north with a population of over 1.6 million to Eugene-Springfield on the south, it is home to nearly 70 percent of Oregon's population. While the vast majority of the population is engaged in commerce, industry and high technology, the Willamette Valley remains a rich, diversified agricultural region of high-value field, nursery, vineyard, seed and tree crops. Salem is not only Oregon's capital city, but with a population of 136,924 it is also the commercial center for Marion County, one of the state's most profitable agricultural regions.

The Puget Lowland is dominated by a vast inland sound with over 1800 miles of shoreline, numerous islands, and deep-water channels and natural harbors. Sheltered from Pacific storms by the Olympic Mountains to the west, the sound offers the advantages of mild climate, deep-water access, and a combination of unique marine and terrestrial landscapes. Many natural and economic advantages have encouraged strong continued growth of the largest urban complex in the Pacific Northwest. Seattle's population is 563,374 and Tacoma's 193,566, but the greater Seattle area is home to more than 3.3 million people.

The Cowlitz-Chehalis Lowland, between the Willamette Valley and the Puget Sound, is an area of wooded rolling hills, steams, rivers, pastures, and croplands. The region occupies a structural depression between the Washington Coast Range and the Cascade Foothills, and the complex hill and valley landscape reflects the meanderings of the Columbia River and its many tributaries. Low-density, rural farm populations occupy the Chehalis, Lewis and Cowlitz River Valleys. The largest urban

Central Oregon Coast. (Photo by Philip L. Jackson)

The Oregon Cascades: Mount Hood. (Photo by Philip L. Jackson)

industrial centers are located at the confluence of the Cowlitz and Columbia Rivers at Longview, and at Kelso and Chehalis along the Interstate 5 corridor.

The Cascade Mountains

The Cascade Mountains sharply divide the Pacific Northwest into two strikingly different climatic landscapes. To the west is a humid, forested, marine-influenced environment, and to the east a much drier, continentally dominated region of lowland shrub and grasslands and highland forests. A volcanic range, the Cascades are 60 to 100 miles wide and extend nearly 500 miles north-south through Oregon and Washington. Much of the region is managed as federal forest and wilderness lands, including national monuments such as Mount St. Helens and Newberry Crater. National parks include the North Cascades, Mt. Rainier, and Crater Lake in southern Oregon. The northern Cascades of Washington are glacially eroded and heavily dissected, but rise to average elevations of 6,000 to 8,000 feet. Distinctive peaks in the northern Cascades include Glacier Peak at 10,436 feet and Mt. Rainier at 14,408 feet. Strato-volcanic peaks within the central Oregon Cascades include Mt. Hood at 11,225 ft., Mt. Jefferson and the Three Sisters, averaging 10,000 ft., and in the south Mt. Theilsen stands at 9,180 ft. just north of Crater Lake.

Historically, the Cascades represented a formidable barrier to transportation and settlement, and except for small towns in the Cascades foothills, and recreation facilities near major transportation routes, population densities remain very low. A number of all-season rail and highway transportation routes accommodate east-west surface movement of people and goods. Stevens Pass at 4,061 feet is an all-season transportation corridor that links Wenatchee to Everett. Snoqualmie Pass at 3,000 feet is the route of Interstate 90 to Seattle. The Columbia River Gorge breaches the Central Cascades, forming a water-level route for barge, rail and highway passage via Interstate 84. Barlow Pass traverses a route along the southern edge of Mt. Hood, Santiam Pass at 4,817 feet connects Bend with Salem and Albany, and Willamette Pass at 5,128 feet provides an east-west connection between Eugene and central Oregon. Hayden Pass at 4,362 feet is the major southern crossing between Klamath Falls and Medford.

The Columbia Basin

The Columbia Basin, to the east of the Washington Cascades, is a broad, arid expanse of volcanic terrain that has been eroded by the tributaries of the middle Columbia River and overlain by airborne glacial silts. The region extends into Oregon on the south and Idaho on the east, and supports a population of just over a million people with a diverse economy based on industry, commerce and farming. The commercial capitol of the "Inland Empire" is the Spokane Metro Area with 417,939 people. The Yakima Valley supports 222,581 people and the Tri-Cities of Kennewick-Pasco-Richland have a combined population of 125,467. Pendleton, Oregon and Lewiston-Clarkston, Idaho have smaller, but locally significant populations. The deeply eroded basalts of the Channeled Scablands at the central and western edge of the basin are thought to be the result of catastrophic floods that occurred toward the end of the Pleistocene glacial period from breached ice-dams in both the Columbia and Snake River drainages. The agriculturally fertile Palouse Hills region on the east side of the basin benefits from a deep mantle of wind-deposited silts and enhanced rainfall at slightly higher elevations. Hundreds of thousands of acres of dryland wheat and peas are grown in a unique crop cycle to conserve soil moisture. In one form or another, settlement patterns throughout the arid Columbia Basin are dependent on water, either from natural rainfall or irrigation. The multi-purpose Columbia Basin Project supplies water for irrigation, power production, navigation, recreation, and fish passage. Rural electrification and irrigation from the Columbia Basin Project support agricultural cropping on over 1.5 million acres in an otherwise arid landscape. Earlier irrigation projects along the Yakima River and its Cascade tributary streams developed high-value orchard, vineyard, and field crops in the Wenatchee and Yakima regions.

The Washington Palouse. (Photo by Philip L. Jackson)

The Central Mountain Complex

A mountainous region known to the Shoshone Indians as the "Ochoco" is a complex of transverse ranges extending from the Cascades to the Rocky Mountains, separating the Columbia Basin from the High Lava Plains. The complex includes, from west to east, the Ochoco, Blue, Strawberry, Aldrich, Elkhorn and Wallowa Mountains, all of which rise 3,000 to 4,000 feet above the surrounding terrain. The elevation of these ranges is sufficient to enhance spring and summer rainfall, and to accumulate winter snow. These mountains are "islands of moisture" that support lush highland meadows and commercial forests of fir and pine. Much of this region is federally managed as national forest and wilderness areas, but the lower-elevation valley environments are privately owned and support ranching, timber and farming enterprises. Winter recreation activities and hunting, fishing, and wilderness packing are seasonally important to the local economy as well. John Day in the central Blue Mountains has a population of 1,821, and La Grande, in the Grande Ronde Valley is the region's largest town with a population of 12,327.

South Central Plateaus and Ranges

From the Oregon High Desert in the west to the Owyhee Plateau in Idaho, this region is characterized by aridity, volcanic tablelands, fault block mountain ranges, and interior drainage basins. Some of the basins contain lakes, some intermittent lakes, and many are dry. The primary land use in the region is stock grazing on hundreds of thousands of acres of range lands. Timber industries utilize the federal forest lands and are large employers in Klamath

Falls, population 19,462, and Lakeview, 2,474. Irrigated crop agriculture is locally important in the Klamath, Harney, and Lakeview Basins. Traditional irrigated agriculture includes alfalfa, onions, grains and potatoes. Because of recurring drought, water use conflicts have developed between agricultural needs and wild life and fish habitat. This situation is most critical in the Klamath Basin, where tributaries to the Klamath River have been regulated to support irrigation, thus limiting stream flow. In central Oregon, the Deschutes and Crooked River watersheds, originally developed to supply water for agricultural settlement and the timber industry, distribute water to fast-growing urban populations in the Bend, Redmond, Madras and Prineville areas.

Tributaries to the Snake, Owyhee, and Bruno rivers in southwest Idaho also support crop and forage production, but most of this area is grazing land. The Owyhee country of southwest Idaho is known as the "Quiet Corner" for good reason; very few people inhabit this strikingly rugged landscape, and access is limited to only a few roads that traverse great distances between settlements.

The Snake River Plain

Nearly two-thirds of Idaho's population lives in the Snake River Plain, a lowland region offering a natural east-west transportation route between the Pacific Northwest and the Rocky Mountain states to the east. This is Idaho's agricultural heartland; the place of "Famous Potatoes" and sugar beets, alfalfa, grains, vegetables, fruits and livestock. Over two million acres of irrigated land support a broadly based agricultural economy. Most of the state's principal cities are found here: Boise, the capital, has a

Snake River in southern Idaho. (Photo by Philip L. Jackson)

population of 185,000; Idaho Falls, 50,730; Twin Falls, 34,469; Pocatello, 51,466, and Caldwell and Nampa have a combined population of nearly 78,000. Transportation services, agricultural processing and agro-chemical industries are strong components of the growing regional economy. The Boise area is one of the Pacific Northwest's rapid growth centers, and in recent years large tracts of prime farmland in the Boise Valley have been converted to residential and commercial use.

The Rocky Mountains

The Northern Rocky Mountains of Idaho are made up of a massive complex of independent mountain ranges. Together the Rockies take their name from the characteristic exposed rock surfaces; deep rocky canyon walls, sheer, glaciated ridges and sharp, rocky peaks. Unlike the mountains of the eastern United States that are covered in conifer and hardwood forests, the Rockies are high mountains with much of the terrain above treeline. The Selkirk Mountains in northern Idaho are separated from the Coeur d'Alene Mountains and the massive Bitterroot Range by the Clark Fork River. The Salmon River Canyon forms the boundary between the Clearwater Mountains in central Idaho and the Salmon River Mountains to the south. Elevations average 6,000 to 9,000 feet, but there are strikingly large elevation differences between adjacent ridges and valleys.

Snow is the dominant precipitation form, with many mountain ranges receiving more than 200 inches a year. In the high elevation basins of the Bitterroots and in the River of No Return Wilderness, summers are very short and winters are long and severe. At lower elevations, winter recreation is very popular. Winter resorts in the Sun Valley and Ketchum area, and in the Sand Point-Lake Pend Oreille area have grown to year-round vacation destinations. Wilderness guiding for hunting, fishing and "back country ecotourism" has become an important mainstay for small towns in the Clearwater, Salmon, and Snake River drainages. Traditional enterprises include silver mining, stock raising and the forest and timber industries. Most of the interior mountain region is under federal management, but the lower-elevation river valleys are settled. Small towns in the Rocky Mountain region are service centers for rural agriculture, mining, and timber industries, inter-mountain transportation, and recreation destinations. Characteristic towns include Sand Point with a population of 6,835; Bonners Ferry, 2,515; and Ketchum 3,003.

Sources

United States Census Bureau, 2000 Census of Population.
State and local data for Oregon, Washington, and Idaho by counties and places.

Chapter 2
Cultural-Historical Geography
Robert Kuhlken

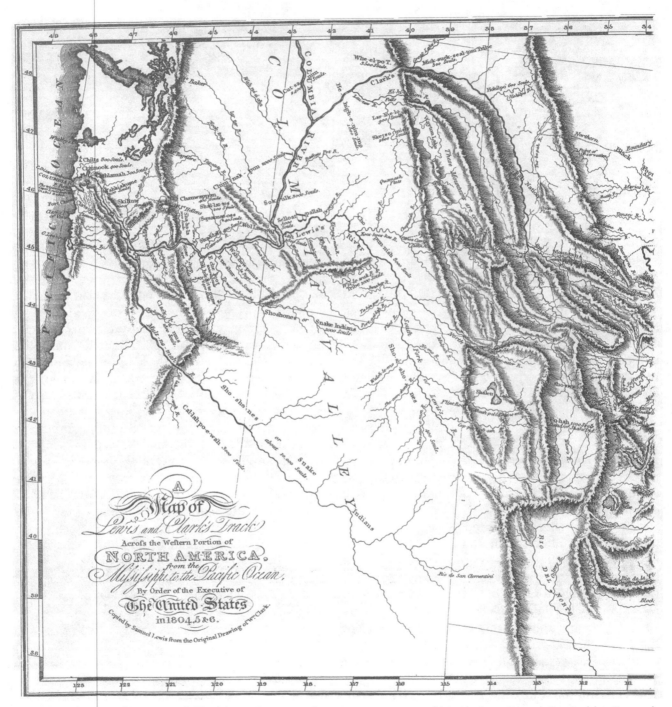

Map 2-1. A map of Lewis and Clark's track across the western portion of North America … Copied by Samuel Lewis from the original drawings of William Clark

The Pacific Northwest has been inhabited by humans for at least fifteen thousand years, according to available evidence. Relative isolation following the Pleistocene Ice Ages allowed formation of identifiably separate cultures, but did not prevent trade patterns and migrations across territory, among various peoples occupying the region and converting its resources. Starting in the sixteenth century the emerging world system encountered the Pacific Northwest, first by coastal visitations from Spanish ships, and later through commercial fur-trading ventures by the British and Americans. Overland expeditions such as that led by Lewis and Clark began to fill in the map, and settlement occurred shortly thereafter. This chapter traces the culture history of the region and charts the many layers of its sequential occupance (see map 2-1).

Prehistoric Occupation of the Pacific Northwest

Among the first humans to inhabit the Pacific Northwest were descendants of Asiatic hunters and gatherers who had either navigated along coastlines or crossed the Bering land bridge during the most recent Ice Ages of the Pleistocene, between twenty-five thousand and twelve thousand years ago. Isolation from ancestral societies and adaptation to the new and rapidly changing environments of an unfamiliar continent resulted in a cultural transformation: these peoples became Native Americans. Several routes of prehistoric migration have been proposed for diffusion into the region, and archaeological investigations have revealed a pattern of widespread activity across mountain, foothill, and river valley environments, beginning about ten thousand years ago. Many early sites identified by archaeologists are located in the interior, along the Columbia River and east of the Cascades. Here, artifacts associated with megafauna hunting, such as the long Clovis-style projectile points found at East Wenatchee, have been excavated and dated to approximately ten thousand years ago. Other important sites include Kettle Falls in northeast Washington; Lind Coulee and Marmes rockshelter in eastern Washington; the Simon site near Fairfield, in south-central Idaho; and central Oregon's Fort Rock cave, where the remains of sandals made from sagebrush have been dated at nine thousand years. A number of important archaeological sites have been documented in the northern Great Basin region of Oregon. Perhaps the most significant concentration of ancient artifactual evidence occurs at the eastern portal to the Columbia River Gorge, along both sides of the river. Thus, the first people in the Pacific Northwest may have traversed interior river basins and the relatively open plateau uplands in search of game and logical dwelling places. This scenario proposes preliminary settlement of the interior and a westward diffusion toward the Pacific littoral. Alternative migration theories suggest a sequence of coastal movements southward, utilizing the broad coastal plain exposed by a lower sea level. But now the waves crash against the mountainous continental edge and any archaeological evidence for such movement and possible colonization has long been submerged and lost. Numerous sites from later occupations, however, dot the Pacific coastline. Across the region, initial cultural ecologies entailed very generalized, broad spectrum, and highly mobile hunting and gathering systems. Over time, settlement occurred where a favorable medley of diverse environments and access to multiple resources enabled livelihood and social reproduction (see map 2-2).

The archaeological record indicates a transition from Clovis points to the shorter but more refined Folsom-style projectile over the period eight thousand to four thousand years before present. Further changes were associated with adoption of the bow and arrow as primary weapon, between three thousand and two thousand years ago. This suggests an evolution of hunting strategies and changing distribution and abundance of prey types. Larger mammals were hunted out, perhaps contributing to their extinction, and people targeted mammals such as deer or bighorn sheep, in some areas even rabbits and smaller game. While coastal populations had most likely already arrived at the advantages of sedentary adaptations, people of the interior Pacific Northwest began a transition toward sedentism about 3,500 years ago, predictably induced by rising populations and diminished hunting resources. This entailed either permanently inhabited villages or fixed camps within an established seasonal round of food procurement activities. A riverine or coastal settlement orientation and a greater reliance on salmon and steelhead in many areas of the region accompanied intensification in harvest techniques, with weirs and traps becoming common, and a requisite elaboration of fish processing and curing techniques and infrastructure. Equally significant was a much greater reliance on plant materials in most areas, especially the carbohydrate-rich roots and tubers which further enabled greater population densities.

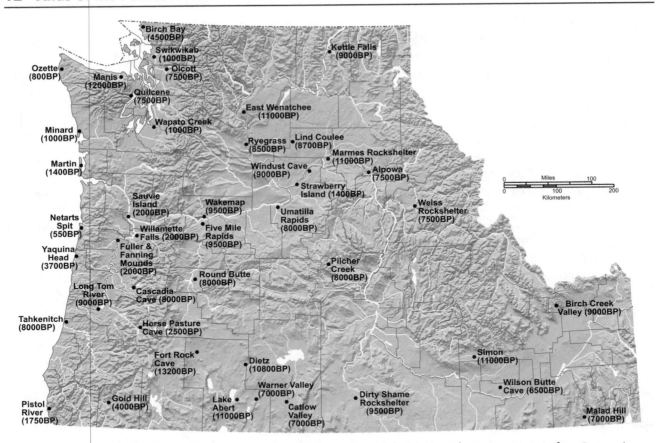

Map 2-2. Major Archaeological Sites, giving site name and age of oldest artifacts (in Years Before Present)

Indian Ways of Life

Native Americans effectively developed technologies and practices that allowed efficient exploitation of a wide variety of environmental settings found throughout the Pacific Northwest. Coastal and riverine tribes west of the Cascades came to depend on the rich bounty of marine resources, chiefly the many species of anadromous fish such as chinook salmon. Likewise in these areas, plentiful timber inspired the elaboration of wood-working skills applied to carving, canoe building, and plank house construction. The western red cedar was an especially useful tree for these peoples. Tribes occupying the Columbia Plateau survived by hunting big game along with smaller animals, gathering ripe berries in the fall, and digging succulent bulbs in the spring, although fish coming far upriver to spawn also afforded a rich food source. The arid areas of southeast Oregon and southern Idaho were home to several desert tribes, organized as highly mobile small bands that successfully adjusted to the harsh conditions and meager subsistence resources of the drylands.

Various comings and goings of tribal peoples interacting with these varied environments resulted in divergent cultural development over several millennia. While many groups shared cultural affinities and lifeways, there were important differences as well. The existence of several major linguistic families and manifold separate languages provides a trait that allows cartographic delineation of the region's complex cultural geography. Tribes claiming territories along the Pacific coast included the Makah, Quileute, Quinault, Chehalis, Tillamook, Alsea, Umpqua, Coos, and Coquille. The Puget Sound littoral was home to numerous groups, including the Lummi, Samish, Swinomish, Snohomish, Duwamish, Muckleshoot, Puyallup, and Nisqually. The Willamette Valley was occupied by tribes such as the Kalapuya and Clackamas, and in the far south central part of what is now Oregon lived the Shasta, Klamath and Modoc peoples. Among the Columbia River tribes, from the mouth proceeding upriver, were the Chinook, Wahkiakum, Cowlitz, Klickitat, Wasco and Wishram, Wyam, Dockspus, Umatilla, Wallawalla, Yakama, Wanapum, Wenatchee, Chelan, Nespelem, Sanpoil, Spokane, and Colville, and in what is now northern Idaho, the

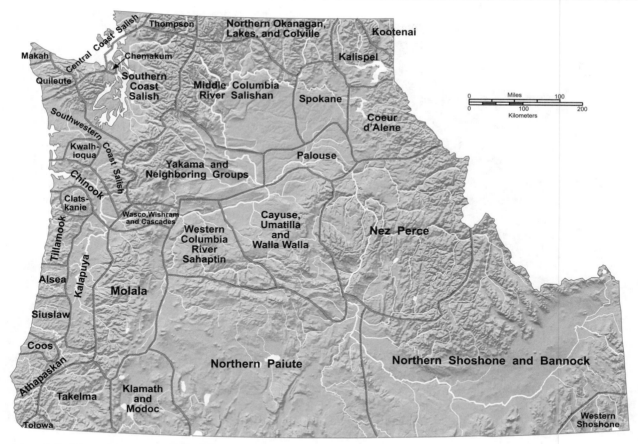

Map 2-3. Native American Tribal Territories

Flathead and Kootenai. The Blue Mountains and Wallowa Mountains were the home of the Cayuse and Nez Perce, respectively, while to the south, the dry desert plains were inhabited by the Paiutes, the Shoshone and Bannock (see map 2-3).

Unlike Native Americans in other areas of the continent, the Indians of the Pacific Northwest never developed full-scale agricultural systems, although modifications of the environment to amplify availability of local food resources certainly took place. These manipulations included setting fire to large valley tracts such as the Willamette to enrich big game habitat, or burning patches of upland forest to generate huckleberry fields. Recent investigations also suggest the probability that some groups attempted to enhance root grounds to stimulate greater yields. Tribal groups from the farthest corners of the region were tied together in a vast trading network, which had as its central locus the constricted reach along the Columbia River near Celilo Falls, just upstream from The Dalles. Here huge quantities of migrating salmon and steelhead were netted, processed, and dried, not only establishing a time and place for people to come together, but also creating a form of currency which facilitated

transactions between tribes as distant as those from the coast or the mountains of Idaho. Dried berries, camas bulbs and other roots, woven baskets, elk and deer skins, marine shells, flint and stone, and even slaves or brides were the typical commodities involved in this enterprise.

Sometime during the early 1700s the horse made an appearance among the Indians of the Pacific Northwest, having diffused from the Spanish settlements along the upper Rio Grande through trade or travel. This animal was adopted most emphatically by the Plateau tribes for greater mobility in seasonal movements and as a strategic advantage in warfare. By the time Euro-American explorers penetrated the region, the horse had also become a form of wealth and status, with chiefs often owning several hundred head. Indians may have known that the arrival of the horse was a portent of things to come, for by that time European trade objects were showing up with increasing frequency. While the geography of the region was well known to those who lived here, it was terra incognita for these mysterious outsiders, and that was about to change.

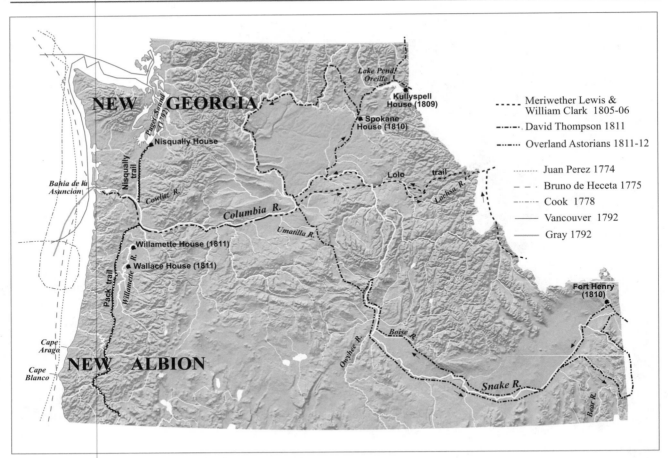

Map 2-4. Exploration by Sea and Land, 1542-1820

European and Euro-American Explorations 1541-1811

The first Europeans to encounter the Pacific Northwest were Spanish seafarers sailing north from Mexico along the coastline. In the year 1541 several ships reached as far north as the forty-second parallel, although they never made landfall. English buccaneer Sir Francis Drake, after looting Spanish galleons off California, may have put in for repairs around the vicinity of Coos Bay, or some say, even further north. The Spanish sent several more maritime exploring expeditions along the Pacific Northwest coast during the first decade of the seventeenth century, but then virtually ignored the region for more than 150 years. Meanwhile, Russian infiltrations from across the Bering Sea followed the continental shoreline south, establishing claims to several places and inaugurating the fur trade. Spain renewed interest after that, and in 1774 Juan Perez erected a small trading establishment at Nootka Sound on Vancouver Island. Other Spanish explorations followed shortly thereafter, including those led by Bruno Heceta and Juan Bodega y

Quadra. In 1778, during his third and final exploration of the Pacific Ocean, the great British navigator James Cook charted the offshore waters of the Pacific Northwest from Oregon to Alaska, finally putting to rest the erroneous theory of a Northwest Passage—the fabled water route across the continent. Ironically, none of the coastal probings up to this time had yet discovered the mouth of the Columbia River. Even George Vancouver, who surveyed most of Puget Sound for the English during 1792, missed identifying the eight-mile wide estuary. Later that same year, it was the American Robert Gray who found the river that now bears the name of his ship. With both Spanish and Russian claims to the region fading, Great Britain and the United States emerged as the leading contenders for territory (see map 2-4).

When the Louisiana Purchase provided a catalyst for the notion that would later become known as Manifest Destiny, President Jefferson appointed a Corps of Discovery, under the command of Meriwether Lewis and William Clark, to traverse the continent from St. Louis to the mouth of the Columbia. Proceeding to the headwaters of the

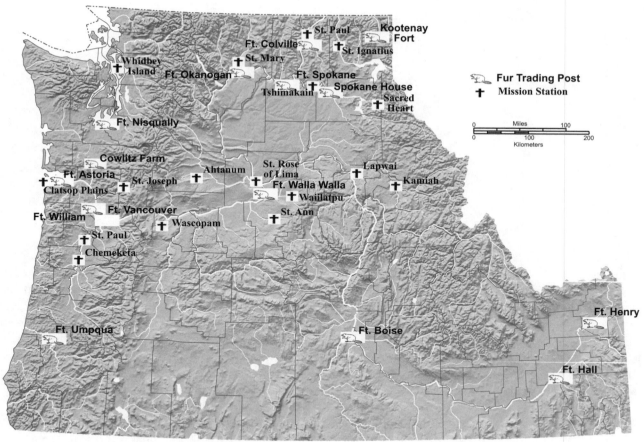

Map 2-5. Fur–trading Posts and Religious Missions

Missouri, they crossed the mountains of Idaho with great difficulty, and then followed the Clearwater, Snake and Columbia Rivers downstream to the Pacific, where they spent the winter of 1805-06 at a small stockade they named Fort Clatsop. The Lewis and Clark expedition added immeasurably to what was then known about the Pacific Northwest. Beginning the very next season, intrepid Northwest Fur Company employee David Thompson took almost four years, between 1807-1811, to explore the vast watershed of the Columbia, thereby helping to activate competing political claims to the region that would only be played out during the commercial frenzy of the fur trade.

The Fur Trade, 1811-1840

The first of the Northwest's natural resources to be injected into the global economic system were the pelts of both marine and freshwater fur-bearing mammals. Beaver, especially, were highly sought after to supply the raw material for trendy headware of European high society. Sea otters and seals, along with river otters and muskrats, were also hunted,

not only by French, Canadian, and American trappers in the employ of competing mercantile establishments, but also by Native Americans seeking to exchange pelts for European trade items. The fur export business lasted only a few decades, but during this time, the landscapes of the Pacific Northwest began a transformation. Fortified trading posts were positioned at various points along the region's major waterways, and various agricultural support activities such as livestock grazing and crop farming ushered in radical new patterns of land use at some locations. Despite its short-lived duration, fur-trading activities in the Pacific Northwest involved four different companies all seeking locational advantage. The Pacific Fur Company was the ill-fated American enterprise of German immigrant John Jacob Astor, who established several outposts, beginning in 1812 with Fort Astoria at the mouth of the Columbia, and followed soon after by Fort Okanogan and Fort Spokane. At the height of wartime hostilities, the Pacific Fur Company sold its holdings to rival Northwest Fur Company, a British firm targeting beaver streams west of the Rockies, which proceeded to build Fort Walla Walla

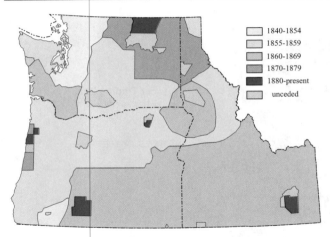

Map 2-6. Indian Land Cessions

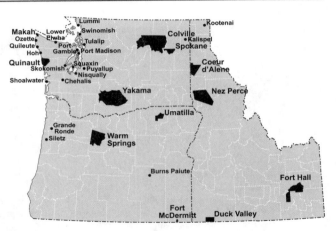

Map 2-7. Indian Reservations

and also maintained several posts in the Columbia headwaters area. In 1821, this company merged with the monopolistic Hudson's Bay Company, which then controlled most trapping and trading activities in the region.

Establishment of Fort Vancouver in 1824 by the Hudson's Bay Company was probably the single most important circumstance in the early historical geography of the Pacific Northwest. Surrounding the palisade were more than two thousand acres cleared and planted to grains and vegetables, along with orchards of apples, pears, and quince. A sawmill was built, and with fishing an additional activity, lumber and salmon joined fur pelts as exports. Roving brigades of trappers based at the fort brought back reports of their explorations and discoveries. For two decades the Company's Chief Factor at Fort Vancouver, Dr. John McLoughlin, not only directed trade activities but also welcomed those bent on permanent settlement. Even after retirement to his home in Oregon City, he remained a major influence on the region's peaceful development right up to the formation of American territorial government. Meanwhile, to the north, other fur trading locations were established, but always with the Company's directive of self-sufficiency. These included Fort Colville, on the upper Columbia River, and Fort Nisqually, near present-day Tacoma. A subsidiary operation was formed, called the Puget Sound Agricultural Company, to foster settlement not only at Nisqually but in the Cowlitz valley as well. Along the Snake River, in what is now southern Idaho, the Hudson's Bay Company also maintained Fort Boise and Fort Hall (see map 2-5).

Subsequently, the activities of Christian missionaries resulted in a number of localized developments across the region during the period between 1834 and 1847. With the ostensible target of converting

Indians, religious outposts run by several Protestant affiliations as well as Catholics appeared throughout the Pacific Northwest. Methodist ministers Jason Lee and his nephew Daniel established the very first mission, in the central Willamette Valley, where in the aftermath of disease epidemics they found few Native Americans but ever-increasing numbers of settlers. Other Methodist operations ensued at Nisqually and at Wascopam, which later became The Dalles. Early Catholic efforts were focused at St. Francis Xavier mission along the Cowlitz River and at St. Paul, near the French Prairie homesteads in the Willamette Valley. Later developments included St. Joseph in the upper Lewis River area, at Willamette Falls, by Oregon City, and first at Sacred Heart, then Cataldo Mission, east of Lake Coeur d'Alene. The interdenominational American Board missions were established with Henry and Eliza Spalding at Lapwai, and with Marcus and Narcissa Whitman at Waiilatpu, in the Walla Walla valley. There followed other teams of spouses attached to missions further north at Tshimakain and Kamaiah. Conversions to Christianity were disappointingly sporadic, and in their attempts to teach farming and other emblems of "civilization," the American Board missionaries met with mixed results, having most notable success at Lapwai. Elsewhere, a series of cross-cultural misunderstandings in combination with a deadly measles outbreak culminated tragically in the so-called Whitman massacre on November 29, 1847, when the Waiilatpu missionaries and a dozen others were killed by Cayuse Indians.

The early Christian missionaries in the Pacific Northwest overall had little effect on the region's development, for the wave of Euro-American immigration was already well under way. Their ultimate failure, epitomized by the fateful turn of events at the Whitman mission, only served to

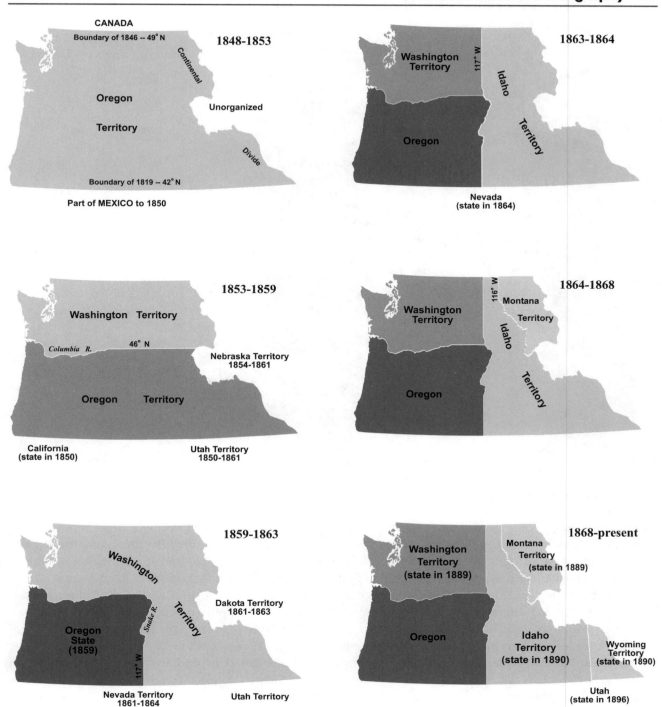

Maps 2-8. Evolution of the Pacific Northwest States

exacerbate the growing tensions between the region's native cultures and the newly arrived settlers. Within the next decade, treaties validating the expropriation of Indian lands were forced upon the tribes of the Pacific Northwest, and the imposed reservation system enabled the settlement frontier to expand without further hindrance or threat from indigenous peoples (see maps 2-6 and 2-7).

Early Settlement and The Agricultural Frontier

Incipient farming centers in the Pacific Northwest were either associated with Hudson's Bay Company endeavors or were more spontaneous concentrations of retired trappers and their families, as occurred around French Prairie and Champoeg just upstream from Oregon City in the Willamette Valley. Here the early settlers found rich soils underlying an open

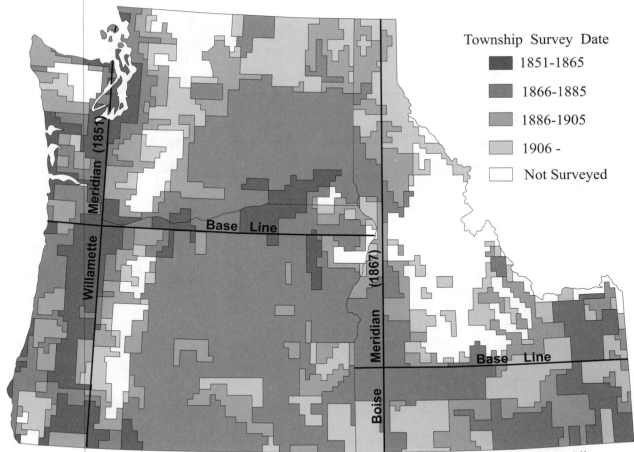

Township Survey Date
- 1851-1865
- 1866-1885
- 1886-1905
- 1906 -
- Not Surveyed

Oregon and Washington surveyed from Willamette Meridian   Idaho surveyed from Boise Meridian

Map 2-9. Public Land Survey

landscape already long cleared and maintained by aboriginal burning practices. Nearby areas naturally became, by virtue of their proximity, the target of subsequent agricultural expansion. These included the Cowlitz Valley and the Tualatin Plains, where wheat soon became a crop specialty. Beginning in the mid-1840s, following establishment of an overland route that became known as the Oregon Trail, a steady influx of immigrants began arriving. Over the next decade, as the number of wagon trains increased so did the population staking land claims in their major destination, the lower Willamette Valley. The California gold rush activated an auspicious market for both crops and livestock from the Northwest, and this further stimulated agrarian expansion. New areas were sought out, and the agricultural frontier progressed across and up the valley, then jumped over and beyond the highlands to the south, into the Umpqua and Rogue River alluvial bottoms. To the north, the glacially leveled plains of western Washington witnessed development somewhat later, with roughly ten years' lag time, but by the mid-1850s the settlement frontier

had enveloped the Puget Sound region, including its islands. More than fifty thousand immigrants arrived between 1840 and 1860. An examination of the chronological schedule of land surveys helps elucidate the pattern of historical settlement (see maps 2-8 and 2-9).

The drylands of eastern Washington and Oregon were perceived by the early overlanders as barren wastes to speed through with all haste. They took to heart the promotional adage that crops never failed in the well-watered western valleys, and so pushed ahead to find their piece of Eden. But once Native American resistance was squelched by military force during the 1850s and 1860s, the remainder of the region was deemed ripe for the taking. The Walla Walla vicinity was one of the first agricultural landscapes to be developed east of the Cascades. The nearby valleys of the Powder, Umatilla, and Yakima River areas were targeted next, although full utilization for field crops or orchards often had to await federal irrigation initiatives. Cattle and sheep ranchers, meanwhile, ran herds over many of these areas that were later converted to farming, such as

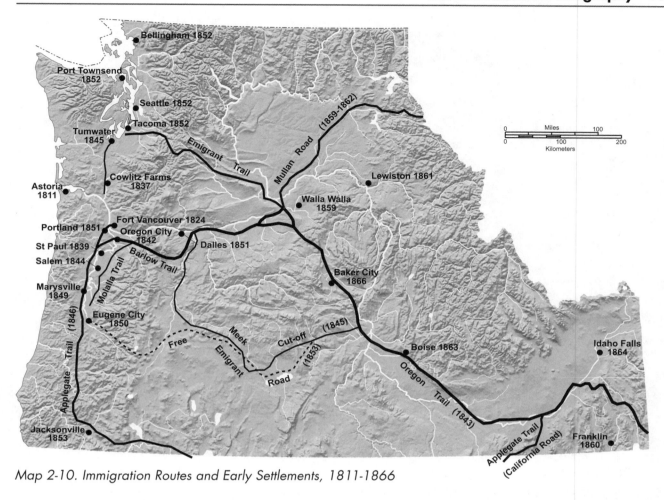

Map 2-10. Immigration Routes and Early Settlements, 1811-1866

the plains of central Oregon, and Washington's spectacular Kittitas Valley. Within myriad watersheds, rudimentary irrigation systems at various scales and levels of complexity were set up by private or cooperative ventures. Federal reclamation projects placed additional acreage under irrigation, sometimes encompassing vast areas such as the Snake River plain during the 1920s, and the Columbia Basin project, beginning in the 1950s. Representing a regional specialty, fruit orchards eventually became established as the dominant agricultural land use in several places, including Medford, Hood River, and Wenatchee.

Urban Developments

While most of the Northwest's early arrivals were agrarian folk seeking lands, it was not long before port functions and agricultural service centers required a merchant class, many of whom arrived by sea to set up shop in the nation's newest land of opportunity. Upstream from the falls at Oregon City, riverboats began to ply the length of the Willamette

during the 1850s, and many of the towns in the valley were platted at that time, including Marysville (now Corvallis), situated at the effective head of navigation on the river. Portland, incorporated in 1851, became the region's leading urban center. Its deep-water anchorage gave it a competitive edge over the upriver settlements of Milwaukie and Gladstone. The shoreline of Puget Sound offered similar port potential, and emerging rivalry between Seattle and Tacoma spurred urban growth, although neither upstart city could catch up with the superior neighbor to the south in terms of population, influence, and developing infrastructure. Political actualities favored Portland as well; even though Tacoma and Seattle were rapidly growing cities, Washington would not be admitted to the union until thirty years after Oregon became a state in 1859. Salem eventually emerged from the Methodist mission station at Chemeketa to become the newest state capital, while far-reaching Washington Territory up until 1863 still included Idaho and parts of Montana. In addition to Seattle and Tacoma, other early towns in western Washington included

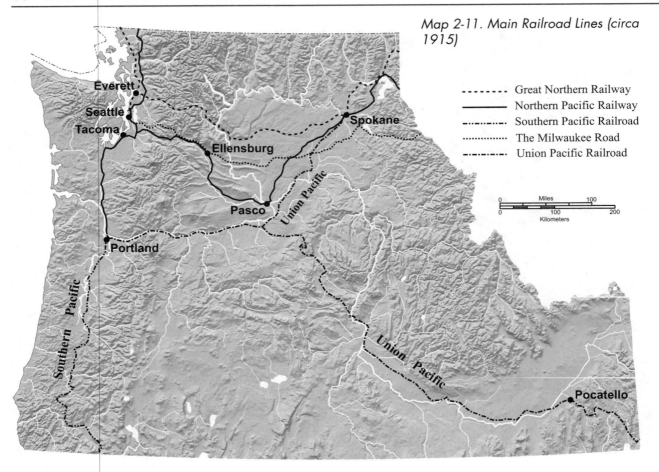

Map 2-11. Main Railroad Lines (circa 1915)

------- Great Northern Railway
——— Northern Pacific Railway
—·—·— Southern Pacific Railroad
··········· The Milwaukee Road
—··—··— Union Pacific Railroad

Tumwater, Centerville (later Centralia), and Port Townsend (see map 2-10).

Beyond the Puget Sound-Willamette Valley core, urbanization on the periphery was characteristically tied to the exploitation of specific natural resources. Spokane looked forward first to developing its water power potential, and later to serving as a farming and mining service center and transportation hub of the so-named "Inland Empire." The discovery of gold in southwest Oregon stimulated development of places such as Jacksonville and Ashland. Similar finds of the precious metal in eastern Oregon and central Idaho in the early 1860s gave rise to towns like Baker City and Boise. At the same time, the agricultural frontier had pushed outward from the western valleys like a backwash east across the Cascades, where the natural grasslands were exploited, first by cattlemen, then sheepherders, and not without conflict between these two groups. Where adequate rainfall permitted, dryland grain farms were established, with the Palouse becoming the most reliable wheat-producing region. Other places beheld attempts at dryland farming, including Washington's Waterville Plateau and Big Bend areas, along with the Deschutes and John Day uplands in

Oregon. Among these locations the standard section of land often proved too small for successful homesteading, as numerous abandoned houses attest even today. Many of the small towns of eastern Oregon and Washington, along with southern Idaho, started as service and market nuclei for the surrounding farms and ranches. Prototypical towns embodying this essential function included Prineville, Pendleton, Yakima, Colfax, Lewiston, and Idaho Falls. In some instances, urban growth in the hinterland compared favorably with the emerging cities of the trans-Cascadia west; by 1880, for example, Walla Walla had become Washington's largest municipality in terms of population. But marketing of an agricultural surplus requires a well-developed transportation system, and it was during the next phase of regional formation that the Pacific Northwest began to articulate a distinct identity.

Railroads and Regional Growth

The completion of the first transcontinental railroad through the region, the Northern Pacific in 1883, set the stage for remarkable change and development. Now the products of rivers, farms, and forests could be shipped to eastern markets in a matter of days. Other connections added to the growing network. In 1887, Portland became linked with San Francisco by rail. And by 1888, the Northern Pacific had headed northwest out of Pasco, threaded through the Yakima Valley, and over (later tunneling underneath) Stampede Pass to connect with the port of Tacoma. In Oregon, the Union Pacific came to dominate freight movements between Portland and Pocatello, while the Southern Pacific expanded its network of tracks extending south of Portland into California. In 1893, another transcontinental line, the Great Northern, linked Seattle with St. Paul, Minnesota. Construction of the electrified Milwaukee Road from Missoula across Idaho and central Washington in 1909 brought to a close this frantic period of establishing routes and competing for the Northwest's freight and passenger traffic (see map 2-11). And it was during the first few decades of the twentieth century that rail networks in the region reached their zenith.

Communities were quick to realize the importance of rail connections, and often took great strides to ensure a position along the mainline or to support a spur. When the Northern Pacific established its station four miles north of Yakima City, many businesses simply placed their buildings on rollers and relocated. Likewise not wishing to be left behind, the City of Prineville built nineteen miles of track to reach the main north-south route through central Oregon, and to this day continues to operate the only municipally-owned railroad in the country. For their part, railroads actively promoted immigration and settlement. This boosterism took the form of exhibits and promotional displays set up around the country, as well as brochures printed in many languages for distribution across Europe. Consequently, many immigrants to the Pacific Northwest after 1890 arrived by rail. Railroad company promotion of the region was not only impelled by anticipation of greater freight or passenger volume but was also tied to lucrative property sales derived from disposal of federal land grants given to the railroads to subsidize construction.

Agricultural land use and settlement patterns responded to the augmented marketing opportunities provided by track linkages. Locomotive service stops became the nodal centers for towns and hinterland homesteads. Shortlines and spurs extended out from the mainlines to create a wider network. With steel rails slicing through the rolling loess, the Palouse developed as a singular dryland wheat region. Here, railroad freight rates were exorbitant and acted to

monopolize and take advantage of the rapid agricultural development. Elsewhere, grazing of rangelands also increased, and Shaniko, in north central Oregon, was for several years the loading terminus for the largest sheep exporting operation in the world. Other natural resources saw accelerated exploitation as well, especially timberlands, which witnessed the narrow-gauge pulse of logging railroads that came and went, leaving little more than abandoned roadbeds graded through the cutover woods.

The influence of railroads on the historical and cultural geography of the Pacific Northwest may be viewed from several perspectives. To be sure, this transportation improvement simultaneously facilitated the marketing and export of products, the phenomenal growth of urban areas, and the rapid settlement of the rural landscape, often by recently arrived immigrants to the United States. But a more disturbing facet of this development may be seen in another light, that of maintaining subordinate dependency relations between the region's new residents and the powerful absentee entities controlling the railroads or the capital required for progress. In that regard, the emerging Pacific Northwest can be recognized as a colony of the country's core areas, supplying raw materials in exchange for finished products. Nowhere was this more apparent than in the historical development of the region's natural resources.

Fishing, Mining, and Logging Activities

Anadromous fish represented a seemingly endless natural resource and formed the basis for an early export from the growing region. Salmon canneries were established at coastal embayments but also along the Columbia River, where large wooden fish wheels rotated or nets were pulled in to shore by horses. Overexploitation during these early years led to diminishment of the anadromous fishery across the Pacific Northwest. Later, construction of dams on the Columbia and its tributaries established barriers to migratory passage and contributed to further deterioration of the industry, as well as limiting the potential of recreational sport fishing. But salmon are also an important cultural resource for Indian peoples, and the exercise of treaty rights has caused considerable conflict and legal maneuvering over open seasons and limits. Coastal fishing towns managed to adapt to taking and processing other species, but even here, overall decline in this activity has been apparent.

Extraction of other minerals besides gold helped spur the growth of the region, and often, as in the case of coal, developed together with railroads. Black Diamond, Newcastle, and Roslyn were early Washington coal-mining towns, while Riddle, Oregon, became synonymous with nickel. The mining frontier reached its fullest elaboration in the panhandle region of Idaho, where lead, zinc, and silver operations dominated the landscape, and the Coeur d'Alene mineral district became of major importance at a national level. Gold was indeed responsible for initial penetration and subsequent settlement of several distinct areas within the Pacific Northwest, and many of these places still vibrate with contemporary life. But perhaps just as many have metamorphosed into dilapidated ghost towns or have vanished altogether, leaving little trace of the rush of such ephemeral activity.

Lumber production has been a signature aspect of Pacific Northwest landscapes ever since the first sawmills were set up by John McLoughlin at Fort Vancouver. As the nation grew, so did the demand for wood products. And when timber supplies dwindled in the eastern and midwestern sections of the country, logging companies looked west for their raw material. Early enterprises in the Pacific Northwest were financed with San Francisco-based capital but often involved the expertise of skilled workers from New England or the Great Lakes. Company towns arose across the region, beginning with highly consolidated locations such as Port Gamble, and later, within the spatial context of larger urban areas like Tacoma and Everett, or Klamath Falls and Springfield, Oregon. Paper mills likewise contributed to the economy of many towns in the region. At the turn of the century, midwest timber magnate Frederick Weyerhaeuser acquired nearly a million acres of prime forest lands from the Northern Pacific railroad to establish an important industrial presence in the region, and the holdings of this one company alone would eventually reach over five million acres. For many years, Oregon was nationally ranked first in timber production, with Washington usually in the top five states as well. Full exploitation of commercial old-growth reserves, combined with shifting public values and perceptions of forest resources, resulted in dramatically reduced logging activities across many areas of the region. Issues such as endangered wildlife species and the export of raw logs have complicated the human-environment equation of Pacific Northwest logging, making it difficult to assign cause or blame to any single factor or variable, and rendering an uncertain future for the industry.

Layers of Immigration History

The peopling of the Pacific Northwest may be seen as a sequence of multiple layers of immigration by different cultures. Following at least ten thousand years of aboriginal occupance, new arrivals coming into the region were first represented by a mixture of French-Canadian, Scots and other British-derived folk associated with the fur-trading operations of the Hudson's Bay Company and its antecedent firms. Pioneer families also included a significant number of métis, offspring of French-Canadian and Native American parents. Owyhees (native Hawaiians) were perhaps the first among a tremendous variety of ethnic groups to settle in the region. Arriving as working sailors aboard ships during the first decades of the nineteenth century, they looked for land-based wage opportunities and were often part of fur-trapping brigades or were employed at forts and missions. The Owyhee River in far southeast Oregon was named after three Hawaiians who disappeared on a fur-trapping foray. Asians, particularly the Chinese, formed the first substantial minority group in the Pacific Northwest. Chinese immigration initially coincided with the discovery of gold in California and then throughout the Northwest. In 1870, they comprised nearly one-third of the entire population of Idaho territory. When the ore played out, Chinese pursued other occupations, such as working in salmon canneries and especially on the railroads. Many settled in the rapidly growing cities, where distinctive "Chinatowns" became part of the urban fabric.

Germans represented the beginning of the second great wave of immigration into the region, with steadily increasing numbers between 1880-1910, followed during the next two decades by Scandinavian peoples, particularly Norwegians and Swedes. Most of these northern European groups were farming folk in search of good land, though the Germans were a diverse lot who found a variety of niches to fill. Fishing and other marine occupations attracted many Scandinavians to the coast and waterfront areas of Puget Sound's urban centers. The rapidly expanding timber industry likewise offered jobs to Nordic peoples proficient in that occupation. Significant centers of Scandinavian settlement included Poulsbo and Gig Harbor, Ballard (now part of Seattle), Astoria, and Junction City, Oregon. Finns put down roots in Astoria and Pendleton, in Naselle and Lincoln County, Washington, and in Idaho's Long Valley, south of McCall. Japanese immigrants were working oyster beds in Washington waters

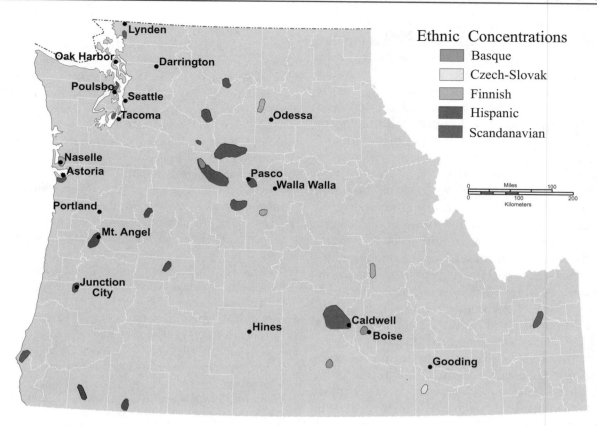

Map 2-12. Ethnic Concentrations and Festival Locations

Astoria—Scandinavian Festival
Boise—Basque Festival, Jaialdi
Caldwell—Cinco de Mayo
Darrington—Bluegrass Festival
Gooding—Basque Festival
Hines—Basque Festival
Junction City—Scandinavian Festival
Lynden—Holland Days, Sinterklass
Mt. Angel—Oktoberfest

Naselle—Finnish American Festival
Oak Harbor—Holland Happening
Odessa—Deutschesfest
Pasco—Cinco de Mayo
Portland—various ethnically related events
Poulsbo—Viking Fest, Skandia Midsommarfest
Seattle—various ethnically related events
Tacoma—Norwegian Heritage Festival
Walla Walla—Italian Heritage Days

during the 1910s, and Japanese farmers had targeted several valleys for settlement—Yakima, White River, and Hood River. Truck gardens surrounding the largest cities also provided opportunities for skillful cultivation of fresh vegetables. But racial prejudice and war-time relocation disrupted the continuity of this particular cultural geography, and a subsequent concentration of Japanese has occurred in Oregon's Malheur County. Another group looking to specialize in market gardening were the Italians, who settled on small farms east of Portland, and south of Seattle, but also in the Walla Walla valley. The agricultural frontier had become fairly saturated by this time, however, and the majority of Italians pursued manual labor with the railroads or in mining towns. Other southern or east Europeans, such as Greeks and Slavic peoples, first arrived in the region during the early twentieth century, and also faced

the reality of earning a living by pursuing wage work not related to farming. Bellingham received the greatest number of Slavic immigrants, while Roslyn's coal mines attracted a host of different ethnic groups. In Idaho, Czech and Slovak settlers could be found in the Buhl-Castleford area, while Basques established communities in Boise, Nampa, and in Jordan Valley, Oregon. During the depression of the 1930s, a unique migration stream arrived in several valleys of the Washington Cascades from the Appalachian highlands. Drawn by the lumber industry and kinship connections, these so-called "tarheels" still form pockets of Southern culture in the areas surrounding Randle and Darrington. African-Americans have been part of the cultural geography of the Pacific Northwest from the beginning, despite a tradition of racial prejudice that tarnishes the region's otherwise egalitarian disposition. Early lawmakers in Oregon excluded blacks from owning land, causing several pioneer families to settle on lands north of the Columbia River. During the late 1800s black workers often found employment on the railroads and coal mines in the region. Industrial wage opportunities during World War Two represented the dominant pull factor for this group, and African-American populations today remain concentrated in the major urban areas of Portland, Tacoma, and Seattle.

Contemporary immigration patterns include a number of cultures new to the region. Southeast Asian ethnic populations, for example, have been settling primarily in urban neighborhoods. Among these groups are Vietnamese, Laotians, and Hmongs, who often specialize in intensive market gardening of fresh vegetables and flowers. Russian "old-believers" form a distinctive farming community around Woodburn and Mount Angel, northeast of Salem, and other agro-religious enclaves may be identified across the region, including German Baptist and Hutterite communities. Indeed, the Pacific Northwest has seemed to attract utopian or communal ventures throughout its history, starting with the Willamette Valley colonies of Aurora and Sublimity, and culminating in the ill-fated social experiment at Rajneeshpuram. Along these same lines, the distinctive Mormon influence on southern Idaho has been decidedly fixed following diffusion from a hearth area along Utah's Wasatch front. But in terms of overall numbers and effective changes to the region's cultural landscape, it is the Hispanic population of the Pacific Northwest that has most dramatically increased in recent years. The first influx was associated with migrant farmworker movements and the *bracero* program, but permanent settlement and U.S. citizenship are now the norm. Significant concentrations of Spanish-speaking folk are currently established in Washington's Columbia Basin and Yakima Valley, around Woodburn, the Klamath Basin, and Malheur County in Oregon, and the western portions of Idaho's Snake River plain.

The cultural geography of the Pacific Northwest thus exhibits unique historical trajectories and identifiable spatial patterns. While overall numbers of minorities háve been relatively low, there is remarkable cultural diversity. Concentrations of ethnic groups are located on map 2-12, while locations of specified folk festivals are an additional attribute that may be represented cartographically. The next chapter examines the region's demographic data in greater detail.

Sources

Aikens, C.M. 1993. *Archaeology of Oregon.* Portland: U.S. Bureau of Land Management, Oregon State Office.

Allen, J. and E. Turner. 1988. *We the People: An Atlas of America's Ethnic Diversity.* New York: Macmillan.

Beals, H. 1985. *For Honor & Country: The Diary of Bruno de Hezeta.* Portland: Western Imprints.

Beals, H. 1989. *Juan Pérez on the Northwest Coast: Six Documents of his Expedition in 1774.* Portland: Oregon Historical Society Press.

Cressman, L. 1977. *Prehistory of the Far West: Home of Vanished Peoples.* Salt Lake City: University of Utah Press.

Dodds, G. 1986. *The American Northwest: A History of Oregon and Washington.* Arlington Heights, IL: Forum Press.

Edwards, G. and Schwantes, C., eds. 1986. *Experiences in a Promised Land: Essays in Pacific Northwest History.* Seattle: University of Washington Press.

Farmer, J. 1973. *An Historical Atlas of Early Oregon.* Portland: Historical Cartographic Publications.

Frederick, R. 1976. *North Pacific Frontiers.* Olympia: The Washington State American Revolution Bicentennial Commission.

Gaylord, M. 1994. *Eastern Washington's Past Chinese and Other Pioneers: A Self-guided Auto Tour to the State's Diverse Heritage.* Winthrop: USDA Forest Service, Okanogan National Forest.

Kilpinen, J. 1994. Finnish Cultural Landscapes in the Pacific Northwest. *Pacific Northwest Quarterly* 86(1): 25-34.

Kirk, R. and R. Daugherty. 1978. *Exploring Washington Archaeology.* Seattle: University of Washington Press.

Loy, W., Allan, S. and Patton, C. 1976. *Atlas of Oregon.* Eugene: University of Oregon.

Meinig, D. 1968. *The Great Columbia Plain: A Historical Geography, 1805-1910.* Seattle: University of Washington Press.

Parker, M. 1988. *Washington and Oregon: A Map History of the Oregon Country.* Fairfield, WA: Ye Galleon Press.

Schwantes, C. 1996. *The Pacific Northwest: An Interpretive History.* Lincoln: University of Nebraska Press.

Sorrels, R. 1991. *Way Out in Idaho: A Centennial Collection of Stories & Songs.* Lewiston: Confluence Press.

Speck, G. 1954. *Northwest Explorations.* Portland: Binfords & Mort.

Stratton, D., ed. 1991. *Spokane and the Inland Empire: An Interior Pacific Northwest Anthology.* Pullman: Washington State University Press.

White, S. and S. Solberg, eds. 1989. *Peoples of Washington: Perspectives on Cultural Diversity.* Pullman: Washington State University Press.

Chapter Three
Population
Robert D. Thompson, Jr.

For over one hundred and fifty years, the Pacific Northwest has been a population growth region, where from 1850 to the final census of the twentieth century there has not been a population decline. At the beginning, Oregon dominated the census statistics, but in 1890 it lost its regional prominence to Washington (see figure 3-1). The relative position of the three Pacific Northwest states, Washington, Oregon, and Idaho, has not varied since then. The overall growth of the region continued at a faster rate than average for the nation. In ten years, Washington has moved from the eighteenth to the fifteenth most populous state, and has four times more people than Idaho, while Oregon continues to occupy a middle position between them.

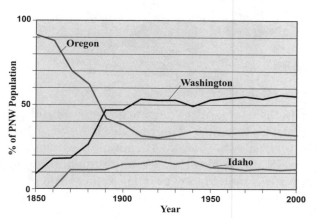

Figure 3-1. Proportional Population by State, 1850-2000

Population Change 1990-2000

The 2000 census showed that the Pacific Northwest region once again outpaced the national rate of population growth. Washington showed a population growth of 21.1 percent, Oregon grew by 20.4 percent, and Idaho, with the greatest proportional growth of the three states, grew by 28.5 percent, while the national population change was 13.1 percent. As shown in map 3-1, by 2000 the region was experiencing, for the most part, a net inflow of people

from all regions of the U.S. and overseas, although there was a slightly larger inflow of people from Canada into the region. California, though, remained the dominant source area and the primary outflow destination. Jointly, the Pacific Northwest states now hold about 3.76 percent of the total United States population.

On the whole, the Pacific Northwest population statistics show the region as a growth area. In the 1990 census this was only because of the state of Washington's strong performance, while Oregon and Idaho both lagged behind the national average

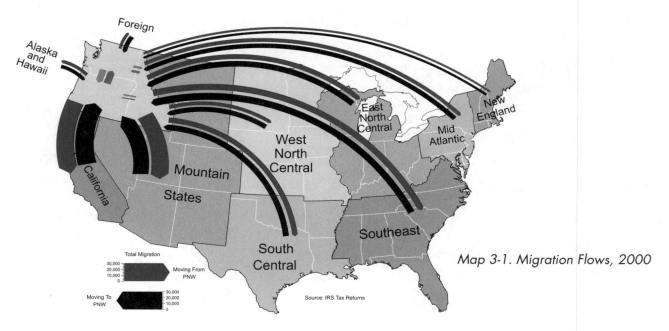

Map 3-1. Migration Flows, 2000

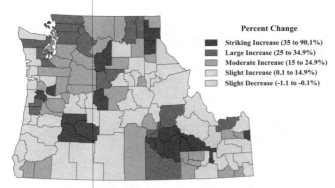

Percent Change

■ Striking Increase (35 to 90.1%)
■ Large Increase (25 to 34.9%)
▨ Moderate Increase (15 to 24.9%)
▨ Slight Increase (0.1 to 14.9%)
□ Slight Decrease (-1.1 to -0.1%)

Map 3-2. Population Change 1990-2000

growth rates and experienced substantial out-migration for much of the decade (1980-1990). In the 2000 census the state of Washington continued to show a strong performance in population growth, but Oregon and Idaho's population growth kept pace with Washington and outperformed the national population growth rate. Oregon's growth rate was 35 percent larger and Idaho's growth rate was more than double that of the 13.1 percent national average.

The news from the 2000 census is that more counties experienced increases in their population, which reversed a population decline that was manifest in thirty-six counties in the 1990 census. As shown in map 3-2, one coastal county in Oregon and two in the state of Washington showed a slight population increase. A larger number of counties in the interior of the two states increased their populations slightly, and three counties in Idaho either had a large or striking increase in their population.

During the past fifty years the two most rapidly growing metropoles have been Seattle and in more recent years Portland. Simultaneously, both the interior and coastal regions experienced population decline, as shown in the 1990 census, subsequently enlarging the two major metropoles of the Northwest. In the last ten years, from 1990 to 2000, certain coastal counties in the region, especially in Oregon, have shown signs of population recovery as their economies gradually shifted from mining, timber, and fishing communities, to gaming (entertainment, gambling) retail/wholesale outlets, and vacation housing business. Map 3-3 shows population losses concentrated in small communities, while larger communities were still growing.

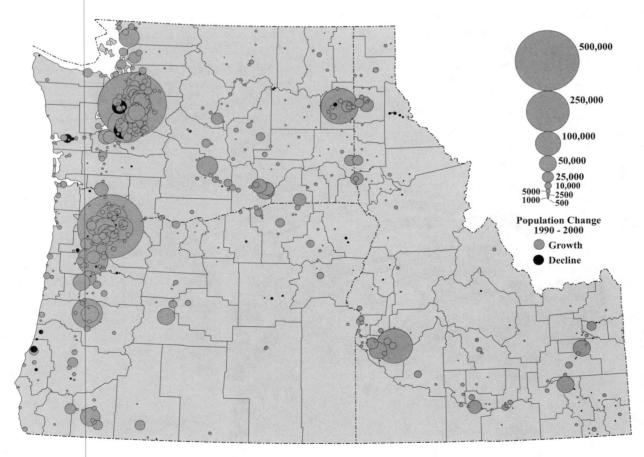

Map 3-3. Population of Incorporated Cities and Towns, 2000

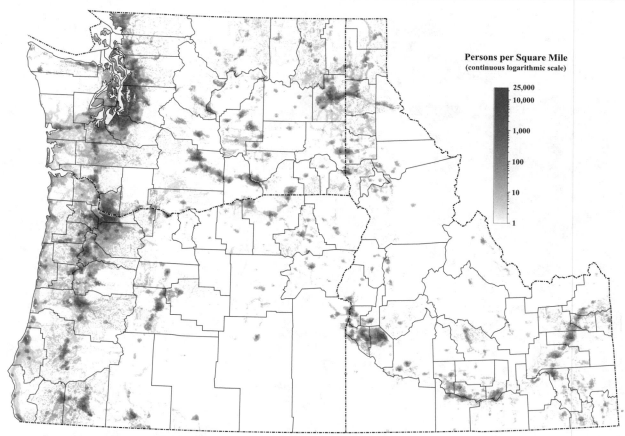

Map 3-4. Population Density, 2000

Population Distribution

As was the case ten years ago in the 1990 census, the population of the Pacific Northwest is very unevenly distributed in favor of a few urban-dominated locations, primarily in the Puget lowland and the Willamette Valley, which together hold more than half of the region's population (see map 3-4). The Puget lowland and the Willamette Valley counties are respectively home to 31 and 21 percent of the Pacific Northwest population.

Unlike the rest of the United States, the region's coastal counties do not have large population centers. Approximately 3.5 percent of the region's population make their home on the coast. Major port facilities, economic and industrial cores are situated more than ninety miles from the Pacific Ocean, with access to and from the ocean via the Columbia and Willamette rivers, serving Portland, and through Puget Sound, serving Seattle, Tacoma, and Everett.

The region east of the Cascades has only a few high-population concentrations. The single biggest population center is the city of Spokane, Washington. Other notable areas that had significant population growth are Boise, Idaho, and the Tri-cities (Richland, Pasco, and Kennewick, Washington). With a total population increase of 159.40 percent, Bend, Oregon, has become in the past ten years a haven for retirees seeking amenities.

Racial Minorities

Over the decades the Pacific Northwest has contained a greater proportion of white residents (84 percent) by comparison with the rest of the U.S. (75.1 percent) The growth rates, however, of people of color in the Northwest continued in the years between 1990 to 2000 at a greater rate relative to the majority white population.[1] While the Asian population in the decade of the 1990s continues to grow, it grew at less than half the rate of the previous decade. Continuing in the nineties, Asians strengthened their economic and cultural ties, both regionally and internationally, on the eastern rim of the Pacific basin.[2] Immigration from California and Latin American countries created an extremely rapid increase of Latino immigrant population into the Pacific Northwest.

The nonwhite population in the region shows substantial distributional variation between races (see map 3-5). Blacks continue to be the most geographically concentrated of all nonwhite groups,

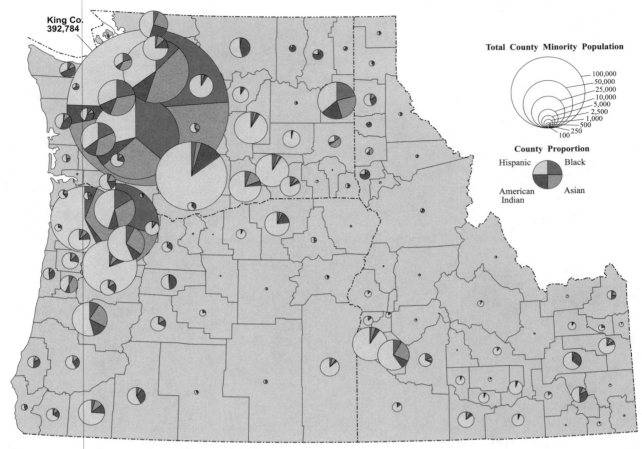

Map 3-5. County Minority Population, 2000

making home in several important urban areas of Oregon and Washington. In the 1990 census Blacks were the most numerous minority group in two counties (Multnomah, Oregon and Pierce, Washington). Black people, however, lost the leading minority group position in Multnomah and Pierce counties in the 2000 census. Nowhere in the Northwest region do they represent a majority of the nonwhite population at the county level. Black urban concentration is so great that they make up less than half a percent of the total population in coastal and inland counties of the Pacific Northwest. Only one county in Idaho (Custer) in the 2000 census recorded no black residents, while in the 1990 census six counties in the three Northwest states recorded no black residents.

Asians are also concentrated in the Northwest urban centers but have expanded their presence by moving to the suburbs and to university communities as well. They represent a majority nonwhite population in two counties of the region and a plurality of nonwhite residents in seven others.

Native Americans, the most represented nonwhite minority group in the rural counties, have for many decades increased their presence in all the major

urban areas of the Northwest. Native Americans[3] continue to have a presence in the rural counties. Although not as prominent in 2000 as they were in 1990, they continue a trend, at a steady rate of increase, of urbanization that began, nationally, in earnest in the early 1940s.

With the 2000 census Latinos are not only the largest nonwhite minority in the region but now also reside in great numbers in all rural counties of the area. Latinos are not only concentrated heavily in the Pacific Northwest urban centers, being the most numerous nonwhite minority in four urban counties (Multnomah, Washington, Marion, and Ada). Of the 119 counties in the region, Latinos are the most numerous nonwhite minority group in over 60 percent of the counties and have a plurality in 15 percent of others. Historically, the Latino presence in the United States reflects the strong attraction of seasonal agricultural work. As in the rest of the United States, the Pacific Northwest agricultural areas have greatly benefited from the steady flow of seasonal agricultural workers into the region. What is significant about the tenth census of the twentieth century is that Latinos not only make up a large segment of agricultural workers but also represent

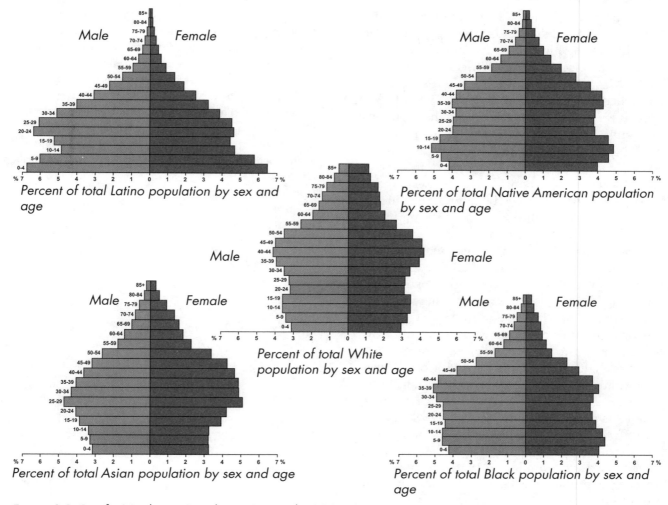

Figure 3-2. Pacific Northwest Population Pyramids, 2000

a growing significant worker presence in the urban centers, concentrated in the service and day-work sectors of the labor force.

Age-Sex Composition

The Pacific Northwest age-sex composition for the majority white population corresponds to the general pattern for the majority population throughout the United States. The 2000 census shows that the "baby boomers" born between 1945 and 1965 are the most numerous age group, while younger age classes show a smaller family size as a consequence of a declining birth rate after 1965. Boys continue to be slightly more numerous than girls at birth, but females substantially outnumber males as differential mortality takes its toll in the older age groups. This pattern is clearly seen in the population pyramid for whites (figure 3-2).

Minority populations in the Pacific Northwest show a somewhat different configuration. As is the

case with the dominant group, Native American boys are slightly more numerous than girls at birth. In the 2000 census, Native Americans show much the same birth rate as Blacks and have a slightly higher birth rate than Whites and Asians. Native Americans, however, still experience a slightly higher mortality rate at all ages, resulting in a smaller elderly proportion of the population, while at the same time the youngest age groups continue to be relatively large, especially in the 10-14 age class.

The black population composition is similar to that of the Native Americans, especially at the younger and elderly ends of the pyramids, except that there is, for Blacks, a strong male dominance in the 20 to 44 age groups. This probably reflects a population strongly influenced by sex-skewed migration streams. The black population, for the most part, is growing from in-migration, and there is commonly a male bias in long-distance migration within the United States. For example, U.S. military personnel are predominantly male and include a disproportionately large black population, and in recent years Blacks have been drawn to the Pacific Northwest for high-paying technical jobs in the aircraft and electronics industries.

The Asian population pyramid also shows the influence of continued migration. The elderly age classes are small, not as small as in the 1990 census, but similar in size to the elderly black female class and slightly larger than the elderly black male class. There is a skewing toward female dominance at a much earlier age than would be expected in a population not influenced by migration, which may suggest a group who are gradually making the Pacific Northwest their home.

The Latino population in the Pacific Northwest shows the largest birth rate of all five groups. This population has the smallest elderly classes (ages 65 to 85) of all groups in the region. There is a strong male dominance in the age range from 15 to 34, historically due to sex-skewed migration flow of Latino males to seasonal agricultural work that enables them to move, as needed, from county to county and in some cases from state to state. Possibly exposure to multiple work and health hazards, in the fields and in dangerous urban work sites, may be reflected in the small elderly class in the Latino population of the Pacific Northwest. It may also reflect a Latino population that, because of close proximity of their homelands and their continual migration into the United States, appears to be a first=generation immigrant group. The elderly have stayed behind in the homeland, and the younger age groups have migrated north to find work, frequently sending money home to their elders and families.

1 The U.S. Bureau of the Census projects that by 2050 Non-Hispanic Whites will be 60 percent of the U.S. population. The Census Bureau projects that in the next five decades the total percentage of minority group Americans will increase from about 25 percent to almost 40 percent. (U.S. Bureau of the Census, 1996, p. 14).

2 Not only accounting for the metropoles along the eastern and western rim of the Pacific basin but also taking into account the population centers, trading, traveling points and various peoples who live on the various islands in the Pacific Ocean.

3 Native Americans are approximately 1.4 percent of the Northwest population, by comparison with .9 percent of the national population.

Chapter 4
Transportation
Steven R. Kale

Rugged terrain, a relatively small number of residents, and long distances between population and economic centers have limited the development and operation of the Pacific Northwest's freight and passenger transportation systems. The region's mountainous topography has contributed to a channeling of highways and rail lines through a few natural corridors and over passes such as Monida in Idaho, Deadman and Willamette in Oregon, and Stevens and Snoqualmie in Washington. Probably the natural corridor of greatest strategic significance is the Columbia River Gorge, the only water-level route through the Cascade Mountains. Highways, rail lines, and the Columbia-Snake inland waterway system provide a vital link via the Columbia Gorge between Portland and the Columbia Basin. Similarly, the construction and operation of transportation routes through the major population centers of southern Idaho, western Oregon, and western Washington have been greatly facilitated by the flat terrain of the Snake River Plain, Willamette Valley, and Puget Trough.

Remoteness from markets nationally and internationally has contributed to efforts to develop the region's multimodal transportation network. Development of marine transportation has helped connect the Northwest with markets overseas, while the rail and interstate highway systems enable Northwest producers to reach domestic markets throughout the United States. The region's rail and highway systems are playing an increasingly important role in trade with Canada and Mexico with ratification of the North American Free Trade Agreement in 1993. Air transportation and pipelines represent additional vital links for the movement of freight or people between the Northwest and domestic and international origins and destinations.

Freight Transportation

In the Pacific Northwest, freight moves by trucks, trains, ships, barges, airplanes, and pipelines. In general, trucks haul a wide variety of commodities over short distances, railroads haul bulk commodities over intermediate distances, and marine carriers haul bulk commodities over long distances. Airplanes are used primarily for carrying mail and high-value or highly perishable commodities over intermediate and long distances. Pipelines move liquids and gases over long distances.

These generalizations break down where modes compete with one another. Barges compete with trucks, railroads, and pipelines for movement of bulk commodities. Short-line railroads compete with trucks for local and regional movements. Long-haul trucks compete with long-haul railroads. Amtrak and intercity bus lines compete with trucks and airlines for moving mail and other time-sensitive commodities. Truck, rail, and marine carriers also work together to move commodities by truck-trailers and containers on rail cars, barges and ships, and through intermodal terminals.

Truck. Most freight moves by truck for all or a portion of its trip. According to data from the U.S. Department of Commerce's *Commodity Flow Survey*, trucks account for at least 69 percent of freight shipments originating in the Pacific Northwest by tonnage, 58 percent by value, and 44 percent by ton miles. The importance of trucks for freight movement is greater in Idaho than in Oregon and Washington, where other modes are more available and modal competition is greater. Average distance per truck shipment was 91 miles in Idaho, 120 miles in Washington, and 182 miles in Oregon.

Interstate highways generally carry the greatest amount of truck freight. Interstate 5 is the most important north-south highway in the Pacific Northwest, running from the Canadian border near Vancouver, British Columbia, into California south of Ashland, Oregon. Other important interstate highways include I-90 from Seattle through central Washington and the Idaho panhandle into Montana; I-84 from Portland through eastern Oregon and southern Idaho into Utah; I-15 between Montana and Utah through eastern Idaho; I-82 between Ellensburg, Washington, and I-84 in northeastern Oregon; and I-86 between I-15 and I-84 in southeastern Idaho. A variety of other interstate, federal, and state highways are important for interstate and intrastate truck freight movements in the region's metropolitan areas as well as smaller urban centers and rural areas.

Trucks carry a wide variety of commodities; data from the *Commodity Flow Survey* show logs and wood products accounting for about one-third of the tonnage originating in the Northwest. Gravel, stone, and related products comprise another 20 percent. "Other," however, is the *CFS* category with the greatest tonnage originating in the region, suggesting the wide diversity of goods moved by truck.

State agencies have designated selected highways and other roads as especially important for truck freight movements. In Idaho, the highways are Intrastate Priority Corridors as established in the *Idaho Highway Plan*. In Oregon, the highways are State Highway Freight System routes as established in the *1999 Oregon Highway Plan*. In Washington, the highways are part of the Freight and Goods Transportation System as designated in the *2003-2022 Highway System Plan*.

Rail Freight. *Commodity Flow Survey* data show that for freight with origins in the Pacific Northwest, rail accounts for 6 percent of shipments by tonnage, 4 percent by value, and 32 percent by ton miles. Rail's greater importance in ton miles than in tonnage or value reflects the relatively long average distances for rail compared to truck. In 1997, the average distance per rail shipment ranged from 1,020 miles in Washington to more than 1,500 miles in Idaho and Oregon.

Large and small railroad companies operated about 7,000 miles of trackage in the Pacific Northwest in 2000 (see map 4-1). The region's two major (Class I) railroads—the Union Pacific (UP) Railroad and the Burlington Northern and Santa Fe (BNSF) Railway Company—accounted for 60 percent of total rail mileage in the Northwest. The UP operated the most trackage in Idaho (858 miles) and Oregon (1,004 miles), while the BNSF operated the most trackage in Washington (1,838 miles).

Regional, local, and switching and terminal railroads operate rail branch lines and other trackage that mostly was owned by the Class I railroads prior to deregulation of the rail industry in 1980. Seven regional, local, and switching railroads operated in Idaho in 2000, eighteen operated in Oregon, and seventeen operated in Washington. Among the smaller railroads, the Eastern Idaho Railroad operated the most trackage (269 miles) in Idaho, the Portland and Western (including the former Willamette and Pacific) operated the most (450 miles) in Oregon, and the Palouse River & Coulee City Railroad operated the most (286 miles) in Washington.

Data from the federal Surface Transportation Board show that total freight tonnage carried in 2000 was highest in Idaho—82 million tons, followed by Washington with 80 million tons and Oregon with 62 million tons. Of rail traffic originating in each state, the following accounted for over half of the total: Idaho—farm products and nonmetallic minerals, Oregon—lumber and wood products and pulp and paper, and Washington—mixed freight, lumber and wood products, and waste and scrap. Of rail traffic terminating in each state, the leading commodities were: Idaho—nonmetallic minerals and farm products, Oregon—chemicals, farm products, coal, and waste and scrap, and Washington—farm products, mixed freight, and food products.

Port of Morrow container yard near Boardman, Oregon. (Photo by Steven R. Kale)

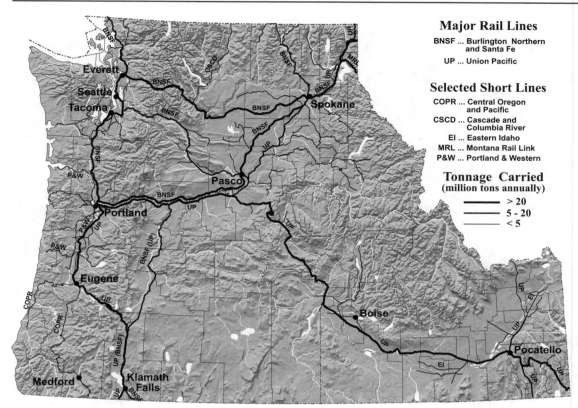

Map 4-1. Railroad Lines

State departments of transportation operate a rail program in all three states. The purpose of the rail programs is to assist in the preservation of essential rail service through statewide planning and various programs. Washington's grain train is an innovative program in which state government and the Port of Walla Walla purchased hopper cars to help relieve shortages of rail cars during harvest season. Other programs in Washington include a fruit express service on Amtrak and short-haul truck-rail inter-modal service.

Ships and Barges. Data from the *Commodity Flow Survey* show water transportation accounting for 9 percent of the tonnage, 2 percent of the value, and 10 percent of the ton mileage of freight shipments with origins in the Pacific Northwest. Waterborne freight is moved by deep-draft ocean-going ships and shallow-draft barges. Ocean ships serve Oregon's and Washington's coastal ports, Washington's Puget Sound ports, and Columbia River ports as far upstream as Portland and Vancouver, just over 100 miles from the river's mouth (see map 4-2). Barges provide service along the Pacific coast and on coastal estuaries, the Puget Sound, and the Columbia-Snake River System. Thirty feet is generally considered the minimum depth for deep-draft service. Fourteen feet

is the minimum depth for shallow-draft barge service on the Columbia-Snake system upriver from the Portland-Vancouver area.

One port district operates in Idaho, twenty-three operate in Oregon, and seventy-six operate in Washington (See table 4-1). The region's port districts are involved in a variety of transportation and non-transportation activities. Marine-related activities include commercial and recreational fishing and moorage, ship repair, channel and harbor maintenance, cruise ship operations, and marine freight terminals. Most port districts own commercial and industrial lands where marine and non-marine businesses operate. About thirty ports own or operate airports and several operate railroads, parks, and recreational vehicle facilities.

Idaho's only port district is located at the confluence of the Snake and Clearwater Rivers in Lewiston, Idaho, just across the state line from Clarkston, Washington. Marine terminals in Lewiston and Clarkston are 465 miles from the mouth of the Columbia River near Astoria, and represent the eastward limit of barge navigation on the Columbia-Snake system.

Fourteen of Oregon's port districts are located along the Pacific Coast, three are on the lower Columbia River, and six are on the Columbia River

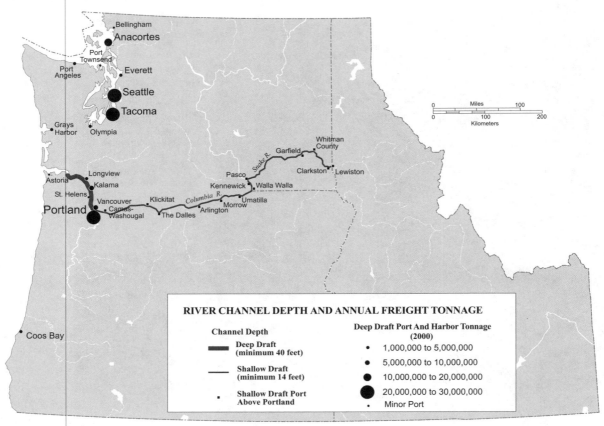

RIVER CHANNEL DEPTH AND ANNUAL FREIGHT TONNAGE

Channel Depth

▬▬▬ Deep Draft
(minimum 40 feet)

──── Shallow Draft
(minimum 14 feet)

▪ Shallow Draft Port
Above Portland

Deep Draft Port And Harbor Tonnage
(2000)

• 1,000,000 to 5,000,000

● 5,000,000 to 10,000,000

⬤ 10,000,000 to 20,000,000

⬤ 20,000,000 to 30,000,000

▪ Minor Port

Map 4-2. Ports and Waterways

Table 4-1. Port Districts in the Pacific Northwest	Idaho	Oregon	Washington
Total port districts	1	23	76
Coastal ports	0	14	3
Deep draft	0	2	1
Puget Sound ports	0	0	34
Deep draft	0	0	7
Columbia River ports downriver from Portland and Vancouver	0	3	8
Deep draft	0	3	3
Columbia River ports upriver from Portland and Vancouver	0	6	7
Ports with barge service	0	4	5
Snake River ports*	1	0	6
Ports with barge service	1	0	4
Other**	0	0	18

*The Port of Pasco has marine terminals on both the Columbia and Snake rivers.

**Other includes dryland ports such as those in Centralia and Chehalis, and waterside and dryland ports in the Columbia River basin upstream from the Tri-Cities area.

Sources: Columbia Snake River Marketing Group, *The Great Waterway*, 2001; Oregon Department of Transportation, *Freight Moves the Oregon Economy*, 1999; Washington Public Ports Association, *Port Directory*, 2001.

Barge on the Snake River. (Photo courtesy of U.S. Corps of Engineers, Walla Walla District)

upriver from Portland. The International Port of Coos Bay is the only major freight port on the Oregon coast. Oceangoing and local freight moves through marine terminals on the Columbia River at Astoria, St. Helens and other locations in Columbia County, and Portland. In terms of marine tonnage in 2000, Portland ranked twenty-second among U.S. ports nationally and third after Los Angeles and Long Beach on the West Coast. Four of Oregon's Columbia River ports upriver from Portland have marine terminals that ship freight by barge.

Of Washington's three ports along the Pacific Coast, only Grays Harbor accommodates ocean-going ships. Seven of Washington's Puget Sound ports accommodate ocean freighters. The Ports of Seattle, Tacoma, and Anacortes ranked twenty-eighth, thirty-second, and fortieth nationally in marine freight tonnage in 2000 and fourth, fifth, and seventh on the West Coast. Marine freight terminals in Longview, Kalama, and Vancouver serve ocean-going ships on the lower Columbia River. Most of Washington's shallow-draft ports on the Columbia River are located just north of the Oregon-Washington state line in the Tri-Cities area. Four ports on the Snake River also provide shallow-draft barge service.

Data from the U.S. Army Corps of Engineers show that 114 million tons of marine freight were shipped in Washington in 2000, followed by Oregon with 40 million tons and Idaho with 1.6 million tons. Commodities varied somewhat, depending on location. Forest products were the primary commodities shipped from coastal ports. Grains, mostly wheat, accounted for about 65 percent of commodity tonnage shipped by barges on the Columbia-Snake

system above Portland. Petroleum products, which are the primary commodities shipped upstream, accounted for another 25 percent of Columbia-Snake tonnage shipped in barges. Grains and petroleum products also were the primary products shipped on the Columbia River below Portland and Vancouver, together accounting for about 60 percent of total tonnage. According to the Columbia Snake River Marketing Group, the Columbia-Snake system handles 40 to 45 percent of U.S. wheat exports, making the system the largest wheat transportation system in the nation.

Grains, petroleum products, and wood products generally are the most important commodities in tonnage shipped through Puget Sound ports. Tacoma is the most dependent on these three commodity groupings, which account for about 50 percent of total tonnage there. About 80 percent of the freight moving between the lower forty-eight states and Alaska moves through the Port of Tacoma, making it the primary Pacific Northwest port handling freight to Alaska.

Unlike most other ports in the Pacific Northwest, Seattle is more dependent on imports than on exports. Seattle terminals focus on petroleum products, aggregates and related products, and manufactured equipment and machinery. Marine terminals in Anacortes mostly handle petroleum products, reflecting the nearby presence of refineries.

Seattle and Tacoma are major ports for shipping higher-value freight in containers. In 2000, together, they ranked sixteenth worldwide and third nationally, after ports in Los Angeles and Long Beach. Portland handles about one-tenth the number of containers that are handled by the Seattle and Tacoma ports.

Environmental and other concerns continue to affect transportation on waterways in the Pacific Northwest. Operation of marine terminals at coastal ports depends on periodic dredging of estuaries and rivers. Federal funding pays for most of the costs of dredging and is subject to changing legal and political priorities. Ports and other business interests along the Lower Columbia are working to deepen the shipping channel from 40 to 43 feet to better accommodate ships requiring greater draft. Groups concerned about salmon migration and recovery argue against channel deepening and in favor of breaching dams on the Snake River between the Tri-Cities and Lewiston. Dam breaching would end barge navigation on the Snake and could lead to more truck and rail traffic, mostly in Washington.

Roads to major terminals in the Portland-Vancouver area and the Puget Sound have become increasingly congested with growth in traffic and economic activity. To help remove bottlenecks in road and rail access to marine terminals in the Everett-Seattle-Tacoma corridor, state and local interests established a Freight Action Strategy for Seattle-Tacoma (FAST) in 1995. FAST Corridor projects focus on improvements where freight is transferred between intermodal rail yards and marine terminals, or where roads and rail lines intersect. A number of FAST Corridor projects received high priority funding through the federal Transportation Equity Act for the 21st Century (TEA 21) in 1998. Funding for FAST Corridor and other projects in Washington has become relatively less available as voters have declined to support a number of transportation funding measures.

Air Freight. *Commodity Flow Survey* data show that air freight accounts for a tiny amount of regional goods movement by tonnage and ton miles, but for 15 percent of the value of freight shipped from origins in the Pacific Northwest. This includes shipments that air freight companies move by truck. In Idaho and Oregon, air freight is less than 5 percent of the total value of freight shipped. In Washington, 25 percent of the value of originating shipments is attributable to air freight, more than any other mode except truck.

Seattle-Tacoma (Sea-Tac) International and Portland International are the leading air freight airports in the Pacific Northwest, with about 1.9 billion pounds and 1.6 billion pounds, respectively, moving through the two airports in 2001. Both airports were among the leading airports nationally in weight of shipments, with Sea-Tac ranking

eighteenth and Portland ranking twentieth in 2001. Sea-Tac's ranking for freight is about the same as its ranking for passenger enplanements. Portland, however, ranks higher as a freight airport than it does as a passenger airport.

Other Pacific Northwest airports ranking in the top one hundred airports by cargo volume in 2001 were King County International at Boeing Field in Seattle (forty-fourth), Spokane International (fifty-sixth), and Boise Municipal Airport (sixty-ninth). While no other airport in the Pacific Northwest ranked among the nation's top one hundred in air freight shipments, about forty have air freight services. For most of the smaller airports, this consists solely of service from small-package carriers such as Federal Express. For the larger airports with regularly scheduled commercial service, freight is carried in the belly of passenger airplanes as well as in airplanes operated by small-package carriers.

Mail is a significant air freight commodity for many airports. Data from the Federal Aviation Administration in the year 2000 showed that mail comprised 20 to 25 percent of air freight for the commercial service airports in the Pacific Northwest. This percentage may now be greater as other types of air freight shipments have decreased following the terrorist attacks of September 11, 2001.

Larger air freight shipments typically move by container or on pallets. Data from the *Commodity Flow Survey* show that transportation equipment accounts for 85 percent of air freight by value in shipments weighing more than 100 pounds. Most shipments of transportation equipment are associated with Boeing and associated businesses in the Puget Sound area. Electrical and electronic equipment and components comprise about 7 percent of the value of air freight over 100 pounds in weight, reflecting the importance of the region's high-technology industry. Considerable amounts of high-technology products also are shipped in lower-weight parcels moving by multiple modes, primarily truck and air.

Increases in air freight shipments, especially those that are time-sensitive, have contributed to the need for expanded airport facilities. This is most notable for the region's larger airports but also has occurred for smaller airports with increased traffic. Expansion of airport facilities, including runways, is controversial where residential areas are located near airports or under existing or proposed flight paths. Concerns about adverse environmental impacts and legal challenges have delayed construction of a proposed third runway at the Seattle-Tacoma International Airport. Construction of the runway is expected to begin no earlier than 2004, with completion no earlier than 2008. Similar issues have arisen during master planning for future runway and other needs at the Portland International Airport.

Pipelines. Petroleum products and natural gas are the two commodities moved by pipeline in the Pacific Northwest. (See chapter 11 for moer detail on petroleum and natural gas supply and consumption.) *Commodity Flow Survey* data show that pipelines account for 3 percent of the tonnage and 1 percent of the value of shipments with origins in the region. All or nearly all of this originates at petroleum refineries in northwest Washington where oil arrives by ship or by pipeline from Canada. Petroleum pipelines from these refineries serve western Washington and western Oregon as far south as Eugene. Petroleum pipelines from Montana, Utah, and Wyoming are located in Idaho, eastern Oregon, and eastern Washington.

Pipelines from Canada supply about 80 percent of the natural gas consumed in Idaho, Oregon, and Washington; the rest comes from Wyoming and other Rocky Mountain states. Williams Gas Pipeline - West serves much of the region with lines roughly following the I-5 and I-84 corridors. PG&E National Energy Group's Gas Transmission Northwest carries natural gas from Alberta to California via northern Idaho, southeastern Washington, and central Oregon. Local distribution companies move natural gas from transmission lines to residential, commercial, and industrial consumers.

Increasing economic and population growth have fueled increased demand for natural gas. To meet this demand, transmission and distribution companies have built and are planning new pipelines and capacity in existing corridors as well as in new locations. This includes constructing lines to serve new residential and commercial developments at the edges of urban areas and lines to new electricity generating plants.

Passenger Transportation

The automobile is the main mode for personal transportation in the Pacific Northwest as elsewhere in the United States. Statewide population surveys in Oregon and Washington reveal that well over 80 percent of commuters use autos, trucks, or vans to drive to and from work. On a per capita basis, residents of Idaho and Oregon travel more miles annually than the national average, while residents of Washington travel less than the national average (see figure 4-1).

Dominance of the auto for commuting and other personal travel reflects the widespread presence of highways and local roads, relatively easy ownership of autos, low gasoline prices as compared to prices in other nations, and personal preferences for the mobility that auto travel allows. Despite the auto's dominance, for a variety of reasons a considerable number of the region's residents rely on other modes. Many travelers use mass transit for some or most of their work, shopping, recreational, and other trips. Ferries, intercity bus, intercity passenger rail, and airplanes also are important non-auto modes of transportation for personal travel.

Usage of non-auto modes, along with transportation demand management, helps reduce impacts of congestion, which is a growing issue in the region's more heavily populated areas. According to a Texas Transportation Institute study of seventy-five metropolitan areas nationally, the Seattle-Everett metropolitan area was seventh worst in annual delay per person in 2000, and the Portland-Vancouver (Washington) area tied for twenty-first. In terms of the amount of daily travel occurring in congested conditions, the Portland-Vancouver area had the highest percentage point increase nationally

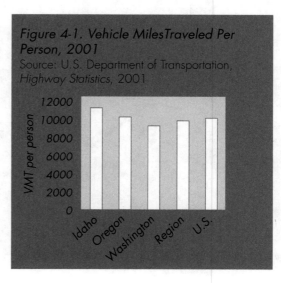

Figure 4-1. Vehicle MilesTraveled Per Person, 2001
Source: U.S. Department of Transportation, *Highway Statistics, 2001*

from 1982 to 2000, and Tacoma tied for eighth highest. The region's other metropolitan areas in the study (Eugene-Springfield, Salem, and Spokane) generally fared better according to the study's congestion measures; however, the Eugene-Springfield area tied for the sixth greatest percentage point increase in the amount of daily travel occurring at congested times from 1994 to 2000.

Mass Transit. In the Northwest, mass transit consists primarily of local bus systems but also includes light rail, commuter rail, demand-response buses, and a monorail. The region accounts for nearly 270 million public transportation trips annually, with 70 percent of these trips occurring in the Seattle and Portland metropolitan areas. In terms of the number of trips annually, King County's Metro Transit in the Seattle area and the Tri-County Metropolitan Transit District (Tri-Met) in the Portland area are among the thirty largest transit systems nationally, with Metro Transit ranking fifteenth and Tri-Met ranking sixteenth in 2001. Among the thirty largest systems, Seattle's and Portland's transit systems rank even higher in terms of the number of trips per person in the transit district service area, with Tri-Met ranking ninth and Metro ranking tenth in 2001. In addition to transit agencies serving metropolitan areas and larger non-metropolitan communities, hundreds of small transit providers serve small towns and rural areas. In

Oregon, for example, more than two hundred agencies provide dial-a-ride and demand-response transit services across the state.

The development of light rail (MAX) in the Portland area has been nationally recognized since completion of the system's first 15 miles in 1986 from downtown Portland to Gresham in eastern Multnomah County. The 1998 completion of the Westside line to Hillsboro in Washington County extended the system to 33 miles; completion of the extension to Portland International Airport in 2001 increased the total another 5.5 miles (see map 4-3). The next extension of the system, a 5.8-mile segment between downtown Portland and the Portland Metropolitan Exposition Center near the Oregon-Washington state line, is scheduled for completion in September 2004. MAX accounted for 27 percent of the Portland area's mass transit trips in 2001.

In 2001, Portland became the first city in the nation to open a modern street car line. Begun in April 1999, the streetcar line extends 2.4 miles in northwest Portland between the Legacy Good Samaritan Hospital and Portland State University. Future development of the line may include an extension from Portland State south to the North Macadam waterfront area near the I-5 Marquam Bridge over the Willamette River. Other passenger rail operations in the Portland area include the Vintage Trolley, operated by Tri-Met between

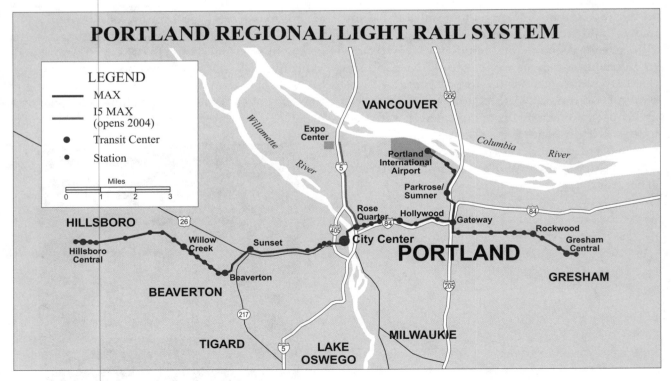

Map 4-3. Portland Regional Light Rail System

downtown Portland and the Lloyd Center east of the Willamette River, and the 7-mile Willamette River Trolley between Portland and Lake Oswego, operated by the Oregon Electric Railway Historical Society. The Vintage Trolley and Willamette River Trolley operate mostly as tourist attractions on weekend and holiday schedules.

Metro Transit operates the George Benson Waterfront Streetcar along Elliot Bay in downtown Seattle. The streetcar operates daily between Jackson Street to the south and Broad Street to the north. The City of Astoria in Oregon runs a waterfront trolley near the Columbia River on a rail line formerly operated by the Burlington Northern and Santa Fe Railway Company. A number of other communities in the Northwest operate rubber-tired trolleys, mostly as tourist attractions.

In November 1996, Everett-Seattle-Tacoma area voters approved *Sound Move*, a 10-year regional transit plan with an estimated capital and operating cost of $3.9 billion. Among the provisions of the plan are a commuter rail system, a light rail system, express buses, and additional park and ride lots and other facilities (**see** map 4-4). Tacoma-Seattle commuter rail (Sounder) service on BNSF lines began September 18, 2000. Sounder service between Seattle and Everett and from Tacoma to Lakewood is scheduled to begin in 2003.

The approximately 25-mile light rail line would extend from the University of Washington on the north to the Seattle-Tacoma International Airport on the south, with extensions farther north and south if funding becomes available. Initially planned to begin in 2006, light rail service has been delayed until at least 2009 because of concerns about higher-than-anticipated costs. Plans for light rail also include a 1.6-mile line in Tacoma between downtown and the Tacoma Dome where connections could be made with local and regional express buses, commuter rail, or Amtrak. Service in Tacoma is scheduled to begin in September 2003.

A competing proposal calls for the construction of a 54-mile elevated monorail in Seattle where voters in 1997 approved Monorail Initiative 41. The measure called for the establishment of an Elevated Transit Company (ETC) to move forward the construction of an electrically powered, rubber-tired, elevated mass transportation system serving the four quadrants of Seattle and running through the downtown. In the November 2000 election, voters approved a follow-up measure, Initiative 53, which required the City of Seattle to provide operating funds for the ETC, the preparation of a Seattle

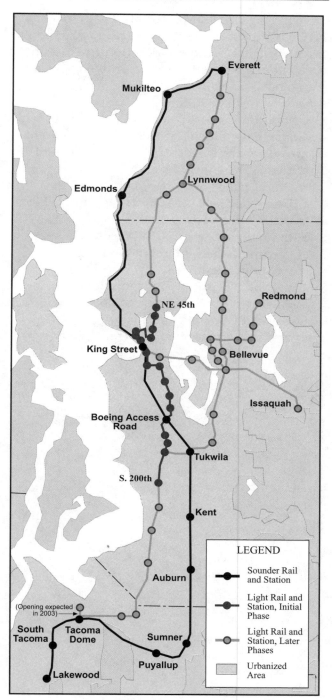

Map 4-4. Commuter Rail in the Central Puget Sound Region

Popular Transit Plan, and $125 to $200 million of bonding capacity for building the system if approved by voters.

On November 5, 2002, Seattle voters again showed their support for the monorail by narrowly passing a ballot measure to create a monorail authority and levy a 1.4 percent motor vehicle excise tax to finance the costs of the monorail system. The first phase of the system, scheduled to begin operation in

December 2007, would extend from approximately NW 85th Street in the Ballard area to SW Morgan Street in West Seattle. Operation for the initial segment of the 14-mile line is scheduled to begin in December 2007, with full operation of the first phase scheduled to begin in 2009.

Demonstration projects or feasibility studies of rail and other emerging mass transit technologies have occurred or are underway in other parts of the Northwest. These include:

- a light rail demonstration project on the Union Pacific's "cut-off" rail line in the Boise metropolitan area,
- the 15-mile Beaverton to Wilsonville Commuter Rail Project in Washington County, Oregon,
- the South Corridor Transportation Alternatives Study between downtown Portland and Oregon City,

- an elevated tram between the Oregon Health and Science University and the North Macadam waterfront area in Portland,
- the Rogue Valley Commuter Rail Study for a 45-mile line between Grant's Pass and Ashland in southwestern Oregon,
- a bus rapid transit project partially on a fixed guideway system between the downtowns of Eugene and Springfield, Oregon (scheduled to begin operations in 2005), and
- the South Valley Corridor light rail project in the Spokane area.

Ferry. Most of the region's ferries operate in the Puget Sound (see map 4-5). Washington State Ferries, a division of the Washington State Department of Transportation, operates the largest ferry fleet in the U.S. In 2001, the fleet consisted of twenty-nine ferries carrying twenty-seven million passengers to twenty different ports-of-call. While the state ferry fleet operates primarily in the Puget Sound, it also includes the Keller Ferry on the Columbia River at the Lincoln-Ferry County line in eastern Washington. A number of other public entities also operate ferry systems in the Puget Sound area. These include Kitsap Transit, Lummi Island Ferry Service, Pierce County Ferry Operations, several seasonal ferry systems, and the Alaska Ferry System, which calls at Bellingham. River ferry systems operate on the lower Columbia River between Cathlamet, Washington, and Westport, Oregon, and at three locations on the Willamette River near Salem and Canby, Oregon.

Intercity Bus. A number of large and small bus companies operate over the region's intercity bus network. Ten intercity carriers, for example, serve Washington, while thirteen serve Oregon. Greyhound Lines is by far the largest carrier, serving all of the region's metropolitan areas and most cities with populations of more than twenty-five thousand outside metropolitan areas. As of spring 2003, Greyhound served about thirty communities in Idaho, eighty-five in Oregon, and fifty-five in Washington. Federal deregulation of the intercity bus industry in 1982 contributed to the pace at which large carriers abandoned services in small communities. The establishment of small bus companies has somewhat compensated for loss of service from the large carriers. Small intercity bus providers generally serve fewer than ten communities although a few provide more extensive services. Some of the intercity carriers also haul packages and

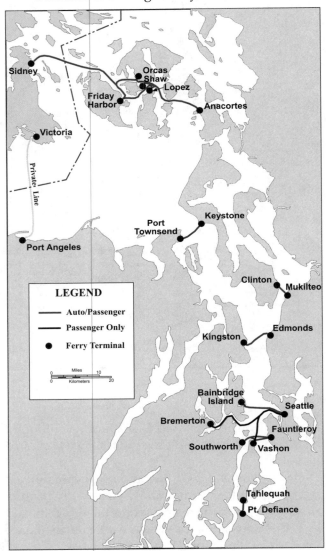

Map 4-5. Washington State Ferry System

other freight. This helps diversify sources of revenue and keep passenger service viable.

Intercity Passenger Rail. Amtrak provides intercity passenger rail service in the region. The Coast Starlight train makes one daily round trip between Los Angeles and Seattle via a route roughly parallel to the I-5 corridor. Amtrak's Empire Builder provides one daily round trip between Chicago and Spokane via northern Idaho. West of Spokane, the Empire Builder provides daily round trip service to and from Seattle via a northern route and to and from Portland via a southern route. The northern route follows Washington State Route 28 and U.S. 2 via Wenatchee and through the 7.8-mile long Cascades Tunnel, the second longest railroad tunnel in the United States. The southern route passes through the Tri-Cities and the Washington side of the Columbia River Gorge. Until 1997, Amtrak also provided service in eastern Oregon and southern Idaho.

Amtrak also runs the Cascades service along the 466-mile Pacific Northwest Rail Corridor between Eugene, Oregon and Vancouver, British Columbia. In 1992, the Federal Railroad Administration designated this corridor as one of five (now eight) high-speed rail corridors nationwide. Since then, Oregon, Washington, and British Columbia have worked with Amtrak and other entities to provide faster, more frequent service. In 2001, an estimated 640,000 passengers rode Amtrak along the corridor, a 150 percent increase from 226,000 in 1993. In early 2003, service on the Cascades route included three round trips daily between Eugene and Portland, four round trips daily between Portland and Seattle, two round trips daily between Seattle and Bellingham, and one round trip daily between Bellingham and Vancouver, British Columbia. Service on the Cascades route is highly dependent on financial support from state governments in Oregon and Washington.

To provide connecting service and build ridership, Amtrak motorcoaches serve numerous locations across the region, including eight in Idaho, thirty-eight in Oregon, and eighteen in Washington as of spring 2003. Private carriers operate the motor-coaches; state or federal funding supports services on some of the routes, helping provide financial stability and build ridership.

Air Passenger. More than 500 private-use and 350 public-use airports are located in the Pacific Northwest, with about 125 public-use airports in Idaho, 100 in Oregon, and 130 in Washington.

Among states nationally, Idaho ranks fourth in the number of public-use airports per capita.

As of spring 2003, regularly scheduled commercial passenger service was available at six airports in Idaho, seven airports in Oregon, and sixteen airports in Washington. Deregulation in the late 1970s, economic recession during the early 1980s, and more recently, high fares and security concerns, have contributed to a decline in air passenger service in some of the region's smaller communities. The loss of a single carrier often means a substantial decline in service.

Despite these challenges, from time to time efforts are made to re-start or begin new services. For example, during the latter half of the 1990s, several small carriers began commercial service in Astoria, Newport, and Corvallis, Oregon. Within a few years of start-up, however, the service had been dis-continued in all three cities.

Seattle-Tacoma International Airport, with 13.2 million enplaned passengers in 2001, is the nation's seventeenth busiest airport. Portland International Airport ranks thirty-third, enplaning just less than half as many passengers as Sea-Tac in 2001. Boise and Spokane have the region's only other airports enplaning more than one million passengers annually.

The Seattle-Tacoma and Portland airports account for more than 80 percent of the region's air passengers. Between 1992 and 2001, the number of enplaned passengers grew by 57 percent regionally, with the Seattle-Tacoma and Portland airports contributing 81 percent of the total increase. Regional totals for 2001 dropped 6 percent from totals in 2000, relecting the nation's soft economy along with travel concerns following the terrorist attacks of September 11, 2001.

Substantial growth in passenger and cargo traffic during the 1990s stretched the capacity of the region's larger airports. Resolving capacity concerns and constraints is a major issue for airport users as well as nearby neighborhoods concerned about adverse impacts from airport expansions expected to be needed in the future.

Transportation Demand Management. According to the National Transportation Demand Management (TDM) and Telework Clearinghouse, TDM is defined as a variety of strategies to influence travel behavior by mode, cost, time, or route in order to reduce the number of vehicles and to provide mobility options.

To help implement TDM strategies, the Washington Legislature passed a commute trip reduction law in 1991. The law requires local governments to develop and implement plans requiring major employers (one hundred or more employees) to reduce single-occupant vehicle commute trips in counties with the greatest automobile-related air pollution and traffic congestion. Commute trip reduction plans are required in all counties with more than 150,000 population, and in cities or towns within these counties containing a major employer. All other jurisdictions have the option, but are not required, to develop such plans.

In Oregon, the state Department of Environmental Quality in 1996 developed a similar commute trip reduction program to achieve and maintain federal ozone standards through the year 2006 in the Portland metropolitan area. The Employee Commute Options Program is authorized by Oregon Administrative Rule and requires employers with more than fifty employees to develop and implement strategies for reducing employee auto commute trips by 10 percent.

Recent estimates show that more than 1,100 employers in Washington and 825 in the Portland area participate in commute trip reduction programs. This is estimated to result in about twenty thousand fewer vehicles in Washington and another twenty thousand fewer vehicles in the Portland area using highways and local roads to and from work on an average weekday.

Congestion pricing, now called value pricing by some observers, has been studied but not implemented in the Pacific Northwest. The regional transportation planning agency (Metro) for the Portland area, however, in November 2000 completed a Traffic Relief Options Study to identify the benefits and costs of peak period pricing options and the possibility of using pricing incentives to reduce traffic congestion. The study authors identified specific roadway segments that may be appropriate for peak period pricing and recommended seeking funds to implement a pilot project.

HOV lanes are an important strategy being pursued to reduce congestion on highways in the Seattle, Tacoma, and Vancouver areas. In general, HOV lanes are intended for usage only by vehicles carrying more than one person, including carpools,

---

Examples of Transportation Demand Strategies

- *Carpooling/vanpooling*
- * *Compressed work weeks*
- *Conngestion pricing*
- *Flexible work hours*
- *High Occupancy Vehicle (HOV) lanes*
- *Mixed use development*
- *Parking management*
- *Staggered work hours*
- *Telework*
- *Trip reduction ordinances*

Source: National Transportation Demand Management and Telework Clearinghouse, "Terminology." Tampa: Center for Urban Transportation Research, University of South Florida, 2000

---

vanpools, and buses. Motorcycles also are allowed to use HOV lanes. About 210 miles of HOV lanes were in operation or under construction in Washington as of 2002, with another 100 miles in the planning stages. The only other HOV lanes in operation were on a 3-mile segment of northbound I-5 in Portland just south of the Oregon-Washington state line.

Efforts to better coordinate transportation and land use policies include encouraging mixed-use zoning along with developing high-density residential and commercial uses near stations along light rail lines or other types of transit routes. Changing single-use zoning to mixed-use zoning is believed to be a strategy for enabling resi-dents to live near workplaces and retail stores, thereby potentially reducing the need for traveling by auto to work or to shop. Various groups have encouraged investments in mixed use, transit-oriented developments (TODs) along light rail lines and other major transit corridors. Tri-Met estimates that $3.0 billion of investment has occurred within walking distance of the light rail lines built in the Portland area.

Parking management strategies include the provision of park-and-ride lots. Users of these facilities typically park their autos and share rides in carpools, vanpools, or public transit. In Washington, approximately 270 park-and-ride lots provide more than 30,000 spaces for commuters and other users. Though fewer in number, park-and-ride lots also are located in a variety of locations in Idaho and Oregon. In the Boise metropolitan area, for example, there are about twenty-five park-and-ride facilities, mostly located in conjunction with local businesses and churches. About 12,600 spaces are available for travelers in Oregon's metropolitan areas.

An emerging TDM strategy is car sharing where, in general, travelers pay a fee each time they use a shared-use vehicle without the costs and responsibilities of ownership. While car sharing is relatively widespread in some parts of Europe, it has developed more slowly in the United States. In 1998, Portland became the first city in the United States to establish a car-sharing program. Seattle followed a year later. As of early 2001, car-sharing services in the Portland and Seattle areas had about seven thousand users with access to 125 cars.

Transportation System Management is similar to TDM in that the intent of both is to more efficiently use the existing transportation system. Intelligent Transportation System (ITS) technologies are among the transportation management system strategies used and planned in the Pacific Northwest. ITS technologies include various types of traveler information systems and vehicle incident detection and response measures. Examples of traveler information systems include:

- Idaho Department of Transportation's (IDOT's) "Ida-Road" internet site on the World Wide Web,
- Oregon Department of Transportation's (ODOT's) "TripCheck" web site,
- WSDOT's "Traveler Information" and "Smart Trek" web sites,
- Tri-Met's "Trip Planner" in the Portland area, and
- RideshareOnline.com in the Puget Sound area.

Incident detection measures include ODOT's "COMET" trucks for helping stranded motorists and clearing debris on heavily traveled highways, especially in the Portland area, and similar incident response teams in Washington.

Issues

Funding for transportation improvements is a major issue in the Pacific Northwest. The region's residents in the late twentieth and early twenty-first century have been reluctant to vote for increased taxes or fees, and have approved ballot measures to reduce existing fees and overturn legislatively authorized increases in fees or taxes. Increases in the usage of alternative fuels and improved fuel economies could lead to further deterioration in the ability to generate adequate revenues based on taxation of fuel consumption. Reluctance to pay for improvements may be a signal that a majority of voters believe too much growth is occurring, at least in some parts of the region. Another possible explanation is that the region's voters believe existing funding is adequate but inefficiently spent.

Worsening transportation conditions adversely affect the region's economy and livability. If mobility and accessibility worsen enough, growth could slow or stop, and residents and businesses may move to other locations where transportation and other conditions are more favorable. Increased reliance on just-in-time manufacturing and e-commerce transactions could lead to even greater concerns about adverse effects from deterioration in transportation infrastructure and increasing congestion, especially congestion that is non-recurring or not predictable.

Environmental concerns will continue to affect the operation of existing and proposed transportation facilities. Increasing numbers of cars and trucks raise concerns about air, water, and noise pollution; similar concerns occur to varying degrees for other freight- and people-moving modes. Reluctance to accommodate transportation improvements likely will grow in areas where new or expanded facilities are perceived as locally unwanted land uses. This will include striving for "environmental justice" in which minority and low-income populations are actively involved in transportation decision-making, and where disproportionately high and adverse social impacts from transportation projects are to be avoided, minimized, or mitigated.

Declining numbers of salmon and other sensitive species may mean less reliance on marine navigation, especially in locations through which threatened or endangered species migrate or where they do or could spawn. Less reliance on marine transportation likely would adversely affect rural economies and mean more reliance on other modes, primarily truck and rail. The presence of other threatened or endangered animal and plant species will continue to affect where new facilities can be built or existing facilities can be expanded.

The ability of the transportation system to accommodate future needs for accessibility and mobility will depend on how the region's residents address funding, environmental, and other issues such as those associated with the need for increased safety and security of travelers and transportation facilities. While resolution of these issues will not be easy, it will become increasingly important to the well-being of residents and businesses in the Pacific Northwest.

Sources

Association of American Railroads. 2003. "Rail Facts and Statistics." Washington, D.C.

Central Puget Sound Regional Transit Authority. 1996. *Sound Move: The 10-Year Regional Transit System Plan.* Seattle.

Elevated Transportation Company. 2003. "Seattle Monorail Project." Seattle.

Greyhound Lines. 2003. "Greyhound Terminal and Agency Information."

Lane Transit District. 2003. "Bus Rapid Transit." Eugene.

Metro. 2000. *Traffic Relief Options Study.* Portland.

Oregon Department of Transportation. 1999. *Freight Moves the Oregon Economy.* Salem.

———. 1999. *Oregon Highway Plan.* Salem.

———. 2002. *Transportation Key Facts.* Salem.

Portland and Western Railroad. 2001. "Home Page." http://members.trainorders.com/dan.sheets/

Quigley, Leo. 2001. "Planning Ahead: Port of Tacoma May Have Important Edge," *Traffic World,* May 20: 31-32.

Sound Transit. 2003. "Sounder Facts." Seattle.

State of Washington. 2000. "Transportation Demand Management." *Revised Code of Washington 70.94.521 to 70.94.551.* Olympia.

Tri-Metropolitan County Transit District. 2001. "Plan Your Trip on Tri-Met." Portland.

———. 2003. "Facts about Tri-Met." Portland.

U.S. Army Corps of Engineers. 2002. "Tonnage for Selected U.S. Ports in 2000." New Orleans: Waterborne Commerce Statistics Center.

———. 2002. *Waterborne Commerce of the United States, 2000.* New Orleans: Waterborne Commerce Statistics Center.

U.S. Department of Commerce. 1999. *1997 Economic Census. Commodity Flow Survey. Idaho.* EC97TCF-ID. Washington, D.C.: Bureau of the Census.

———. 1999. *1997 Economic Census. Commodity Flow Survey. Oregon.* EC97TCF-OR. Washington, D.C.: Bureau of the Census.

———. 1999. *1997 Economic Census. Commodity Flow Survey. Washington.* EC97TCF-WA. Washington, D.C.: Bureau of the Census.

U.S. Department of Transportation. 2000. "Enplanement and All Cargo Data." Washington, D.C.: Federal Aviation Administration.

———. 2003. *Highway Statistics.* Washington, D.C.: Federal Highway Administration.

Washington Public Ports Association, *Port Directory,* 2003. Olympia.

Washington State Department of Transportation. 1996. *Public Transportation and Intercity Rail Passenger Plan for Washington State, 1997-2016.* Olympia.

———. 2002. *Key Facts: A Summary of Transportation Information for Washington State.* Olympia.

Chapter 5
Landforms and Geology
Charles L. Rosenfeld

The Pacific Northwest comprises five physiographic provinces, which in turn are subdivided into one or more terranes as shown in map 5-1. The following is a brief description of the major physiographic features of each province.

The Pacific Border Province

The Pacific Border Province includes the Klamath-Siskiyou terrane, Coast Range, Olympic Mountains, and Willamette-Puget Lowlands.

The Klamath Mountains section is defined on a partially geologic and partially topographic basis. The steep topography, dense vegetation, and structural complexity have produced a confusing geologic record. Metamorphic recrystallization masks much of the deposition history of the ancient sedimentary and volcanic strata of the region. This section has been folded, uplifted a few thousand feet, and dissected by erosion. Topographically, these

mountains merge with the younger Coast Range to the north and with the southern end of the Cascade Range.

The Coast Range of Oregon and Washington consists of moderately folded marine tuffaceous sandstones and shales together with basaltic volcanic rocks and related intrusives. These also have been uplifted 1,000-2,000 feet or more, and then eroded by streams to form rounded mountains of moderate relief. Resistant igneous rocks account for certain summits and for several capes projecting seaward. Sea terraces, sand dunes, and other shore features occupy narrow strips along the coast. Drowned valleys provide many harbors and the drowned lower course of the Columbia River offers a route through the Coast Range.

The Olympic Mountains consist of a mass of folded and metamorphosed rocks eroded into sharp, steep-sided ridges standing 4,000-8,000 feet above sea level. The highest peaks bear perpetual snow-

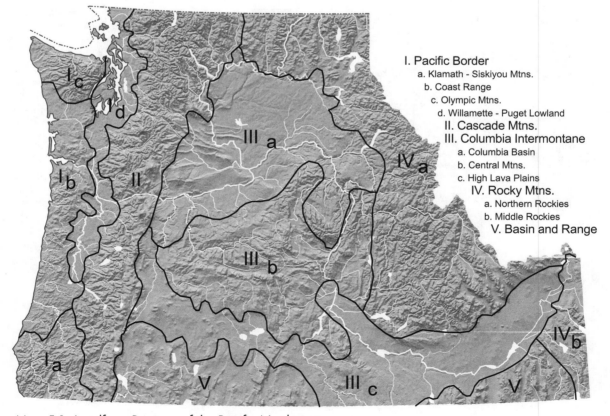

I. Pacific Border
    a. Klamath - Siskiyou Mtns.
    b. Coast Range
    c. Olympic Mtns.
    d. Willamette - Puget Lowland
II. Cascade Mtns.
III. Columbia Intermontane
    a. Columbia Basin
    b. Central Mtns.
    c. High Lava Plains
IV. Rocky Mtns.
    a. Northern Rockies
    b. Middle Rockies
V. Basin and Range

Map 5-1. Landform Regions of the Pacific Northwest

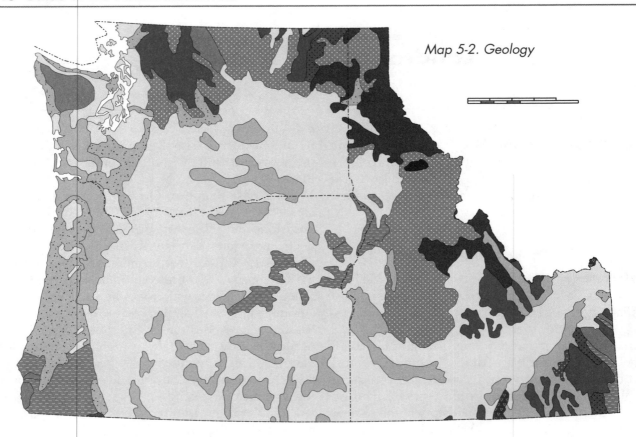

Map 5-2. Geology

Sedimentary Rocks

Quaternary: Recent and Pleistocene

Upper Tertiary: Pliocene and Miocene including Recent and Pleistocene

Lower Tertiary: Oligocene, Eocene, and Paleocene

Cretaceous: in parts of Rocky Mountains includes Jurassic and Triassic

Jurassic and Triassic

Upper Paleozoic: Permian, Pennsylvanian, and Mississipian; parts of Rocky Mountains are middle and lower Paleozoic

Middle Paleozoic: Devonian and Silurian

Lower Paleozoic: Ordovician and Cambrian

Younger Precambrian

Older Precambrian: Metamorphic and igneous rocks

Volcanic Rocks

Quaternary and Tertiary: includes small areas of intrusive rocks

Intrusive Rocks

Lower Tertiary and Mesozoic: chiefly granitic rocks

banks and several small glaciers. The mountains were severely glaciated during the ice age.

The Willamette and Cowlitz Lowlands are primarily stream valleys eroded to low elevations in belts of relatively nonresistant tilted or folded Tertiary rocks (see map 5-2). Resistant rocks locally form hills and watergaps. Both valleys contain alluvial terraces. The Puget Lowland, eroded by streams and Pleistocene glaciers, is a partially drowned system of valleys. Bordering Puget Sound are hummocky plains of till and fairly smooth sheets of glaciofluvial gravel.

The Cascade Mountains

The Cascade Mountains of Oregon and the southern half of Washington are a broad upwarp composed of (1) underlying layers of early Tertiary tuffs, breccias, lavas, and mudflows, exposed in the Columbia River Gorge and other deep valleys; (2) a thick middle section of Tertiary basalts that form the deeply eroded Western Cascades; and (3) an upper section of Tertiary and Quaternary andesites and basalts that form the less dissected High Cascades lava platform, which is generally 15-25 miles wide and 4,000-6,000 feet high along the crest of the range. Crowning the range are a number of well-known snow-capped volcanic peaks in various stages of dissection— Mount Rainier, Mount St. Helens, Mount Adams, Mount Hood, Mount Jefferson, Three Sisters, Mount McLoughlin, and others. Crater Lake occupies a caldera which resulted from the eruptive collapse of the summit of Mount Mazama about 6,600 years ago.

The northern half of the Cascade Range of Washington is a dissected upland underlain mainly by upper Paleozoic sediments that have been folded, metamorphosed, and intruded by granites with ridges rising to elevations of 6,000-8,000 feet. Above them rise several volcanic cones (Mount Baker and Glacier Peak). The northern Cascades were extensively glaciated, and the mountains now harbor many small glaciers.

The Columbia Intermontane Province

The Columbia Intermontane Province, often inappropriately called the Columbia Plateau, includes the Columbia Basin, Central Mountains, Harney High Lava Plains, Malheur-Owyhee Upland, and Snake River Lava Plain.

The Columbia Basin is an irregular structural and topographic basin underlain by Tertiary basalt flows that have been depressed below sea level in the Pasco area and upwarped on the flanks of the surrounding mountains. Fluvial, lacustrine, eolian, and glacial sediments overlie much of the basalt, and locally form terraces or other subordinate physiographic features.

The portion in north central Oregon is partly a plateau incised by canyons and partly a low plain of sand and gravel. The portion in south central Washington comprises a series of anticlinal ridges (partly faulted) and synclinal valleys. The outstanding features include Horse Heaven Hills, Yakima Valley, Saddle Mountain, Kittitas Valley, and the Wenatchee Mountains-Frenchman Hill. The

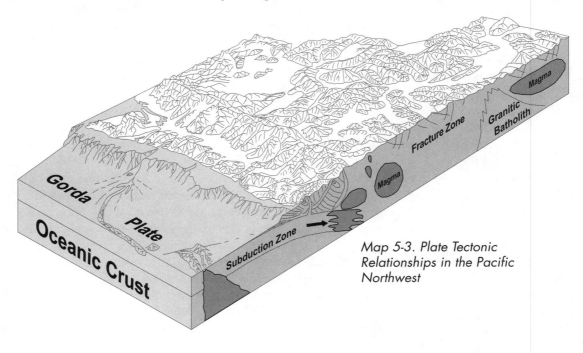

Map 5-3. Plate Tectonic Relationships in the Pacific Northwest

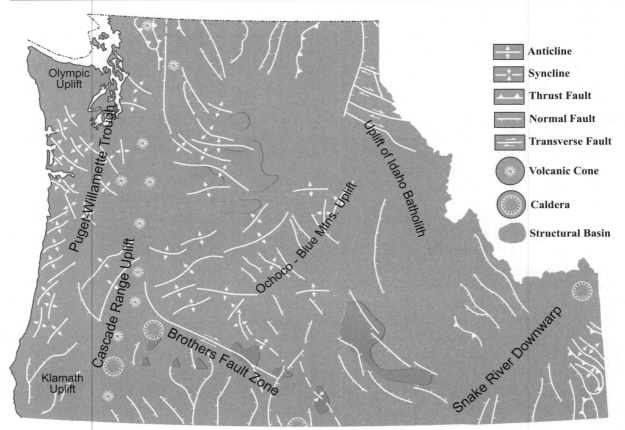

Map 5-4. Major Tectonic Features

Columbia and Yakima rivers cross several of these ridges, forming watergaps. Most of the remainder is a plateau with steeply incised stream valleys. Noteworthy are the Waterville Plateau, Quincy Basin (alluvium filled), Palouse Hills (loess covered), and Tristate Upland (on the southeast). The northern edge of the plateau was glaciated and the channeled scablands reflect the drainage ways of ice-age floods. The Grand Coulee is the most spectacular of these channels.

The Blue Mountains comprise a complex group of folded and faulted uplifts, including the Seven Devils, Wallowa, Elkhorn, Greenhorn, Aldrich, and Ochoco mountains. They rise 2,000-5,000 feet above their surroundings and reach elevations of 6,000-10,000 feet. They include various rocks of differing resistance to erosion. Because of orographic rainfall, the mountains are well dissected. The higher portions, especially the Wallowa mountains, were glaciated. Alluvium-filled fault troughs occur within the mountains, as at La Grande, Oregon.

The Harney High Lava Plains are situated between the Central Mountains, the Basin and Range area, the Cascade Mountains, and the Malheur-Owyhee Upland. They are mainly a flattish tract of recent lavas, ranging in elevation generally from

about 4,000-5,000 feet. The surface is lower near the Deschutes River canyon, the only major stream in the area. Volcanoes are abundant in the western portion. Chief among them is Newberry Volcano (Paulina Mountain), with its breached caldera. Hundreds of faults, mostly of small throw, are present; they become more pronounced southward toward the Basin and Range Province.

The Malheur-Owyhee Upland occupies parts of southeastern Oregon and southwestern Idaho. It is a partly dissected, warped plateau, mostly 4,000-8,000 feet high and underlain mainly by Cenozoic lava flows, tuffs, and lakebeds. Most of the area is poorly mapped and little studied. The Owyhee River and its tributaries drain much of the area in deeply incised canyons.

The Snake River Lava Plain is an arcuate downwarp 30 to 60 miles wide and about 400 miles long. It descends gently from an elevation of about 6,000 feet above sea level at its east end to about 2,200 feet on the west. The eastern part is a more or less silt-covered recent lava plain, almost featureless except for low lava domes and occasional cinder cones. Very young lavas occur at Craters of the Moon, Hell's Half Acre, and elsewhere. The western part of the plain is underlain by lakebeds and alluvium as well as

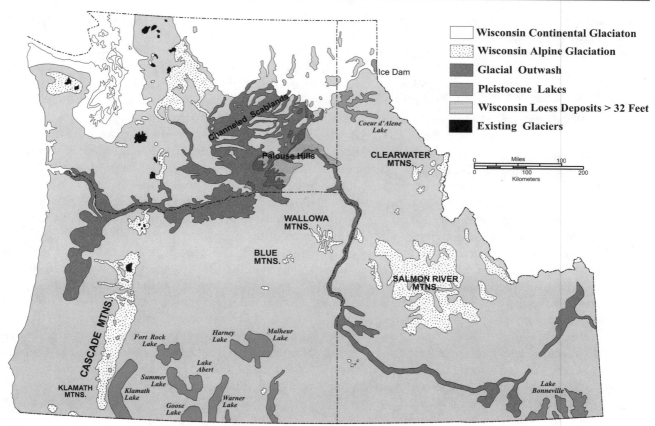

Map 5-5. Glacial and Periglacial Features

lava, and is partly dissected to terraces, box canyons, and open valleys.

The Rocky Mountains Province

The Northern Rocky Mountains Province includes parts of northeastern Washington, northern and central Idaho, and western Montana. It is characterized by high mountain ridges and deep intermontane valleys eroded from rocks of moderately complex structure. Where the rocks have been folded and faulted, the ridges are aligned as in the Selkirk ranges. Some valleys (e.g., Bitterroot and Purcell) are 10 to 20 miles wide and favor settlement and transportation. The mountains of central Idaho, developed by erosion of massive granite rocks (the Idaho batholith), are irregular and resist exploration and settlement.

Most of the province drains into the Columbia River and its tributaries, although the eastern part outside the Pacific Northwest drains into the headwaters of the Missouri River system. Although much of this section is well dissected, Pleistocene glaciation has produced some of North America's most spectacular mountain scenery.

A part of the Middle Rocky Mountains section extends into southeastern Idaho, where northerly to northwesterly trending mountain ridges and valleys have eroded from folded, thrust-faulted, or tilted rocks. The valleys are about 6,000 feet above sea level, and the ridges reach 2,000-4,000 feet higher. Block faulting, characteristic of the Basin and Range Province, extends into this area also; therefore, the boundary is somewhat arbitrary.

The Basin and Range Province

The northern edge of the Great Basin section of the Basin and Range Province extends into south central Oregon and into southern Idaho. The part in Idaho consists of a series of tilted fault blocks and parallel stream valleys developed in a region of folded rocks. By contrast, the part in Oregon is a high lava plain interrupted by fault block mountains and by fault troughs. Representative of the high-standing blocks are Steens Mountain, Hart Mountain, Abert Rim, and Winter Ridge. Typical fault troughs are Alvord Basin, Warner Valley, and the basins of Abert, Summer, Goose, and Klamath lakes. The western part of this province is covered by the ash and pumice of the Mount Mazama and Mount Newberry eruptions, which greatly alter the appearance, drainage, and vegetation of the area. The presence of so many young faults attests to the recency of tectonic activity in the region, as do the numerous hot springs and geothermal areas.

The Tectonic Setting of the Pacific Northwest

The geologic deformation of the earth's crust has undergone radical re-examination in light of discoveries linking such movement with sea-floor spreading and continental drift, which have been combined to form a body of theory called plate tectonics. Submarine volcanic activity produces new sea-floor material, forcing older oceanic crust to spread laterally away from the activity. In some cases, the sea floor is thrust beneath the margins of a continent, back into the mantle of the earth. This process is called subduction. At present many earth scientists believe such a process is active in the Pacific Northwest; however, it appears to be a complex and rather special case.

The digrams of plate tectonic relationships in maps 5-3 and 5-4 illustrate the concept of subduction as applied to this region. The movement of the oceanic Gorda Plate has been indicated by seismic and paleomagnetic evidence, providing a source of tectonic stress and material. This results in the continued volcanic activity of the Cascades and the moderate seismic activity of the region. The 1980 eruption of Mount St. Helens generated considerable scientific inquiry into the mechanisms of Cascade volcanism and its relation to plate tectonics. The creation of the Cascades Volcanoes Observatory and the regional seismic network promise to yield new insights into the tectonic origins of the region.

Glacial Features

The complexity of the landscape history of the Pacific Northwest is well illustrated by the sequence and variety of landforms related to the Pleistocene ice ages. Lobes of ice pushed southward from the Cordilleran ice in western Canada, forcing their way along river valleys and lowland areas (see map 5-5) Although we have identified several periods of glaciation during the Pleistocene, the complexity of glacial activity within the region has masked any simple sequence. For example, the large lobes were part of a continental ice sheet of great thickness which advanced by pressure flow, whereas the local glaciers in the mountains contained much less ice and moved down their valleys by gravity. The mechanics and volume of these different glacial systems indicate that they responded differently to

changes in climate, and their respective advances were not necessarily synchronous.

Glacial features also include all the modifications brought about by glacial meltwater and associated climatic changes. These effects include glacially diverted rivers, large inland lakes, and the effects of frozen ground upon the landscape. Among the most dramatic effects were the sequence of mammoth floods which formed the Channeled Scablands of eastern Washington. Glacial Lake Missoula formed when the Clark Fork of the Columbia River was dammed by a Cordilleran ice lobe. When the lobe began to melt, the ice dam burst, releasing up to 50 cubic miles of water which rushed westward over the Columbia Plateau near Spokane. As the floods raged over the plateau, the water ripped off the soil cover and cut channels into the basalt bedrock.

Other features include the shorelines of lakes that were greatly expanded during the wetter, cooler glacial periods of the Pleistocene. Some of these lakes have dried up completely, while others, like Summer Lake and Goose Lake in Oregon, remain as small remnants of their former extent.

Geologic Hazards

The dynamic landscapes of the Pacific Northwest have been influenced by catastrophic geologic events throughout earth history. Fortunately, few of these events have occurred during the period of intensive human occupation. These northwest cataclysms have included the explosive eruption of Mount Mazama that created Crater Lake about eight thousand years ago, the massive Missoula floods which scoured the northwest over twenty thousand years ago, and massive undersea earthquakes which have inundated the coastline with tsunamis at three to five hundred year intervals. The fact that such events were not recorded by European settlers over the past two hundred years does not mean that similar events will not occur in the future.

Natural processes become hazards when populations and resources are vulnerable to damage or displacement by such occurrences.

Mount St. Helens' eruptive behavior in 1980 captured the attention of many citizens of the Pacific Northwest. Fortunately, the monitoring of eruptive precursors, and the steps taken to isolate the at-risk population, reduced the death toll, despite billions of dollars in damages. Map 5-6 shows the distribution of potential risk factors directly related to volcanic events, based upon the geologic history and tectonic behavior of the region. Lava flows, hot ash

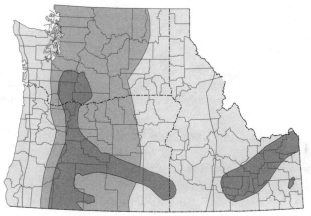

Map 5-6. Lava Flow and Ashfall Hazard

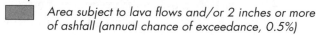 Area subject to lava flows and/or 2 inches or more of ashfall (annual chance of exceedance, 0.5%)

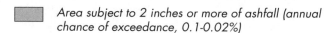 Area subject to 2 inches or more of ashfall (annual chance of exceedance, 0.1-0.02%)

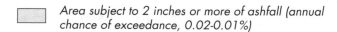 Area subject to 2 inches or more of ashfall (annual chance of exceedance, 0.02-0.01%)

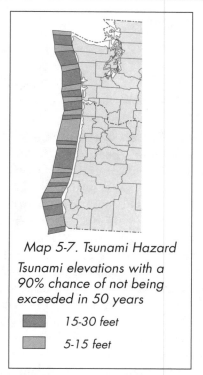

Map 5-7. Tsunami Hazard

Tsunami elevations with a 90% chance of not being exceeded in 50 years

15-30 feet

5-15 feet

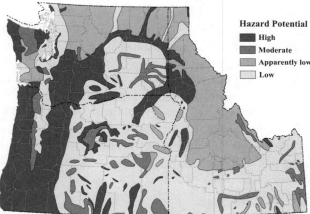

Hazard Potential
High
Moderate
Apparently low
Low

Map 5-8. Landslide and Debris Flow Hazard

clouds, and heavy ashfall are restricted to the volcanic Cascade Range, the Brothers Fault Zone and the Snake River Plain, where geologically recent eruptions have occurred. However, mud flows in river valleys and ashfall on cities, watersheds, and agricultural areas could result in significant losses throughout large areas of the region.

The Pacific coast has sustained significant damage from tsunami flooding in the past. The 1964 Alaska earthquake caused damage and deaths in the region, but was minor compared to the effects of past Magnitude 9+ events that resulted from subduction subduction zone earthquakes at three to five hundred year intervals over the past thirty-five hundred years. Evidence indicates that the last of these large events occurred in 1700, thus leaving the possibility that a similar event could occur within the next century. Factors such as proximity to the subduction boundary, off-shore bathymetry, and coastal landforms affect the estimated height of wave run-up. Map 5-7 shows areas of high tsunami run-up potential, but other factors such as soil stability and saturation will also influence damage from ground shaking.

Steep slopes, intense precipitation and deep soils are all factors that affect the potential for landslide damage. Map 5-8 illustrates the frequency of past landslides throughout the region. Human activity, such as construction and forestry, also influences the probability of such events.

Chapter 6

Land Use

Philip L. Jackson

The geography of land use in the Pacific Northwest has evolved over time in response to location, technology, economy and society. The regional settlement patterns we observe today reflect a pragmatic adherence to classic location and resource use principles, focusing on the attributes of the land necessary for commodity procurement, trade, transportation, housing and communication. However, a striking factor in the evolution of land use in the Pacific Northwest, in contrast to the eastern United States, is the status of land ownership: the majority of land is publicly managed, and consequently land use on millions of acres is determined by government management plans rather than by individual land owners. The regional land base of the Pacific Northwest is 157.1 million acres; 83.4 million acres, roughly 53 percent of the land, is under federal, state, and local management; 73.7 million acres, (47 percent), is privately owned (tables 6-1 and 6-2). A legacy of public land management and public access to enormous tracts of forests and rangelands dates from the federal land policies of the late nineteenth and early twentieth centuries. Millions of acres of timber and rangelands were reserved in the pubic interest under federal conservation and preservation policies that established thirty-one national forests, four national parks, and numerous federal rangelands and wildlife refuges. During the late twentieth century, new management designations added national recreation areas, national monuments, national historic sites and parks, national scenic areas, and wilderness areas.

Land Use/Land Cover Types

The map of land use/land cover types on page 58 (map 6-3) depicts the regional distribution of land surface characteristics, including vegetation cover and settlement patterns. Land cover patterns reflect the Pacific Northwest's unique geographic com-bination of climate, topography, geology, soils, and the availability of surface and ground water. Generalized land cover types are derived from digital analysis of year 2000 satellite AVHRR (advanced very high resolution radiometer) data. The most extensive land cover type observed is evergreen forest, found at moderate elevations throughout the Coast Ranges, Cascades, Blue-Ochoco-Wallowa Mountains, and Rocky Mountains. The arid interior is dominated by grasslands and shrub lands from the Columbia Basin on the north, through the central High Lava Plateaus, and southeast into the Snake River Plain. Cropland and pasture, both dryland and irrigated, cover the Willamette, Umpqua and Rogue valleys of western Oregon, the three-state Columbia Basin and Palouse Hills region, the Snake River Plain and its eastern Idaho tributary valleys. The vast expanse of rural lands dominates geographic scale in the Pacific Northwest, but urban land use is highly visible on AVHRR imagery, especially the metropolitan regions of Seattle and Portland and their associated north-south urban settlement corridors. While urban land cover occurs with much less frequency in the eastern portion of the region, the contrasts are easily discernable for Spokane, Tri-Cities, Boise, and Twin Falls-Pocatello.

Table 6-1. Public Land Ownership

	Oregon		Washington		Idaho	
	acres	%	acres	%	acres	%
Owned by federal government	31,982,600	51.9	12,952,900	30.4	32,519,000	61.5
Owned by state government	1,662,059	2.7	2,461,850	5.6	2,629,633	4.9
Total land area	61,557,760	100.0	42,604,800	100.0	52,913,280	100.0

Sources: *Washington County Yearbook*, 1999; *County Profiles of Idaho*, Idaho Department of Commerce, 2000; *Oregon Blue Book*, 1999-2000.

Land Use Policy

Historic land use policies of the federal government provided settlers of largely European descent the opportunity to claim rich farmlands in the Oregon Territory. Throughout the region, but primarily in central Oregon, eastern Washington, and southern Idaho, land was also reserved by treaty for Native Americans. With Congressional passage of the Donation Lands Act of 1850, settlers were assured title to millions of acres of farmlands in the Willamette Valley and Puget Lowlands. Subsequent land acts which included federal homestead, timber, stock raising, reclamation, and desert land settlement acts, transferred millions of acres of forest and rangelands across the region, from public to private ownership. The "Inland Empire" of the Columbia Basin and the Palouse Hills region was settled for grain farming, ranching and forestry. Farming, mining, ranching, and forestry land uses evolved in the mountains and valleys of northwestern Idaho, and in the eastern Snake River Plain. To support the development of intensive land use, a regional infrastructure of local irrigation associations and

power cooperatives was established. Rail, water, and highway transportation corridors were developed to provide passage across the Rocky Mountains to the Pacific. These linkages effectively connected the resource-rich regions of the Snake River Plain, the Columbia Basin and the Willamette Valley and Puget Lowland. The establishment of the Bonneville Power Administration in the early 1930s expanded land use opportunities throughout the Pacific Northwest by greatly improving rural electrification and assuring low-cost power supplies for growing urban, industrial and agricultural uses.

From 1850 to 1934 the United States General Land Office conducted the legal transfer of millions of acres of public domain lands to individuals. By the end of the nineteenth century, much of the land settlement activity shifted to the semi-arid and arid lands under stock raising, desert land entry, and arid-land reclamation policies. Outside the reclamation projects, settlement failure rates were high, and federal land resource studies in the early 1930s concluded that much of the land in the arid region was simply too dry, rugged, and remote, and could not support sustained agricultural settlement. To

Table 6-2. Land Ownership by Federal Agencies (in acres)

	Oregon	Washington	Idaho
Department of Agriculture			
Forest Service	14,687,631	8,902,434	20,743,088
O&C Lands	492,533	–	–
Other agencies	14,607	394	32,462
Department of Commerce	9	123	–
Department of Energy	4,889	370,,872	571,744
Environmental Protection Agency	21	18	–
General Services Administration	377	372	175
Department of Health, Education & Welfare	2	–	–
Department of the Interior			
Bureau of Indian Affairs	401	102	687,272
Bureau of Land Management	13,579,528	370,110	11,996,646
O&C Lands	2,132,940	–	–
Bureau of Mines	44	21	–
Bureau of Reclamation	66,308	100,818	283,391
Fish & Wildlife Service	479,712	128,713	140,908
National Park Service	169,372	1,811,070	97,508
Department of Justice	–	4,456	4
Department of Labor	801	–	–
Department of Transportation	1,066	1,067	624
U.S. Postal Service	71	140	10
Veterans Administration	614	255	67
Department of Defense	176,267	472,574	133,301
Total	31,982,600	12,952,900	32,519,000

Source: *Public Land Statistics*, Bureau of Land Management, 2000, Volume 185.
Note: Figures may vary from Census, other sources, and other tables in this *Atlas* due to differences in definitions and data-gathering methods.

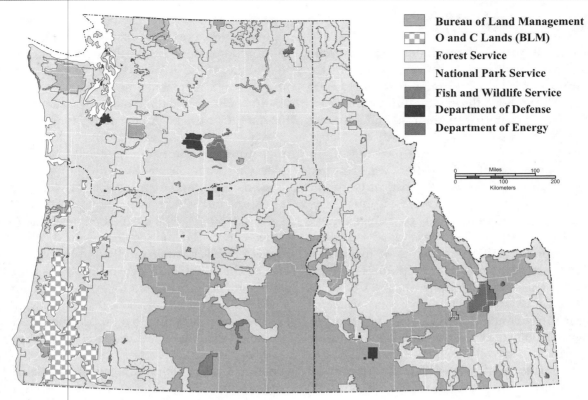

Bureau of Land Management
O and C Lands (BLM)
Forest Service
National Park Service
Fish and Wildlife Service
Department of Defense
Department of Energy

Map 6-1. Land Under Federal Management

prevent overgrazing and consequent landscape deterioration due to land clearing and abandonment, Congress authorized the retention and management of these lands by the Soil Conservation Service, and later by the Bureau of Land Management. Except for the 1954 Veteran's Lottery in Idaho, the passage of the 1934 Taylor Grazing Act largely signaled the end of public land settlement in the Pacific Northwest. As a result largely of federal land use policies that attempted to organize unsettled public domain lands for conservation purposes, federal and state governments became the majority land holders, managing nearly 54 percent of the total land base for sustainable resource use, defense, and environmental, scenic, and recreational purposes (map 6-1).

Patterns of private land ownership across the region strongly reflect the selection of land parcels on the basis of economic opportunity, and potential for financial profit. Over time, as society and technology have evolved, amenity, recreation, and other personal location values have somewhat altered the selection criteria of the private land market. Land market forces and employment opportunities have greatly increased the demand for land close to the region's major urban centers. Commuting by auto and public transportation has extended urban residential land use, merging smaller, formerly rural communities into the larger metropolitan realms of Seattle, Portland, Boise, Salem, Eugene, and Spokane.

Present-day Land Use

The scenic beauty of the Pacific Northwest has attracted electronics and communications corporations, business and professional organizations and large numbers of retirees from adjacent states who seek a more rural lifestyle but demand urban services close by. The demand for rural amenity land has resulted in the conversion of forest and farm resource lands to residential and commercial developments. During the mid-1990s developed lands (urban and transportation uses), increased by 12.1 percent in the Pacific Northwest. The largest relative percentage increases for this period were in Washington with 13.2 percent and Idaho with 13.9 percent (table 6-3). Some of the region's highest-quality agricultural soils, including prime farmlands, were converted to developed uses during the period. In Washington, 10.3 percent of prime farmland, largely used for pasture, was converted from 1992 to 1997, and in Oregon 5.8 percent was lost to urbanization.. In Idaho, the largest percentage of prime farmland conversion occurred on high-quality croplands, at 2.6 percent (table 6-4).

As a percentage of total land area, urban uses make up only 2.3 percent (1.9 million acres) of the regional land base. As a percentage of privately-owned land, urban and developed lands constitute 5.6 percent of Oregon, 5.3 percent of Idaho, and 6.8 percent of Washington. The distribution of large urban areas is spatially biased to areas favored by locational advantages relative to transportation, commerce, industry, technology, and commodity production. The largest concentrations of high-density settlements are found west of the Cascade Range in Washington's Puget Sound Lowland and in Oregon's Willamette Valley. Idaho's Boise Valley in the middle Snake River Plain and the Spokane metro area in far eastern Washington represent smaller but significant contiguous concentrations of high-density settlement.

Large areas of the Pacific Northwest remain unsettled or at very low settlement densities. Forest lands cover nearly 47 percent, (73.5 million acres), of the Pacific Northwest, with commercial forest management representing the largest use of these lands (see table 6-5). The U.S. Forest Service is responsible for managing 46 percent of the forest lands, the federal Bureau of Land Management oversees about 5 percent, and state governments manage 6 percent of forest lands. Large timber corporations own and manage nearly 20 percent of the commercial forests, particularly in the highest timber-producing regions of western Oregon and Washington. Smaller timber corporations and individual farm and forest owners manage 18

Orchard lands in the Hood River Valley. (Photo by Philip L. Jackson)

Table 6-3. Land Use Change, 1992-1997			
	Federal Lands	Developed Lands	Rural Nonfederal Lands
Pacific Northwest			
1992	76,678,200	36,056,000	76,652,400
1997	76,747,100	40,427,200	75,984,000
Change	+0.1%	+12.1%	-0.9%
Oregon			
1992	31,275,400	1,118,400	29,109,000
1997	31,260,400	1,222,300	28,858,100
Change	-0.05%	+9.3%	-0.9%
Washington			
1992	11,921,900	1,824,200	28,750,400
1997	11,923,400	2,065,000	28,508,200
Change	0.01%	+13.2%	-0.8%
Idaho			
1992	33,480,900	663,000	18,793,000
1997	33,563,300	754,900	18, 617,700
Change	+0.2%	+13.9%	-0.9%

Source: Summary Report, 1997 *National Resources Inventory*, Statistical Bulletin, USDA, Natural Resources Conservation Service, 1999

percent of the commercial timberland. Native American tribal corporations own approximately 3.5 percent of the region's forest lands.

Rangelands, used for stock grazing and wildlife habitat, consist of sub-humid grasslands and desert shrublands. At 56.8 million acres, rangelands constitute the second largest use of land in the Pacific Northwest. Fifty-four percent of these lands are administered by the BLM as large tract pastures, predominantly in central and southeast Oregon and in southern Idaho.

Agricultural lands used for cropping constitute over 25.3 million acres, or 24 percent of the non-federal lands in the region. Dry-land crops are grown on 18.5 million acres, and 6.8 million acres are irrigated. A greater percentage of total cropland is irrigated in Idaho (37 percent) than in either Washington (18 percent) or Oregon (24 percent).

Land Capability and Prime Farmlands

"Land Capability" is a classification system used by the Natural Resources Conservation Service (NRCS) to rate soil suitability for cultivated agricultural use. The classification is not based on inherent soil productivity, but rather on the potential for erosion from continued use. The classification is often used

as a proxy for high-quality farmland because soils with low erosion potential can be intensively farmed. Classes I—IV have the fewest limitations and are generally considered high-quality farmland. Classes V and greater are generally not well suited to crop agriculture due to higher erosion potential. The greatest amount of land in the Pacific Northwest is Class VI or greater, unsuitable for cultivation, but those suited to cultivation are extensive and well-distributed across the region (map 6-2).

As might be expected, the region's "prime farmland", land with the best combination of climate, slope, and soil attributes, is heavily utilized for cropping. More than two-thirds of the nine million acres classed as prime farmland is intensively cropped; the remaining 2.2 million acres is in pasture, rangeland, and forest uses. Nearly one-half million acres classified as prime farmland is in urban or developed use. During the most recent ten-year period, the regional average rate of prime farmland conversion to built-up uses amounted to 7,500 acres per year. The conversion of prime farmland reflects the strong economic demand for residential, commercial, and industrial land use, particularly in the Puget Lowland and the Willamette Valley. Washington leads the region in prime farmland conversion, at nearly 9,200 acres per year.

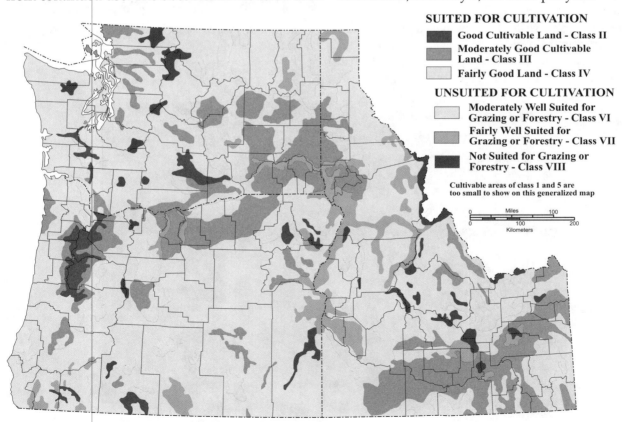

Map 6-2. Land Capability Classes

Table 6-4. Prime Farmland by Land Cover/Use, 1992-1997

	Crop	Pasture	Range	Forest	Minor	Totals
Pacific Northwest						
1992	6,398,400	1,171,300	334,100	802,400	187,000	8,893,200
1997	6,280,800	1,101,900	343,400	791,500	222,400	8,740,000
Change	-1.8%	-5.9%	+2.8%	-1.4%	+18.9%	-1.7%
Oregon						
1992	2,207,100	579,600	253,300	267,000	77,400	3,384,400
1997	2,171,000	545,700	252,400	257,000	100,500	3,327,000
Change	-1.6%	-5.8%	-0.4%	-3.6%	+29.8%	-1.7%
Washington						
1992	1,299,800	364,600	25,800	507,500	84,802	2,282,500
1997	1,293	327,100	28,000	503,202	95,800	2,247,100
Change	+0.5%	-10.3%	+8.5%	-0.8%	+13.0%	-1.6%
Idaho						
1992	2,891,500	227,100	55,000	27,900	24,802	3,226,300
1997	2,816,800	229,100	63,000	30,900	26,100	3,165,900
Change	-2.6%	+0.9%	+14.5%	+10.8%	+5.2%	-1.9%

Source: Summary Report, 1997 *National Resources Inventory*, Statistical Bulletin, USDA, Natural Resources Conservation Service, 1999

Table 6-5. Land Use in the Pacific Northwest

	Pacific Northwest		Oregon		Washington		Idaho	
	acres	%	acres	%	acres	%	acres	%
Non-federal lands								
Cropland	15,935,100	19.8	3,760,700	12.8	6,656,100	19.7	5,517,300	27.8
Irrigated land	9,031,100	10.9	2,082,200	7.1	4,877,200	14.5	2,071,700	27.8
Forest land	29,415,100	35.4	12.642,800		42.912,824,500		38.1	
3,947,800	19.9							
Pasture	3,257,000	3.9	482,600	1.6	1,420,500	4.2	1,353,900	6.8
Rangeland	21,643,700	26.0	9,286,300	31.5	5,856,900	17.4	6,500,500	32.7
Developed land (urban and transportation)	3,764,000	4.5	1,222,300	4.2	2,065,000	6.1	476,700	2.4
Total	83,045,000*	100	29,476,900	100	33,700,200	100	19,867,900	100
Federal lands								
Commercial forest land	28,587,000	36.9	13,811,000	43.2	5,214,000	40.2	9,562,000	29.4
Other forest land	16,244,700	21.1	4,866,900	15.3	4,260,300	32.9	7,177,500	29.4
Rangeland	30,485,800	39.3	13,135,800	41.0	1,667,600	12.9	15,682,400	48.2
National parks	2,077,000	2.7	169,372	0.5	1,811,000	14.0	97,508	0.3
Total	77,454,500	100	31,982,600	100	12,952,900	100	32,519,000	100

*This total includes state lands

Sources: Summary report, 1997, *National Resources Inventory*, USDA Natural Resources Conservation Service, updated 2000; *Forest Resource Facts*, USDA Forest Service, www.fs.fed.us/gov 2002; Public Land Statistics, USDI Bureau of Land Management, www.or.blm.gov 2002.

Note: Figures may vary from census, other sources, and other tabbles in this *Atlas* due to differences in definitions and data-gathering methods.

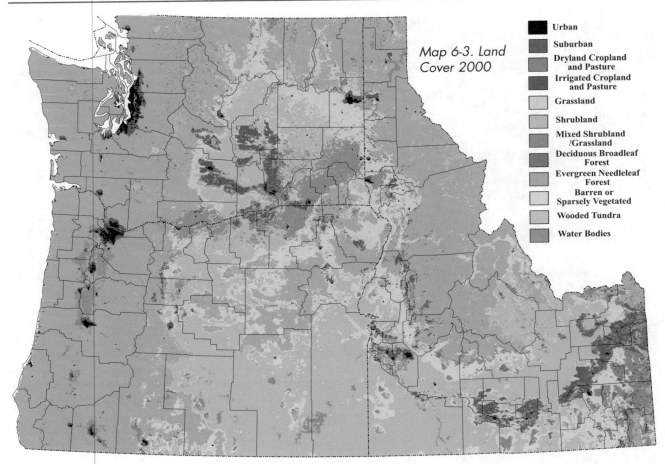

Map 6-3. Land Cover 2000

■	Urban
■	Suburban
■	Dryland Cropland and Pasture
■	Irrigated Cropland and Pasture
▫	Grassland
▫	Shrubland
▫	Mixed Shrubland /Grassland
▫	Deciduous Broadleaf Forest
▫	Evergreen Needleleaf Forest
▫	Barren or Sparsely Vegetated
▫	Wooded Tundra
■	Water Bodies

The people of the Pacific Northwest take great pride in the "livability" of the region. No matter how "livability" is defined, the term draws significantly on the natural amenities and resource values of the land. Throughout the region, there is a strong belief in private property ownership rights and for the responsible use of the land. In Oregon and Washington public concern over the rapid conversion of prime farmlands, forests, shore lands and wetlands has resulted in state legislation to regulate the use of private land to achieve environmental and resource goals. Oregon's statewide land use program is one of the most comprehensive in the nation, seeking to maintain a rational balance between conservation and development. The program focuses on restricting the spread of urban uses into surrounding farm and forest land by creating exclusive farm and forest zoning, establishing urban growth boundaries around cities, coordinating city and county planning policies, and legislating farm property tax incentives and right-to-farm laws. Washington has enacted growth-management legislation, which requires rapid growth counties to enact land use regulations to protect resource and environmentally sensitive lands, and to designate specialized intensive development zones. While Idaho has experienced relatively less demand for development of rural resource lands, growth management as a planning tool is practiced in rapid growth areas such as the Boise Valley, the Coeur d'Alene-Spokane I-90 corridor, and the Sun Valley winter recreation area.

Sources

County Profiles of Idaho. 2000. Boise: Idaho Department of Commerce.

Forest Statistics of the United States. W.B. Smith, J. Faulkner, D. Powell. 1994. GTR-NC 168. USDA, Forest Service.

Land Ownership Statistics. 2002. USDI. Bureau of Land Management. Web pages: http://www.id.blm.gov and www.id.blm.gov.

Oregon Blue Book. 1999-2000. Salem: Oregon State Archives.

Public Land Statistics. 2000. USDI. Bureau of Land Management

State of the Land. 1997 National Resources Inventory (Updated 2000). USDA, Natural Resources Conservation Service.

Summary Report, Statistical Bulletin 185, 1997 National Resources Inventory. USDA, Natural Resources Conservation Service, 1999.

Washington State Yearbook. 2001. Sammamish: Electronic Book Publishers.

Chapter 7
Climate
Philip L. Jackson

The regional climatography of the Pacific Northwest is distinguished by contrasts, perhaps more than by similarities. There really is no distinctive Pacific Northwest climate, but rather there are several climates that share similar seasonal characteristics. While climate stations in far eastern Oregon, Washington, and Idaho show bi-modal spring and summer patterns, the most striking climatic feature of the Pacific Northwest is the summer-dry, winter-wet seasonality of precipitation. It is the dominance of winter season precipitation, in the form of rain and snow, that unifies a variety of subregional climates influenced by the unique interactions of subtropical and high latitude air masses, the Pacific Ocean and the landforms of Western North America. A linear transect drawn from west to east, some 600 miles along the forty-fifth parallel (figure 7-1), includes climate types that range from the mild marine environments of the Pacific shores to the lusty continental climates of the Rocky Mountains. In between, are found Mediterranean-like climates, steppes, deserts, and alpine climates. It is this diversity and complexity of climate types, in a mid-latitude position, that makes the region geographically unique, supporting a rich natural ecology and a superb fundamental resource base for human activities.

Climate Elements

Geographic position has much to do with the climatic character of the Pacific Northwest. The geographic position of the region may be described as "West Coast-Mid Latitude". This seemingly general description has important climatic implications, however. The Pacific Ocean has a moderating effect on the western portion of the region in terms of the seasonal stability of air temperatures and humidity. The North Pacific Current reaches its eastern terminus in the offshore waters of the Pacific Northwest, then spreads north and south along the coastal zone, effecting similar surface temperatures from Tatoosh, Washington to Brookings, Oregon. The relatively consistent year-round ocean surface temperatures also serve to reduce seasonal air temperature extremes throughout the far western portion of the region. The marine influence extends throughout the coastal littoral, the coastal valleys and into the Puget Lowland of Washington. Modified marine air characteristics are also observed in the Willamette Valley and over 140 miles inland at Cascade Locks in the Columbia River Gorge.

Mid-latitude position brings region-wide distinctive seasonal contrasts in temperature and precipitation. Extending from 42 to 49 degrees north latitude, the region is roughly half-way between the north pole and the equator, and consequently, there are seasonal variations in the length of the daylight period, and in the receipt of solar radiation. Temperatures increase during the high-sun period (summer) and decline in the low-sun period (winter). The region is also positioned as the meeting ground for transient air masses originating from source areas much farther to the north and south. Both marine and continental air masses seasonally dominate the western and eastern portions of the region, but when strongly contrasting air masses of subtropical and polar origins converge, the resulting weather extremes can include high winds, snow and ice storms, torrential rainfall, alpine blizzards and widespread flooding when warm subtropical rain falls on massive mountain snow packs.

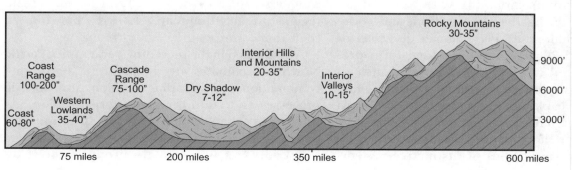

Figure 7-1. Topography and Precipitation

Rocky Mountains
30-35"

Coast Range 100-200"

Cascade Range 75-100"

Interior Hills and Mountains 20-35"

Dry Shadow 7-12"

Interior Valleys 10-15'

Western Lowlands 35-40"

Coast 60-80"

9000'
6000'
3000'

75 miles   200 miles   350 miles   600 miles

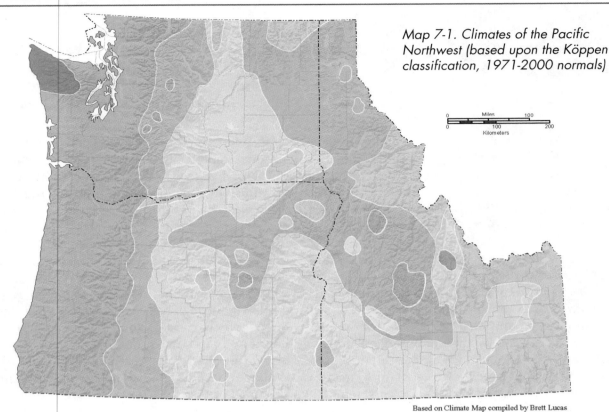

Map 7-1. Climates of the Pacific Northwest (based upon the Köppen classification, 1971-2000 normals)

Based on Climate Map compiled by Brett Lucas

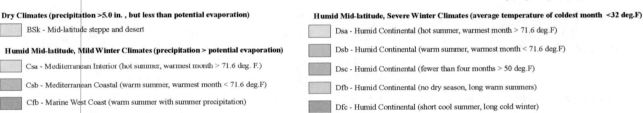

Dry Climates (precipitation >5.0 in. , but less than potential evaporation)

BSk - Mid-latitude steppe and desert

Humid Mid-latitude, Mild Winter Climates (precipitation > potential evaporation)

Csa - Mediterranean Interior (hot summer, warmest month > 71.6 deg. F.)

Csb - Mediterranean Coastal (warm summer, warmest month < 71.6 deg.F)

Cfb - Marine West Coast (warm summer with summer precipitation)

Humid Mid-latitude, Severe Winter Climates (average temperature of coldest month <32 deg.F)

Dsa - Humid Continental (hot summer, warmest month > 71.6 deg.F)

Dsb - Humid Continental (warm summer, warmest month < 71.6 deg.F)

Dsc - Humid Continental (fewer than four months > 50 deg.F)

Dfb - Humid Continental (no dry season, long warm summers)

Dfc - Humid Continental (short cool summer, long cold winter)

Characteristically, the Pacific Northwest has dry summers and wet winters. But there are also identifiable cycles of drier and wetter periods that may last for several years in succession. The wettest year on record across the region was 1996. The average for 107 years of record is 27.57 inches; in 1996 the regional average was 37.30 inches. The two succeeding years were also well above normal. However the recent period from 2000 to 2002 has been much drier than normal, with some areas receiving only one-half of normal precipitation. Maps 7-11 and 7-12 illustrate the features of region-wide precipitation variability with near normal precipitation in the 1997-1999 period, and wide-spread drought for most PNW climate divisions for the 2000 and 2001 period. The long-term precipitation trend from 1950 to 2001 indicates an increasingly large range of variability in contrasting dry and wet years, and on average, a trend toward slightly higher annual precipitation amounts.

Climates of the earth are often described by regionalizing similarities of distinctive meteor-ological elements and seasonal weather patterns. A widely recognized rule-based system of climate classification developed by Köppen and Geiger (1930) delineates regional climate patterns based on long-term observations of monthly temperature and precipitation averages, with seasonal characteristics designed to reflect the adaptive responses of natural vegetation. The Pacific Northwest can be classified into three broad Köppen climate regions, with nine sub-regional variations (see map 7-1). The regional patterns of temperature and precipitation are illustrated by graphs for twenty Pacific Northwest climate stations on map 7-2. The Köppen climate regions presented on map 7-1 are discussed in the context of corresponding landform regions.

As indicated in the preceding paragraphs, Pacific Northwest climates are the result of the unique combination of geographic position, atmospheric processes and landform characteristics. The distinctive seasonal changes in precipitation and temperature, characterized by warm, dry summers and cool, wet winters, are brought about by

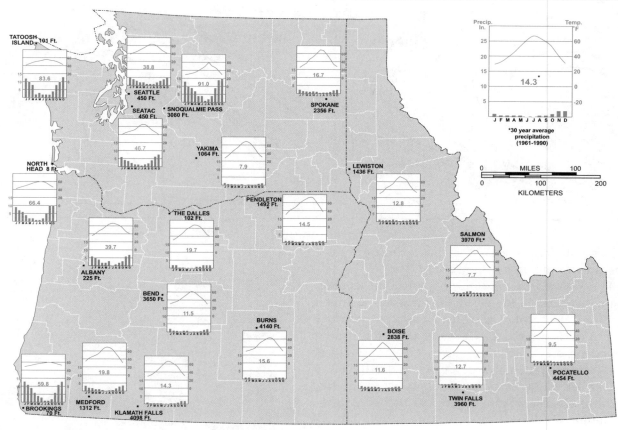

Map 7-2. Variations in Temperature and Precipitation

corresponding latitude shifts in solar radiation, the positions of the Hawaiian High and the Aleutian Low atmospheric pressure systems, and the seasonal trajectories of the polar and subtropical jet streams (see maps 7-3, 7-4, and 7-5). Mid-latitude cyclonic storms are formed along distinctive air mass boundaries; the contact zone between cold air to the north and warmer air to the south. In summer, the polar front jet stream and its storm tracks are pushed northward by the Hawaiian High. As illustrated in map 7-3, the seasonal migration of the high pressure ridge into the region corresponds to the high-sun period, with longer daylight hours and more direct solar radiation in the mid-latitudes. In summer, the southern margin of the polar front generally extends through British Columbia and southern Alaska, leaving all but the far northwest coast of Washington under the influence of generally stable, drier air from the northwest. In winter, the Hawaiian High migrates south, and is replaced by the Aleutian Low. Moist air from the central Pacific is drawn into the semi-permanent low pressure region, and vast cloud sheets materialize as the warmer marine air from the south cools and condenses on its curving, northward trajectory. In contrast to the higher latitude summer storm tracks, winter storms pass with great fre-

quency through the coastal zones of northern California, Oregon and Washington en route to the Rocky Mountains of Idaho and beyond. Major landforms strongly affect the climates of the region (figure 7-1). The Coast Range, the Cascade Mountains and the Rocky Mountains are aligned perpendicular to prevailing atmospheric flows. They act as semi-permeable barriers to surface-level marine and continental air masses, allowing moderating marine air to invade the western coastal zone and proximate interior valleys, while protecting much of the Pacific Northwest from the more extreme hot summer and cold winter temperatures that characterize North American regions to the south and east. During winter, these ranges orographically lift on-shore cyclonic systems, greatly enhancing rain amounts on the lower slopes and building snow packs at higher elevations in the interior mountain ranges. From December through March precipitation is widespread throughout much of the Pacific Northwest, but totals are much greater in the region west of the Cascades. Rain falls abundantly on the Coast Range and western slopes of the Olympic Mountains and the Cascades, with some areas receiving more than 150 inches. At higher elevations, snowfall generally exceeds 300 to 500

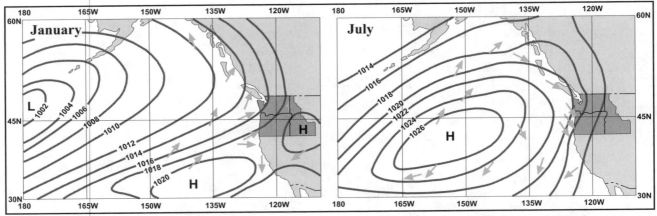

Map 7-3. Generalized Pressure and Winds

inches, with more than 1000 inches recorded in some Cascade Mountain locations (map 7-6).

The Cascade Range, along with the coastal Klamath-Siskiyou Ranges in the far south, creates a significant regional moisture and temperature divide. In some areas the Cascades are 90 to 100 miles wide, and elevations range from 7,000 to 9,000 feet with some strato-volcanic peaks rising 10,000 to 14,000 feet. Immediately west of the Cascade divide, stations average from 55 to 110 inches of precipitation. To the east, the average is only 8 to 18 inches. Summer and winter temperatures are more extreme in the eastern interior as well. Some of the highest average summer temperatures in the region are found at low elevation interior sites in the intermontaine Columbia Basin and the Snake River Plain. Oregon's High Lava Plateau, on the northern margin of the Basin and Range Physiographic Province, often records some of the region's lowest winter temperatures. The interior also has fewer rainy days, more bright, clear days, lower humidity, and fewer days with fog than on the west side of the Cascade Range (maps 7-7 to 7-13).

Interior ranges, rising to peak elevations exceeding 8,000 feet, share distinctive mountain climates. The Ochoco-Blue Mountain-Aldrich-Wallowa complex arcs east then north, from central Oregon into southeastern Washington, and eventually connects with the Rocky Mountains of Idaho, where peak elevations exceed 12,000 feet. The interior mountain climates are characterized by winter snow accumulations, and large seasonal temperature ranges resulting from differences in altitude, slope and aspect. Distinctive vertical temperature and moisture contrasts are observed between alpine and lowland climate stations located in close geographic proximity, but varying by thousands of feet in local relief.

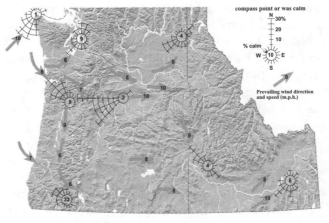

Map 7-4. Prevailing Surface Wind Direction and Speed, January

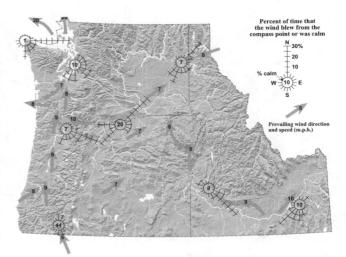

Map 7-5. Prevailing Surface Wind Direction and Speed, July

Climatic Regions

Regional climate types that emerge from Köppen's classification (map 7-1) include *mesothermal* "Ocean-influenced Marine West Coast" and "Dry-summer Mid-latitude" classifications, which feature substantial precipitation and moderate seasonal temperature ranges. Several sub-types of microthermal climates are found in high mountain complexes where seasonal temperature extremes are the norm, snow is the principal form of precipitation, and winters are long. Dry climates are represented in the Pacific Northwest by the "Mid-latitude Steppe" classification; a climate type found to the lee of high mountains, which features low precipitation amounts in all seasons.

The climates of the Pacific Northwest may be described in the context of five major geographic regions. This spatial typology is based on a combination of landform features, natural vegetation patterns, and climate observations that illustrate the region's distinctive climate characteristics.

The Coast Region. A mild, wet, marine climate extends along a narrow coastal strip, into the river valleys and western foothills of the Coast Ranges of Oregon and Washington. This cool summer climate is moderated by coastal fog that forms as the result of cold water upwelling into humid marine air. The coastal climate is described by the Köppen classification as "Marine-influenced Dry-summer Subtropical Mid-latitude," in the Pacific Northwest. The summer months from June through August are much drier than winter months, receiving only about 10 percent of annual rainfall totals. Summer average temperatures range from 55 to 59 degrees Fahrenheit, but in August, maximums may exceed 70 degrees, and Astoria, Oregon, has recorded 100-degree temperatures. Fog conditions generally reduce the duration of sunshine by nearly one-half of that possible. Cape Disappointment, Washington, has the distinction of being the foggiest place on the U.S. Pacific Coast, averaging 2,552 hours a year (map 7-7). However, during the summer months, due to strong solar radiation and advection winds, fog generally "burns off" by mid-day. The climate of the far northwest coast of Washington is more closely associated with that of Vancouver Island, British Columbia. It is classified as "Marine West Coast," and is distinguished by year-round rainfall, high total precipitation, and slightly cooler summer and winter average temperatures.

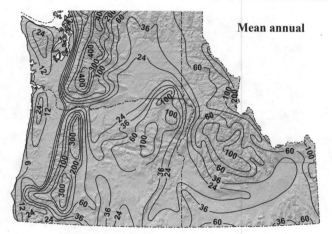

Mean annual

Map 7-6. Snowfall, mean annual in inches

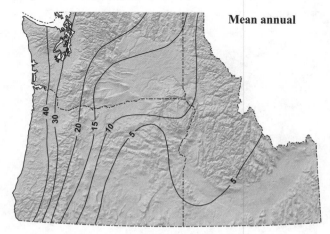

Mean annual

Map 7-7. Days with Dense Fog, mean annual number of days

Due to the marine influence and moderate year-round temperatures, the freeze-free season is long; varying from 300 days at Brookings, Oregon, to over 240 days at Ocean Shores, Washington (maps 7-14 to 7-16). Winter temperatures in the coastal zone are generally mild, but the weather is cloudy, windy and wet, and successive storm days may last for over a week in duration. Depending on the location, rain may fall over two hundred days a year. Average precipitation ranges from 60 to 80 inches on the southwest Oregon coast to 80 to100 inches in the far north.

The windward slopes of the Coast Range receive the most rainfall at elevations from 500 to 2,000 feet, as a result of orographic lifting. Laurel Mountain, at the head of the Siletz River canyon, is one of the wettest places in the Oregon Coast Range, receiving nearly 200 inches of precipitation a year. Snow is common at higher elevations during winter months, though snow on the beaches is less common. To the far north, the Olympic Mountains tower 4,000 to

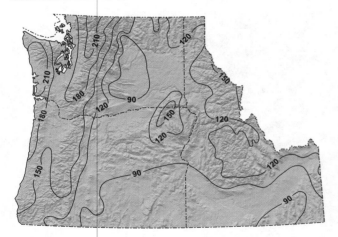

Map 7-8. Days with Precipitation, mean annual number .01 inches or more

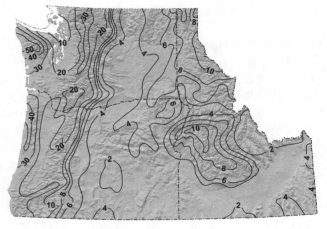

Map 7-9. Winter Precipitation, mean number of inches December, January, February

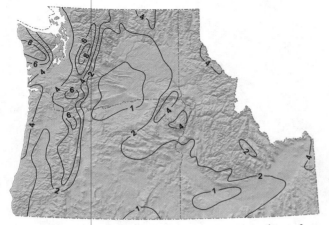

Map 7-10. Summer Precipitation, mean number of inches June, July, August

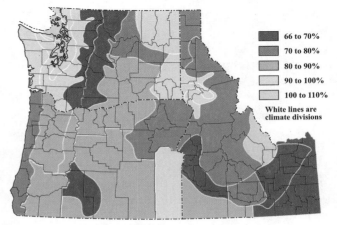

66 to 70%
70 to 80%
80 to 90%
90 to 100%
100 to 110%

White lines are climate divisions

Map 7-11. 24-month Percentage of Average Precipitation through the End of September, 2001

8,000 feet above sea level. Year-round rainfall occurs at lower elevations, and snowfall exceeds 100 inches on the higher slopes.

The Western Lowlands extend from the Rogue Valley in the south to the Willamette Valley and the Puget Sound Lowlands in the north. This region is characterized by lower precipitation totals and greater seasonal temperature ranges than found on the coast. The western lowlands have dry, sunny summers, and moist mild winters. This region is classified as the interior phase of Köppen's "Marine-influenced Dry-summer Mid-latitude" climate. The Rogue Valley is in the lee of the Klamath Mountains and consequently has hotter summer temperatures and lower winter precipitation amounts than the lowlands to the north. The Willamette Valley is linked by many low terrain gaps to coastal marine air, and the Puget Lowland, in the lee of the Olympic Mountains, is nevertheless strongly influenced by

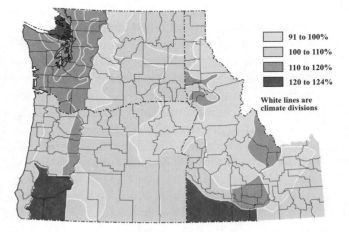

91 to 100%
100 to 110%
110 to 120%
120 to 124%

White lines are climate divisions

Map 7-12. 60-month Percentage of Average Precipitation through the End of September, 2001

AVERAGE ANNUAL PRECIPITATION*

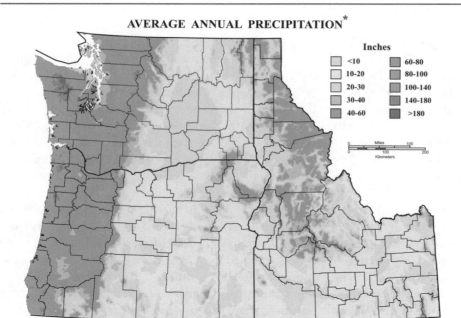

Inches

<10	60-80
10-20	80-100
20-30	100-140
30-40	140-180
40-60	>180

Map 7-13. Average Annual Precipitation
This map is a composite of Average Annual Precipitation maps for Idaho, Oregon, and Washington produced and copyrighted (2000) by the Spatial Climate Analysis Service, Oregon State University

* This map is a composite of Average Annual Precipitation maps for Idaho, Oregon and Washington produced and copyrighted (2000) by the Spatial Climate Analysis Service, Oregon State University

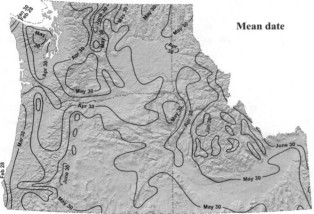

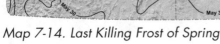

Mean date

Map 7-14. Last Killing Frost of Spring

Mean date

Map 7-15. First Killing Frost in Fall

the waters of the Sound and the marine air entering the region through the Straits of Juan de Fuca (maps 7-17 and 7-18).

In the Rogue Valley, hot summer days in excess of 90 degrees are not uncommon, whereas in the north, summer daytime averages are much more moderate. The July maximum average temperature for Portland is 78 degrees and for Seattle; 75 degrees. Because winter is the dominant rainfall season, daytime summer humidity averages only 40 to 50 percent. In the Willamette Valley, moderate humidity and daytime temperatures in the upper seventies create a favorable human comfort level. Land mass heating during the daylight hours develops a strong on- shore breeze that draws marine air into the Willamette Valley and the Puget Lowland to produce cooler nighttime temperatures. On occasion how-

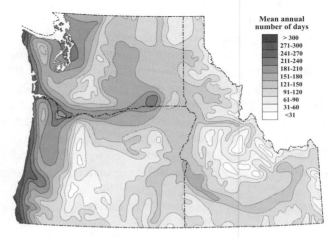

Mean annual number of days

> 300
271-300
241-270
211-240
181-210
151-180
121-150
91-120
61-90
31-60
<31

Map 7-16. Freeze-free Period

ever, dry hot winds from the Columbia Basin invade this region in summer, funneling through the Columbia Gorge (maps 7-3 to 7-5). Clear, hot and dry conditions may last for several days, elevating daytime temperatures, reducing humidity and increasing demands for water and electricity. Dry spells may last 30 to 50 days especially in the months of July, August and September. When these weather conditions occur in late summer, the threat of wildfire hazard is greatly increased (maps 7-19 to 7-22).

The dry season generally merges into the rainy season by late October. Winter in this climatic region is mild, cloudy, and wet. Cloud cover reduces possible sunshine to 25-30 percent, and low-intensity gentle rains last an average of 16 to 18 days a month in December and January (maps 7-8 to 7-10). The wettest month is December, with rainfall totaling from six to ten inches. In the south, the Rogue Valley receives only about one half the totals of the northern lowlands, but winter inversion fog may cloak the narrow interior valleys for days at a time. Throughout this region, some winters may pass without appreciable snowfall on the valley floors, but it is not uncommon for up to 10 inches to fall in a winter season. The snow does not remain on the ground for extended periods, however. Total annual precipitation ranges from 19 inches at Medford to 47 inches at Eugene, 36 inches at Portland and 35 inches at Seattle. Corvallis, located on the western edge of the valley, midway between Eugene and Portland, receives 43 inches on average, a relatively small amount of precipitation considering that rainfall is recorded more than 150 days a year.

The Cascades form a sharp temperature and precipitation gradient separating the marine influenced climates of the western region from the continental climates to the east. The mountain range itself is classified as a "Microthermal, Dry-summer Continental" climate, with warm summers and cold winters. Similar to the two previous regions discussed, winter precipitation is dominant. The western slopes of the Cascades receive copious amounts of low elevation rainfall from November through March. Detroit Dam, Oregon, at 1220 feet elevation, averages 87 inches, primarily rainfall. At Crater Lake Headquarters, in the Oregon Cascades, at 6,500 feet, the average snowfall is 495 inches. Government Camp, at 4,000 feet on the slope of Mt. Hood, averages 278 inches, and at Paradise Ranger Station, at 5,500 feet on Mt. Rainier, totals up to 1000 inches are not uncommon (map 7-6). Just east of the High Cascades crest, snow amounts rapidly decline,

but accumulations are sufficient for high-quality winter recreation enhanced by a greater frequency of clear weather and sunshine. Year-round snow fields and glaciers are found on the highest peaks; in other areas, snow fields may last from April to the end of July. Winter temperatures are distinctly colder at high elevations, but the Pacific slopes of the Cascades have mean minimum temperatures above 30 degrees. The average January temperature at Snoqualmie Pass, Washington (3,080 feet) is 27 degrees F.

Summer is brief in the higher Cascades; in some areas the length of the freeze-free season is less than thirty days (map 7-16). The northern Cascades have a higher frequency of summer storms than do the more southerly mountains. Yet only about 8 to 10 percent of the total annual precipitation falls during summer. Temperature maximums generally range from the 70s to 80s during the day, but may drop to freezing at night due to clear, a relatively thin, dry atmosphere found at high elevations.

The Intermontaine region covers an extensive area of interior plains and plateaus between the Cascades and the Rocky Mountains. The region extends from the Columbia Basin on the north to the Basin and Range on the south, from the Oregon High Lava Plateau on the west to Malheur-Owyhee Uplands and the Snake River Plain on the east. The distinguishing features of this region are few cloudy days, low precipitation amounts and large seasonal temperature ranges. Classified as "Dry Interior Steppe" climates, precipitation totals range from less than 7 inches to slightly more than 20 inches. Yakima, Washington, at 1064 feet averages 7.9 inches, Bend, Oregon, at 3,680 feet averages 11.5 inches, Twin Falls, Idaho, at 3,960 receives 12.7, and Spokane, Washington, and Moscow, Idaho, in the eastern edge of the Palouse Hills, average between 18 and 22 inches of precipitation. The Alvord Desert, in the lee of Oregon's Steens Mountains, barely totals 4 inches. Across this vast region, there is a shift from a dominant winter season precipitation regime to a spring season maximum, characteristic of the Rocky Mountain region. Another feature of precipitation in the interior region is annual variability. Drought has many definitions, but generally refers to a short-term negative departure from the mean expected precipitation. Maps 7-12 and 7-13 illustrate the relative percentage of average (normal) precipitation. Two examples illustrate the spatial and temporal variability of this phenomenon. Drought cycles are more frequent and more severe east of the Cascades

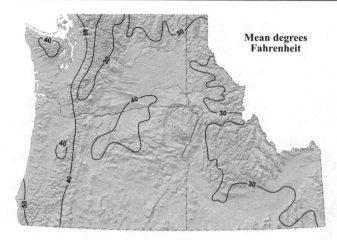

Mean degrees
Fahrenheit

Map 7-17. January Maximum Temperature

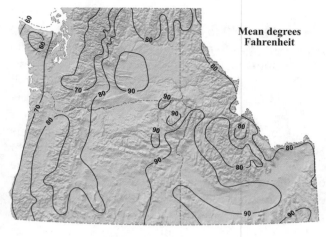

Mean degrees
Fahrenheit

Map 7-18. July Maximum Temperature

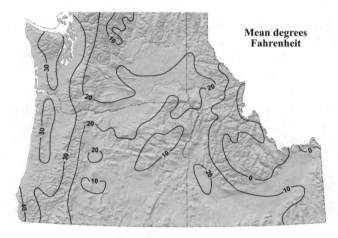

Mean degrees
Fahrenheit

Map 7-19. January Minimum Temperature

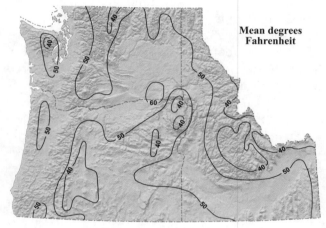

Mean degrees
Fahrenheit

Map 7-20. July Minimum Temperature

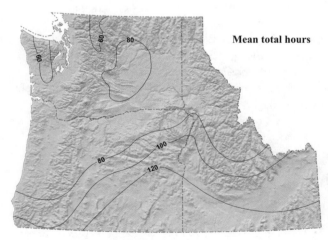

Mean total hours

Map 7-21. January Sunshine

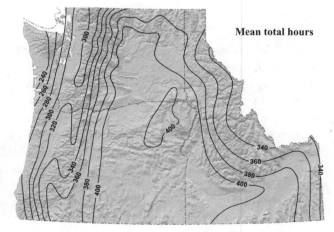

Mean total hours

Map 7-22. July Sunshine

range. During the twenty four-month period (September 2000 to September 2002), only 50 to 70 percent of normal precipitation was recorded in the areas of southeastern Idaho, central Washington, and south central Oregon. During this drought period, much of the eastern portion of the Pacific Northwest recorded only 70 to 90 percent of normal precipitation. Taking a longer-term view, the previous sixty-month period somewhat conceals the drought cycles. Western regions appear to be at or above the expected average precipitation totals, but central and eastern regions generally exhibit below average precipitation, characteristic of prolonged drought.

In contrast to the humid evergreen forest environments west of the Cascades, the interior vegetation associations include short grass, bunch grass, sage, juniper, and greasewood. These characteristic "steppe" and "xeric" species have adapted to a regime featuring high summer maximum temperatures, low winter minimums, and extended dry periods. In mid-summer, daytime temperatures at Pendleton may reach 105 degrees and drop into the upper 50s by morning. January mean temperatures at Burns are 25 to 30 degrees, and occasionally winter temperatures drop to minus 15 to 20 degrees under the influence of frigid continental air masses flowing out of the Rocky Mountains. Along the Columbia River, solar radiation in the summer months is intense, and the freeze-free period is generally greater than two hundred days. Due to the elevation of the High Lava Plateaus, the freeze-free season above 4,000 feet may be reduced to less than 80 days.

The Northeastern Mountains and Valleys region extends from the Ochoco Mountains eastward into the Blue Mountains of Oregon and Washington, and finally to the Rocky Mountain complex of Idaho. Classified as "Microthermal Climates, under Continental Influence," the great variance in relative elevations and landform positions results in several sub-regional climate types. The Blue Mountains are generally characterized as "Warm, Dry-summer Continental." Higher peaks in the Wallowa Range, Seven Devils, Bitterroot, and Salmon River Mountains are described as "Continental with Short, Cool Summers." On the highest mountain peaks, snow falls 70-90 days a year and early snows may fall by mid-September. Mid-elevation northwest facing slopes may be classified as "Warm-summer, Humid Continental" climates. The primary winter precipitation form is snow, and in these mountains, total snowfall may reach 40 to 80 inches a year. Spring

and summer thunderstorms are frequent, and while much of the summer rainfall quickly evaporates, it serves to cool down temperatures (map 7-11). The most striking climatic feature of the eastern mountains is the difference between temperature and moisture conditions at nearby mountain and valley locations. Vertical zonation is highly apparent in the east-central mountains of Idaho. Salmon, Idaho, in a valley location, gets barely 8 inches of precipitation at an elevation of 3,949 feet, but nearly 25 inches is recorded at Leadore, 6,115 feet elevation, on the nearby ridges of the Lemhi Range. Cold air drains off the high slopes and into the deep canyons in winter, resulting in lower minimum temperatures. In summer, the deep canyons register high afternoon temperatures, then begin to moderate as the sun leaves the upper slopes, winds pick up, and cooler air drains into lower elevations.

The Pacific Northwest is a region of diverse and distinctive climate patterns, yet uniquely among the climates of North America, there is the unifying feature of mid-latitude seasonal temperature regimes, and a tendency toward contrasting wet winters and dry summers. Distinctive climate patterns contribute to the geographic character of the Pacific Northwest, a region rich in variety and contrasts.

Sources

Climatic Atlas of the United States. 1992. Environmental Sciences Services Administration. U.S. Department of Commerce

Climatological Data :Climates of the States. 1993. Asheville, North Carolina: U.S. National Weather Service, NOAA.

Climatic Data for Oregon,Idaho,Washington 1961-1990 Normals. Oregon, Idaho, Washington: Offices of the State Climatologists:.

Koppen W. and R. Geiger. 1930. Map of Koppen climates for the Pacific Northwest composed by Brett Lucas and P.L. Jackson for: J.M. Castro and P.L. Jackson, 2001. *Bankfull Discharge Recurrence Intervals and Regional Hydraulic Geometry Relationships: Patterns in the Pacific Northwest, USA.* American Water Resources Association, Vol. 37, No. 5.

Taylor, G. and R. Hattan. 1999. *The Oregon Weather Book: A State of Extremes.* Corvallis: Oregon State University Press.

Western Regional Climate Center. 2002. Reno, Nevada: National Climate Services Program, NOAA. http://www.wrcc.dri.edu/

Chapter 8
Vegetation
Robert E. Frenkel

The vegetation of the Pacific Northwest exhibits a complex pattern reflecting diversity in climate, soils, relief, incidence of fire, biotic interaction, and history. Recent impacts on pristine vegetation by logging, agriculture, grazing, industrial development, and urbanization have greatly altered the natural pattern. Although it is possible to map this altered pattern and create a map of actual vegetation, map 8-2 shows the natural plant cover as it might appear if the effects of logging, agriculture, and urban-industrial use were not present.

Major vegetation differences, especially those determined by regional climate, are reflected by three vegetation provinces—Forest, Shrub-Steppe, and Alpine—embracing fifteen vegetation zones or zone complexes. As used here, a vegetation zone is the area within which maturely developed soils support a specific climatic climax vegetation. It is a broad area of relatively uniform regional climate and typical

regional topography within which one plant association is capable of becoming dominant under prevalent climatic conditions over a long period of time. In practice, alteration of plant cover has been profound. As a result, the potentially dominant species characteristic of the mapped vegetation zones may not currently prevail.

Numerous plant communities exist within a given vegetation zone. When fully described by their species composition and structure, these plant communities are called plant associations. The classification and description of these localized plant associations and related habitat types has been well developed in the Pacific Northwest under the leadership of the U.S. Forest Service research scientists.

Despite much research, the vegetation of the region is imperfectly known. A general review of the plant cover of Oregon and Washington was con-

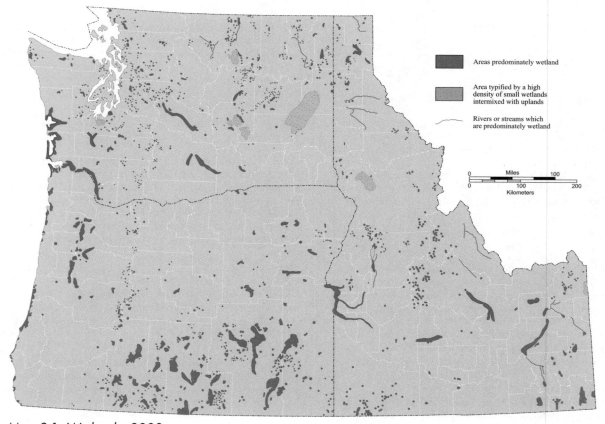

Areas predominately wetland

Area typified by a high density of small wetlands intermixed with uplands

Rivers or streams which are predominately wetland

Map 8-1. Wetlands, 2000

Map 8-2. Vegetation Zones

Forest Province

Sitka Spruce Zone. Confined to the coast, this coniferous zone extends from Alaska to southwestern Oregon and has been extensively altered by logging and fire. Sitka spruce (*Picea sitchensis*) characterizes the zone although in many places western hemlock (*Tsuga heterophylla*) and Douglas-fir (*Pseudotsuga menziesii*) dominate. Red alder (*Alnus rubra*) often forms patches in disturbed areas and riparian situations, while western redcedar (*Thuja plicata*) characterizes swampy habitats. Besides stabilized dune communities in which shore pine (*Pinus contorta*) is a prominent successional species, there are salt marsh communities in estuaries and communities associated with shifting dunes. The Sitka Spruce Zone grades into Western Hemlock Zone to which it is closely related.

Western Hemlock Zone. Mantling both the Coast Range and western slopes of the Cascades, this zone is one of the most extensive in the region, stretching from British Columbia to California. Although named for the shade-tolerant western hemlock characterizing the persistent vegetation, the dominant tree is often the seral Douglas-fir. Extensive logging has occurred throughout the area. Communities within this zone have been studied in detail and have been related to site characteristics. Some important species are western redcedar in moist sites and, in the south, ponderosa pine (*Pinus ponderosa*) and incense cedar (*Calocedrus decurrens*). In disturbed moist sites, red alder and bigleaf maple (*Acer macrophyllum*) are common. Western hemlock gives way to Douglas-fir in drier sites and Pacific silver fir (*Abies amabilis*) at higher elevations.

Cascade Subalpine Forest Zone Complex. A group of zones marked by heavy snow flanks the Cascades and Olympics and extends into British Columbia. This group includes the Pacific

Silver Fir Zone marked by *Abies amabilis*. At higher elevations, silver fir gives way to a more stunted forest of mountain hemlock (*Tsuga mertensiana*) and subalpine fir (*Abies lasiocarpa*) and forms a parklike pattern of open meadow and forest stringers. In areas of volcanic ash or areas recently disturbed by fire, even-aged stands of lodgepole pine (*Pinus contorta* var. *murrayana*) prevail. In southern Oregon, the zones bear close relationship to the California red fir forest.

Grand Fir and Douglas-fir Zones. Mesic coniferous forests occur in interior areas and exhibit a broad distribution. Often both grand fir (*Abies grandis*) and Douglas-fir occur in mixed stands, although Douglas-fir tends to be more prevalent in Idaho. Other trees of importance, in order of increasing moisture tolerance, are ponderosa pine, western larch (*Laris occidentalis*), and lodgepole pine, the latter two species are fire-responsive pioneers. In northern Idaho, western redcedar and western hemlock are prominent. Oregon boxwood (*Pachystima myrsinites*) and common snowberry (*Symphoricarpos albus*) dominate two prevalent understory communities.

Ponderosa Pine Zone. In a broad belt below the Grand Fir and Douglas-fir zone, is an open coniferous forest dominated by *Pinus ponderosa*. Understory vegetation varies from shrubby mats of bitterbrush (*Purshia tridentata*) and snowbrush (*Ceanothus velutinus*) in central Oregon to meadows of Idaho fescue (*Festuca idahoensis*) further to the east. This zone has been severely altered by timber harvest.

Western Redcedar Zone. At moderate altitudes in moist locals in the northeastern portion of the region, this zone occurs between the more xeric Grand Fir and Douglas-fir zones and the spruce-fir type. Dominant trees include western redcedar, western hemlock, and western white pine (*Pinus monticola*), but grand fir and western larch are found in drier sites. Understory unions in this zone are often similar to those of the Grand Fir and Douglas-fir zones.

Engelmann Spruce and Subalpine Fir Zones. Confined to higher elevations to the east, this type if the counterpart of the Cascade Subalpine Forest. Varying from dense to open parklike stands of subalpine fir and Engelmann spruce (*Picea engelmannii*), the zone has occasional intrusions of subalpine larch (*Larix lyallii*) and whitebark pine (*Pinus albicaulis*) at higher elevations and Douglas-fir at lower elevations.

Mixed Needlefleaf-Broadleaf Forest Zone Complex. A highly intricate set of zones closely related to plant communities in California, this mixed evergreen forest straddles the Siskiyou Mountains in southwestern Oregon. Edaphic, fire history, and climatic contrasts lead to sharp breaks in plant cover. Douglas-fir dominates the upper canopy, but various sclerophyllous trees and shrubs are found in the understory including tanoak (*Lithocarpus densiflorus*), canyon live oak (*Quercus chrysolepis*), Pacific madrone (*Arbutus menziesii*), and golden chinquapin (*Castanopsis chrysophylla*). Serpentine soil bears a distinctive flora and sparse vegetation, and other dry rocky areas support sclerophyllous broadleaf chaparral.

Rogue-Umpqua Forest-Shrub Zone Complex. Occupying valleys in the rainshadow of the Siskiyou Mountains is a vegetation mosaic exhibiting many xeric characteristics. Woodlands are dominated by Oregon white oak (*Quercus garryana*), with California black oak (*Q. kelloggii*) on mesic sites. Pacific madrone, ponderosa pine, sugar pine (*Pinus lambertiana*), and incense cedar distinguish this zone from Willamette Valley forest. On shallow soils, south slopes and recently burned areas, sclerophyllous shrub communities are found with narrow-leaved buckbrush (*Ceanothus cuneatus*) and white-leaved manzanita (*Arctostaphylos viscida*).

Willamette Forest-Prairie Zone Complex. Confined to bottomland and adjacent slopes of the Willamette Valley is a mosaic of forest, woodland, open savanna, and prairie. Prairie and oak savanna at the time of first settlement was maintained by aboriginal burning. Woodlands dominated by Oregon white oak have since been invaded by Douglas-fir and grand fir, with bigleaf maple important on north-facing slopes. Grasslands maintained by grazing include many introduced species and occupy drier sites. Lacing this mosaic of forest and prairie are bands of riparian woodland in which Oregon ash (*Fraxinus latifolia*), black poplar (*Populus trichocarpa*), and willow (*Salix* spp.) are prominent.

Western Juniper Zone. This open woodland dominated by western juniper (*Juniperus occidentalis*) is the northern counterpart of the Pinyon-Juniper type of the Great Basin. Shrub-steppe dominated by big sagebrush (*Artemisia tridentata*) and Idaho fescue typically comprises the understory of this zone. Throughout the arid regions of interior Oregon, juniper woodland characterizes rimrock habitat where local moisture supplies permit establishment of this xerophytic tree.

Shrub-Steppe Province

Steppe Zone Complex. Grassland without shrubs mantles areas of north-central Oregon and the Palouse of southeastern Washington and adjacent Idaho. Among the various communities within this grassland is the *Agropyron-Festuca* type characterized by bluebunch wheatgrass (*Agropyron spicatum*) and Idaho fescue. In moister situations, Sandberg's bluegrass (*Poa sandbergii*) and Idaho fescue are prominent together with many forbs and shrubby common snowberry. The steppe type is intermediate between ponderosa pine forest and more xeric shrub-steppe, and the communities of the Steppe Zone Complex form understory unions in these adjacent vegetation types.

Big Sagebrush Zone. This most widespread vegetation zone in the Pacific Northwest extends from Canada to Nevada and from the Cascades to the Rockies. Dominated by big sagebrush, the zone intermingles with juniper woodland in central Oregon and supports nonintensive grazing. Plant communities have been identified based on understory grasses, shrub cover, soils, and slope. Two prominent communities are *Artemisia tridentata/Festuca idahoensis* and *Artemisia tridentata/Agropyron spicatum* associations, the former with greater moisture requirements. Low sagebrush (*Artemisia arbuscula*) frequently replaces big sagebrush in eastern Oregon on shallow stony soils. Other prominent shrubs include several species of sagebrush and rabbit brush (*Chrysothamnus* spp.). Commonly referred to as "high desert," this shrub-steppe in this zone consists of nondesert species and exhibits a shrub-grass structure which is distinct from true desert.

Desert Shrub Zone Complex. Occupying pockets within the Big Sagebrush Zone, the Desert Shrub Zone Complex is the most xeric of the region. Frequently the type occupies playas where saline conditions prevail, but also occurs in the rainshadow of several mountain ranges in southeastern Oregon and southern Idaho. Important shrubs, most of which are halophytic, include shadscale (*Atriplex confertifolia*), salt sage (*A. nuttalli*), greasewood (*Sarcobatus vermiculatus*), and spring hopsage (*Grayia spinosa*). Grasses and forbs are occasionally found in this open vegetation.

Alpine Province

Alpine Zone Complex. Found near and above the tree line, this zone complex is narrowly represented in the Cascades and more extensively in the Rocky Mountains. Mainly comprising herbaceous plants and low shrubs, these zones contain a few trees displaying krummholz form and occupying protected habitats. Alpine health communities of the subalpine park land extend into the alpine zones, and glaciers, permanent snow fields, and extensive areas of talus and rock cover much of the area.

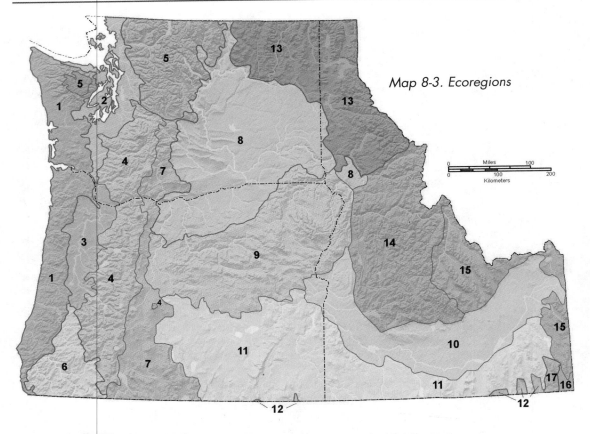

Map 8-3. Ecoregions

1 Coast Range	**10** Snake River Plain
2 Puget Lowland	**11** Northern Basin & Range
3 Willamette Valley	**12** Central Basin & Range
4 Cascades	**13** Northern Rockies
5 North Cascades	**14** Idaho Batholith
6 Klamath Mountains	**15** Middle Rockies
7 Eastern Cascades Slopes & Foothills	**16** Wyoming Basin
8 Columbia Plateau	**17** Wasatch & Uinta Mountains
9 Blue Mountains	

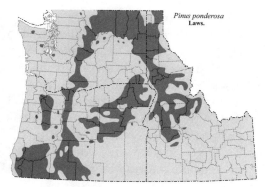

Pinus ponderosa
Laws.

Map 8-4. Ponderosa Pine

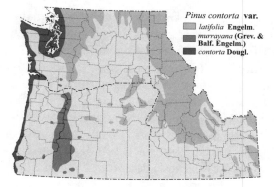

Pinus contorta **var.**
 latifolia **Engelm.**
 murrayana (**Grev. &
 Balf. Engelm.**)
 contorta **Dougl.**

Map 8-5. Shore Pine/Ponderosa Pine

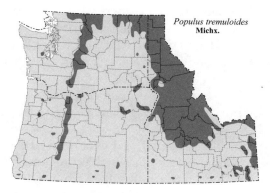

Populus tremuloides
Michx.

Map 8-6. Quaking Aspen

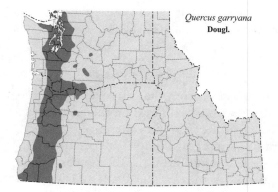

Quercus garryana
Dougl.

Map 8-7. Oregon White Oak

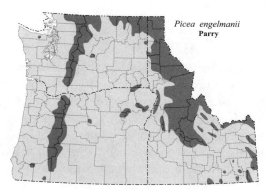

Picea engelmanii
Parry

Map 8-8. Engelmann Spruce

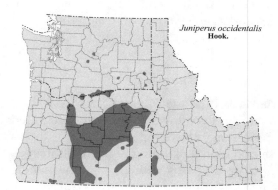

Juniperus occidentalis
Hook.

Map 8-9. Western Juniper

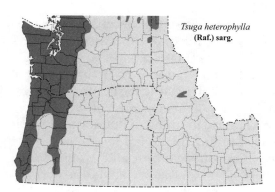

Tsuga heterophylla
(Raf.) sarg.

Map 8-10. Western Hemlock

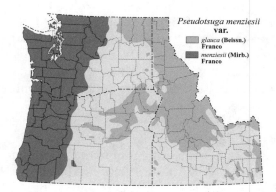

Pseudotsuga menziesii
var.
 glauca (**Beissn.**)
 Franco
 menziesii (**Mirb.**)
 Franco

Map 8-11. Douglas-fir

ducted by Franklin and Dyrness (1988). Other major works introducing the interested individual to broad aspects of Pacific Northwest vegetation include a detailed study of steppe vegetation (Daubenmire 1970), a description of the forest vegetation of eastern Washington and northern Idaho (Daubenmire and Daubenmire 1968), and many comprehensive technical reports for Oregon and Washington issued as "Regional Guides" by the U.S. Forest Service, Pacific Northwest Region 6, Portland, Oregon, such as the report by Henderson et al. (1989). For Idaho, comparable studies are published as "General Technical Reports" by the U.S. Forest Service at the Intermountain Research Station, Ogden, Utah, such as the report by Steel et al. (1981).

Species Range and Ecotype

A quite different concept from that of vegetation zones concerns the distribution of individual plant species within the region of their occurrence, termed a species' range. An organism does not occupy all the area within its range, through differences in soil, topography, and local climate. Plant species often consist of a series of races, genetically adapted to localized ecological conditions, called ecotypes. Maps 8-4 to 8-11 show the ranges of eight prominent tree species and some major ecotypes in the Pacific Northwest.

Ecoregions

Regional variations in climate, vegetation, soil, and landforms in the Pacific Northwest are integrated into a single map of ecoregions (map 8-3). An outgrowth of regional planning at the federal level, ecoregion mapping helps with (1) planning where broad management problems must be considered; (2) organizing and retrieving resource inventory data; and (3) interpreting and analyzing these data. This system has been useful in assessments required under the Resources Planning Act and the National Forest Management Act, and for various regional and national studies conducted by the U.S. Environmental Protection Agency, and in the National Wetlands Inventory conducted by the U.S. Fish and Wildlife Service.

Although combining different kinds of physical and biological data into a single system of regionalization is not new, the ecoregion map developed by R. G. Bailey (1976 and 1978) establishes a hierarchical system based on independent databases. Since broad similarity in zonal heat and moisture availability is the major control on physical systems, the Pacific Northwest is first divided into two domains, the Humid Temperate Domain and the Dry Domain. Each domain includes several divisions based on more specific macroclimatic criteria at the level of broad climatic types, e.g., Warm Continental Climate Division. At the third level, each division is divided into several provinces reflecting bioclimatic and soil criteria as generally expressed at the level of soil order and vegetation formation, e.g., Douglas-fir Forest Province.

This hierarchical system of regionalization may be refined at lower levels; for example, provinces are subdivided into sections reflecting potential natural vegetation types, and sections are broken down into districts based on land surface form. Ultimately, the system is capable of defining a site, a more or rless homogeneous unit of land with respect to local climate, landform, soil, and vegetation for which a management prescription can be effectively prepared (Bailey 1982).

A very similar system has been refined by Omernik and Gallant (1986) in which ecoregions in the Pacific Northwest are synthesized from independent regional data sets describing (1) land surface form, (2) potential natural vegetation, (3) land use, and (4) soils.

Wetlands

Wetlands are those transitional lands between terrestrial and aquatic environments in which water saturation is the dominant factor governing soil development and plant and animal communities. Seasonal wetlands are saturated only for short periods of time during the growing season; other areas such as marshes and many swamps are saturated, or even inundated, throughout the year. In the Pacific Northwest wetlands constitute a very small proportion of the total land area, less than 1.5 percent (see map 8-1).

Once considered waste places, many wetlands have been drained, filled, or otherwise destroyed. Nationally, the United States has lost approximately 50 percent of its wetland resources (Tiner 1984, Dahl et al. 1991, Frayer et al. 1983). In the Pacific Northwest losses are about 39 percent, most of which were caused by historical draining of interior freshwater wetlands for farming. Idaho has lost 56 percent of its wetlands, Oregon 38 percent, and Washington 31 percent (Dahl 1990). Coastal wetlands, the majority of which are salt marshes, constitute probably less than 5 percent of the total wetland acreage.

Conversion of coastal wetlands has nonetheless been profound, with losses varying from 30 to 90 percent per estuary.

In the early 1970s, the multiple values of wetlands began to be recognized. These resources provide critical habitat for wildlife, help purify polluted water, reduce flooding, and provide important areas for recreation, education and research. Today, many practices that damage wetlands are regulated as required under federal and state legislation, yet still the region continues to lose wetlands, particularly by the conversion of wetlands to urban and commercial uses.

The U.S. Fish and Wildlife Service is in the process of inventorying the wetlands of the nation. The National Wetlands Inventory is based on the interpretation of aerial photographs, and identified wetlands are classified and mapped at the scale of U.S. Geological Survey quadrangles. The inventory is complete for Oregon and Washington and is in progress for Idaho. The small-scale map of Pacific Northwest wetlands (map 8.11) is based on the national map of Wetland Resources of the United States (Dahl 1991). In part, mapped wetlands represent aggregated data from the National Wetlands Inventory and the judgement of staff in the regional offices of the U.S. Fish and Wildlife Service. Mapped are (1) areas that are predominantly wetland and (2) areas within which there is a high density of small wetlands. Deepwater habitats are excluded from the map.

Sources

Bailey, R. G. 1976. *Ecoregions of the United States.* Ogden, Utah: U.S.D.A. Forest Service Intermountain Region.

Bailey, R. G. 1978. *Description of the Ecoregions of the United States.* Ogden, Utah: U.S.D.A. Forest Service Intermountain Region.

Bailey, R. G. 1982. "Classification systems for habitat and ecosystems," p.16-26 in *Research on Fish and Wildlife Habitat.* U.S. Environmental Protection Agency. EPA 600/8-82-022.

Cronquist, A., et al. 1972. *Intermountain Flora, Vascular Plants of the Intermountain West, U.S.A.,* Vol. 1. New York: Hafner Publishing Company.

Dahl, T. E. 1990. *Wetland Losses in the United States 1780s to 1980s.* Washington, D. C.: U.S. Department of the Interior Fish and Wildlife Service.

Dahl, T. E. 1991. *Wetland Resources of the United States.* (Map at 1:3,168,000). St. Petersburg, Florida: U.S. Department of the Interior Fish and Wildlife Service, National Wetlands Inventory.

Dahl, T. E. et al. 1991. *Status and Trends of Wetlands in the Conterminous United States, mid-1970s to mid-1980s.* Washington, D.C.: U.S. Department of the Interior Fish and Wildlife Service.

Daubenmire, R. 1970. *Steppe Vegetation of Washington.* Washington Agricultural Experimental Station Technical Bulletin 62.

Daubenmire, R. and J. B. Daubenmire. 1968. *Forest Vegetation of Eastern Washington and Northern Idaho.* Washington Agricultural Experimental Station Technical Bulletin 60.

Franklin, J. F. and C. T. Dyrness. 1973. *Natural Vegetation of Oregon and Washington.* U.S.D.A. Forest Service Pacific Northwest Forest and Range Experimental Station General Technical Report PNW-8. Reprinted Corvallis: Oregon State University Press, 1988.

Frayer, W. E. et al. 1983. *Status and Trends of Wetlands and Deepwater Habitats in the Conterminous United States, 1950s to 1970s.* Washington, D. C.: U.S. Department of the Interior Fish and Wildlife Service.

Henderson, J. A., D. H. Peter, R. D. Lesher, and D. C. Shaw. 1989. *Forested Plant Associations of Olympic National Forest.* U.S.D.A. Forest Service Pacific Northwest Region R6 Ecological Technical Paper 001-88.

Kuchler, A. W. 1964. *Potential Natural Vegetation of the Conterminous United States.* American Geographical Society Special Publication No. 36.

Little, e.L., Jr. 1971. *Atlas of United States Trees. Vol 1. Conifers and Important Hardwoods.* U.S.D.A. Forest Service Miscellaneous Publication No. 1146.

Omernik, J. M. and A. L. Gallant. 1986. *Ecoregions of the Pacific Northwest.* U.S. Environmental Protection Agency, Research and Development Report, EPA/600/3-86/033.

Steele, R., R. D. Pfister, R. A. Ryker, and J. A. Kittams. 1981. *Forest Habitat Types of Central Idaho.* U.S.D.A. Forest Service Intermountain Forest and Range Experimental Station, General Technical Report INT-114.

Tiner, R. W. Jr. 1984. *Wetlands of the United States: Current Status and Recent Trends.* Washington, D. C.: Department of the Interior, Fish and Wildlife Service.

Chapter 9
Agriculture
Philip L. Jackson

From the Pacific shores of Oregon and Washington where high-quality cranberries flourish, to barley and alfalfa fields high in the mountain valleys of Idaho, the rich diversity of climate, soils, and topography of the Pacific Northwest provide a wide range of crop environments and agricultural opportunities. The region annually produces well over $11 billion in crops and livestock on more than forty-four million acres of farmland. Innovative agricultural technology and product development has increased the efficiency of harvested croplands and introduced new high value crops to complement traditional crop production.

Pacific Northwest crops enjoy national and international market recognition for high quality. Perhaps the best-known regions include: Oregon's Tillamook County dairy products; apples and grapes from Washington's Yakima Valley; apples and pears from Oregon's Hood River Valley; wheat, and dry peas from the Palouse of Washington and Idaho; Idaho potatoes and sugar beets from the Snake River Plain; onions and potatoes from Oregon's Treasure Valley; and vegetable crops from Washington's Walla Walla region. The Willamette Valley is known as the "grass seed capital of the world," but such a favorable agricultural environment produces everything from berries to vegetables and from nursery stock to grape vineyards. The extensive rangelands of eastern Oregon and southern Idaho are well known for forage and cattle production.

Approximately 29 percent of the land area of the Pacific Northwest is in farms (see maps 9-1 and 9-2). The total acreage of farmland has continued a slight decline in recent years, as has the acreage of cropland. It is not unusual for farmland acreages to fluctuate from one census period to the next; the longer- term trends in farmland growth and decline for the period 1987 to 1997 are shown in table 9-1. Short- term trends from 1992 to 1997 are illustrated by county in map 9-3. For the most recent period, a new trend in farmland use has appeared. The 2000 State and County reports indicate that more available cropland is being harvested than previously observed. This trend was noted in the 1997 Census of Agriculture. Oregon posted the highest percentage increase in harvested cropland, 11.4 percent, of all three states from the period 1987 to 1997 (table 9-2). Washington increased harvested acreage by 6.5 percent, and Idaho, 2.9 percent. Significant increases in irrigated acreage account for some of the increased efficiency in harvested cropland use. Oregon added 300,534 acres of irrigated croplands, an 18.2 percent increase from 1987 to 1997. Idaho added 274,350 irrigated acres (8.5 percent), and Washington posted an increase of 186,341 acres (12.3 percent). The regional historical record for irrigated acreage stood at 6,995,412 in 1978; however the 1997 total betters this acreage by 151,849. Maps 9-4 and 9-5 illustrate the geographic distribution of irrigated lands and irrigated land as a percentage of land in farms, by county (see also map 9-6).

Farm values continue to rise. The majority of farms in the Pacific Northwest, 60 percent, are valued at between $100,000 and $499,999 (see table 9-3).

Table 9-1. Farmland growth and decline by selected county, 1987-1997			
	1987	1997	% change
Oregon (acres)			
Jefferson	506,590	783,466	+54.7
Curry	79,555	84,781	+6.6
Crook	860,738	916,451	+6.5
Morrow	1,115,683	1,118,226	+1.0
Harney	1,519,876	1,358,883	-10.6
Malheur	1,381,625	1,257,201	-9.0
Washington	150,130	130,887	-12.8
Washington (acres)			
Chelan	115,566	123,731	+7.1
Ferry	760,670	809,816	+6.5
Kitsap	9,576	19,129	+99.8
Pacific	34,870	40,228	+15.4
Kittitas	403,338	177,815	-55.9
Klickitat	698,453	588,732	-15.7
Okanagan	1,339,306	1,178,850	-11.9
Idaho (acres)			
Benewah	115,100	125,988	+9.5
Custer	137,022	147,913	+8.0
Cassia	653,525	656,658	+1.0
Bannock	358,189	307,281	-14.2
Bingham	1,406,990	796,065	-43.4
Boise	66,811	45,461	-31.9
Idaho	802,746	649,851	-19.1

Source: 1997 Census of Agriculture

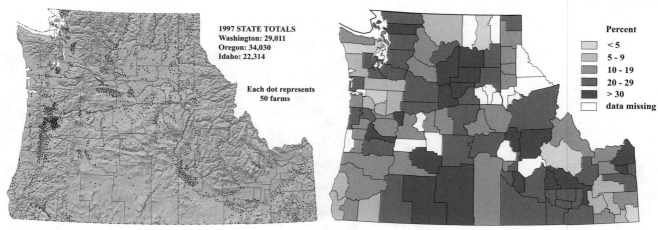

Map 9-1. Number of Farms, 1997

1997 STATE TOTALS
Washington: 29,011
Oregon: 34,030
Idaho: 22,314

**Each dot represents
50 farms**

Map 9-2. Percent of Lands in Farms Operated by
Corporations, 1997

Percent
	< 5
	5 - 9
	10 - 19
	20 - 29
	> 30
	data missing

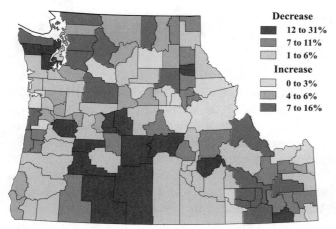

Map 9-3. Percent Change in Number of Farms,
1992-1997

Decrease
	12 to 31%
	7 to 11%
	1 to 6%

Increase
	0 to 3%
	4 to 6%
	7 to 16%

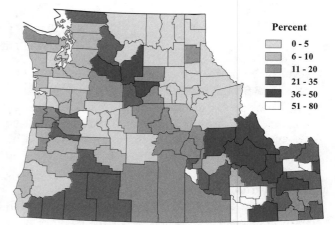

Map 9-4. Irrigated Land as a Percentage of Land in
Farms, 1997

Percent
	0 - 5
	6 - 10
	11 - 20
	21 - 35
	36 - 50
	51 - 80

Table 9-2. Land in Farms and Farmland Use, 1978-1997

	1978 acres	1987 acres	% change	1997 acres	% change
Oregon					
Land in farms	18,414,484	17,809,165	-3.3	17,449,293	-2.0
Total cropland	5,427,487	5,236,393	-0.3	5,287,136	+1.0
Harvested	3,280,005	2,832,663	-13.7	3,154,523	+11.4
Woodland	1,786,919	1,636,531	-8.4	1,832,176	+12.0
Irrigated land	1,920	1,648,205	-14.2	1,948,739	+18.2
Washington					
Land in farms	17,002,288	16,155,568	-6.2	15,179,710	-6.0
Total cropland	8,410,749	8,168,454	-3.1	7,893,449	-3.4
Harvested	5,073,078	4,597,476	-10.1	4,895,633	+6.5
Woodland	2,683,874	2,541,513	-6.2	1,851,925	-26.9
Irrigated land	1,681,268	1,518,684	-11.2	1,705,025	+12.3
Idaho					
Land in farms	14,869,911	13,931,875	-7.1	11,830,167	-14.9
Total cropland	6,631,994	6,742,285	+2.1	6,308,877	-6.5
Harvested	4,877,569	4,349,122	-12.4	4,476,890	+2.9
Woodland	891,162	1,153,837	+23.2	520,527	-54.4
Irrigated land	3,508,254	3,219,192	-9.2	3,493,542	+8.5

Source: 1997 Census of Agriculture

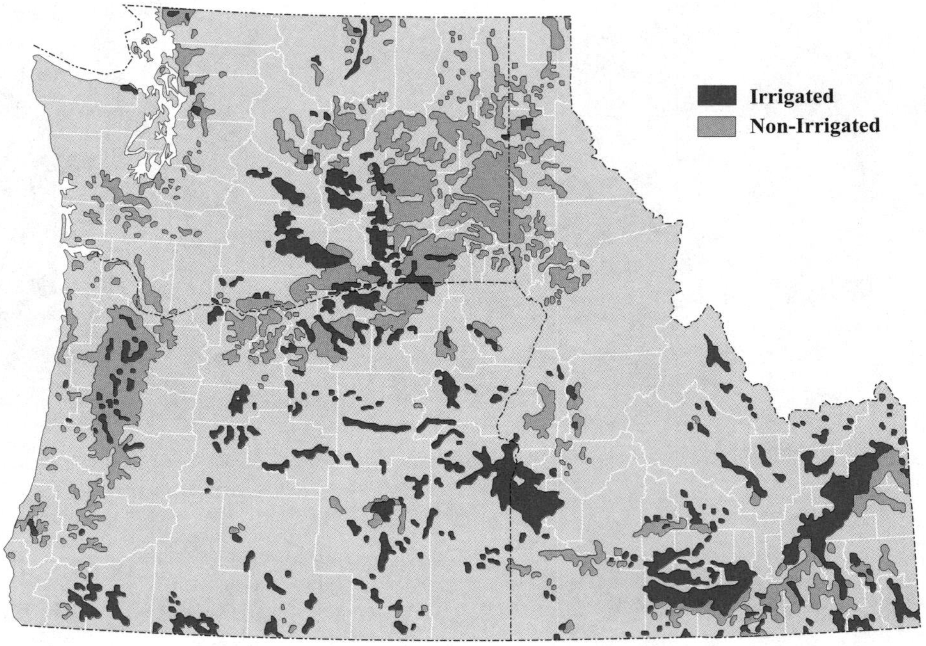

Map 9-5. Croplands

Irrigated
Non-Irrigated

Twelve percent of farms are valued at over $1,000,000 and only 8.5 percent are valued at $40,000 or less. Maps 9-7 and 9-8 provide county level data on farm size and farm values. Map 9-9 illustrates relative values of agricultural products sold by county. Value of agricultural products sold per farm is shown on map 9-10, and value per acre of agricultural products sold by county is found on map 9-11.

Livestock grazing is the most extensive agricultural land use in the Pacific Northwest, and cattle and calves produce the highest agricultural revenue, exceeding $2 billion per year. Cattle production has increased in Idaho, but slightly declined in Oregon and Washington.

Grazing utilizes a significant proportion of private farmlands; exceeding 26 million acres region-wide, with an additional 46 million acres of federal timber and rangelands under seasonal grazing permits.

Cropland represents nearly 44 percent of total farmland in the Pacific Northwest. While total cropland acreage has declined slightly in Washington and Idaho since the 1987 Agricultural Census, there has been a slight gain in Oregon. The increase in

irrigated cropland acreage region-wide (from 6.4 million acres in 1987 to 7.2 million acres in 1997) is a land use trend that has significantly increased productivity on today's proportionally smaller farmland base. Over 56 percent of harvested cropland in the Pacific Northwest was irrigated in 1997. The largest increases in irrigated acreage are in north central and south central Oregon, central Washington, and south central Idaho.

Wheat, barley and other grain crops account for $1.5 billion of the region's $11.2 billion annual agricultural production; roughly 13.4 percent of total revenues. Washington continues to lead the region in wheat production with over 2.4 million acres, and Idaho produced 1.4 million acres of wheat and over 770,000 acres of barley. However, the annual sales for these traditional farm crops have been bettered in recent years by $1.6 billion in sales for fruit, nuts and berry crops, with Washington leading the three state sales receipts at nearly $1.3 billion alone. As enumerated in table 9-4, the rapid growth in annual sales of nursery and greenhouse products is perhaps a most significant trend in Oregon, accounting for nearly 23 percent of that state's total agricultural sales in 1997. Washington and Idaho have also seen rapid sales growth in nursery and greenhouse products. Revenue for field seeds, hay and forage crops increased 131 percent in Oregon from 1987 to 1997, and nearly doubled in Washington and Idaho as well. Over fifty additional crops are grown in significant quantities, and several are important in national production totals.

Table 9-3. Pacific Northwest farms by value of land and buildings			
	Oregon	Washington	Idaho
$39,999 and under	2,586	1,886	2,410
$40,000 to $99,999	3,539	3,075	3,236
$100,000 to $499,999	23,821	15,637	10,979
$500,000 to $999,999	4,254	4,352	2,879
$1,000,000 and over	3,301	4,062	2,849
Source: 1997 Census of Agriculture			

Harvesting grass seed in the Willamette Valley. (Photo by Philip L. Jackson)

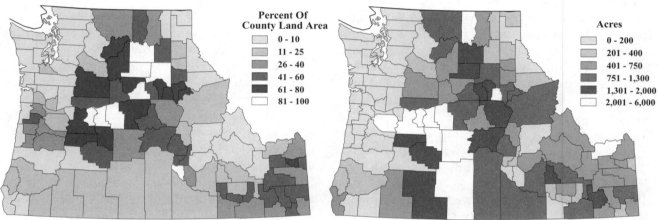

Map 9-6. Land in Farms

Map 9-7. Average Farm Size

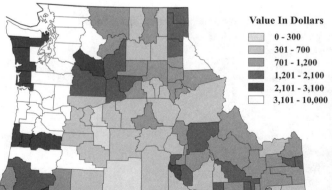

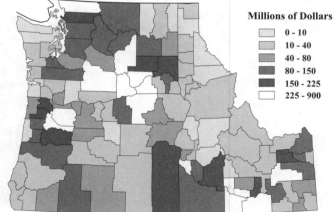

Map 9-8. Value of Farmland per Acre

Map 9-9. Value of Agricultural Products Sold, 1997

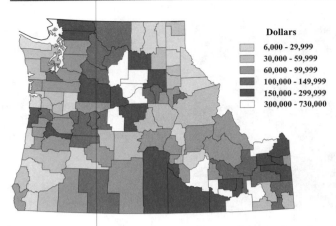

Map 9-10. Average Value per Farm of Agricultural Products Sold, 1997

Dollars
	6,000 - 29,999
	30,000 - 59,999
	60,000 - 99,999
	100,000 - 149,999
	150,000 - 299,999
	300,000 - 730,000

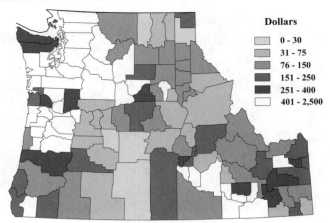

Map 9-11. Average Value per Acre of Agricultural Products Sold, 1997

Dollars
	0 - 30
	31 - 75
	76 - 150
	151 - 250
	251 - 400
	401 - 2,500

Hops, wine grapes, dry peas, peppermint, spearmint, grass seeds, apples, winter pears, hazelnuts, blueberries, cranberries, and potatoes are but a few of the crops of special note. Washington produces nearly 75 percent of the nation's spearmint oil and the three Pacific Northwest states together account for nearly 90 percent of the nation's peppermint production. Thirty-five percent of all hops grown in the U.S. come from the Yakima Valley, and the northern Willamette Valley produces another 18 percent of the nation's annual production. Washington's Columbia Valley region, encompassing the Yakima and Tri-Cities areas, has doubled its vineyard acreage to over 40,000 acres since the 1987 Census. Oregon's Willamette Valley specializes in cool-climate wine grape varieties, and acreage has also nearly doubled, totaling nearly 10,000 acres. Vineyard acreage in Idaho has declined in recent years from 730 in 1987 to 280 acres in 1997.

Cranberries grown on Oregon's south central coast and Washington's Long Beach Peninsula are of exceptional color and flavor, and are used to enhance the quality of many cranberry products.

Orchard crops are an important agricultural feature of the Pacific Northwest. Fruit quality and production is favored by cool wet winters, hot summer days, cool summer nights and favorable spring blooming conditions. Major centers of apple, pear and cherry production include Washington's Wenatchee, Yakima, and Okanogan Valleys, and Oregon's Hood River Valley. Southwest Oregon's Rogue Valley produces high value pear crops. The Payette area's Emmet Valley of Idaho produces apples, and the Willamette Valley contributes significantly to cherry production. Hazelnuts are grown almost exclusively in the Willamette Valley, where acreage continues to grow. More than 32,000 acres are currently under production. These orchard

Table 9-4. Value of commodity groups, 1997 (in thousands of dollars)

	Oregon	Washington	Idaho
Total sales	2,969,194	4,767,727	3,345,860
Grains	240,290	673,641	573,088
Field seeds, hay, forage	444,541	252,478	255,411
Vegetables, sweet corn, & melons	213,101	270,260	50,636
Fruits, nuts, & berries	307,917	1,240,242	24,408
Poultry & poultry products	99,215	170,322	15,000
Dairy products	207,871	622,226	557,339
Cattle & calves	480,260	646,919	910,865
Sheep, lambs, & wool	25,806	3,559	29,977
Hogs & pigs	5,544	7,645	4,473
Other livestock & livestock products	36,302	65,725	54,572
Nursery & greenhouse products	676,429	271,580	57,189

Source: 1997 Census of Agriculture

Nursery stock and greenhouse products account for nearly 25 percent of Oregon's total agricultural revenue. (Photo by Philip L. Jackson)

regions benefit from ample irrigation water, hot summer days, and cool summer nights. In the Okanogan region, the best orchard sites are located on lake shore terraces where spring blooming is safely retarded by nearby cold lake surface temperatures. Orchard valley locations benefit from mountain-valley air drainage and mixing to reduce the freeze hazard on spring nights.

The Willamette Valley of Oregon represents one of the largest concentrations of diversified cropland in the Pacific Northwest. As mentioned previously, the Valley produces orchard crops, vegetable seeds and vegetables for the fresh, frozen and canned markets. It produces a wide variety of grain crops, forage crops, berries, mint, wine grapes, grass seeds, Christmas trees, nursery stock, flower bulbs, dairy products, livestock and poultry. Willamette Valley nursery stock and greenhouse products accounted for the highest value sector in Oregon's agricultural economy in 2000, nearly 25 percent of total annual

revenues. Grass seeds, primarily rye, fescue, and orchard grasses, are planted on nearly 300,000 acres and account for annual revenues of $450 million.

Idaho is the "gem state," but the Snake River Plain is known for "famous potatoes." Centers of production extend from Caldwell-Nampa to Twin Falls, Pocatello, and Idaho Falls where potatoes are planted on nearly 400,000 acres. Significant acreages of mint, field corn, alfalfa, onions, melons, sweet corn, wheat, and barley are also grown in this rich agricultural region. In several of these Idaho counties, over 80 percent of the land is in farms, and irrigated cropland accounts for more than 75 percent of production.

The Columbia Basin of Washington is the most important grain-producing area in the Pacific Northwest. It accounts for roughly two-thirds of the region's wheat production with more than 2.4 million acres planted in 1999. It leads the region in field corn production, and contributes significantly to the

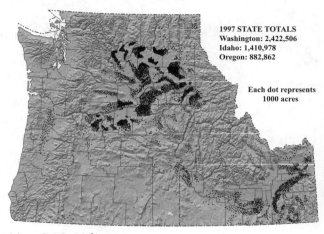

1997 STATE TOTALS
Washington: 2,422,506
Idaho: 1,410,978
Oregon: 882,862

Each dot represents
1000 acres

Map 9-12. Wheat

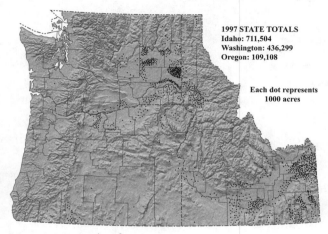

1997 STATE TOTALS
Idaho: 711,504
Washington: 436,299
Oregon: 109,108

Each dot represents
1000 acres

Map 9-13. Barley for Grain

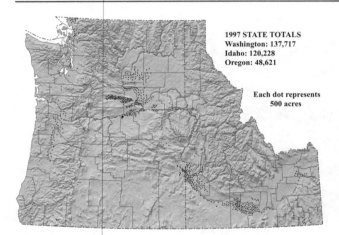

1997 STATE TOTALS
Washington: 137,717
Idaho: 120,228
Oregon: 48,621

Each dot represents
500 acres

Map 9-14. Field Corn for All Purposes

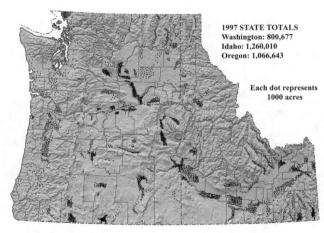

1997 STATE TOTALS
Washington: 800,677
Idaho: 1,260,010
Oregon: 1,066,643

Each dot represents
1000 acres

Map 9-15. Hay

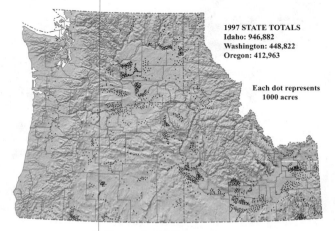

1997 STATE TOTALS
Idaho: 946,882
Washington: 448,822
Oregon: 412,963

Each dot represents
1000 acres

Map 9-16. Alfalfa and Alfalfa Mixtures

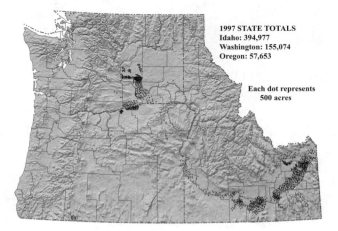

1997 STATE TOTALS
Idaho: 394,977
Washington: 155,074
Oregon: 57,653

Each dot represents
500 acres

Map 9-17. Irish Potatoes

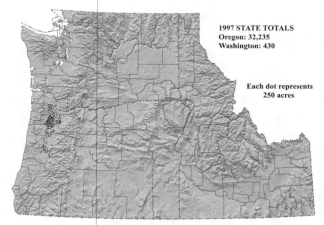

1997 STATE TOTALS
Oregon: 32,235
Washington: 430

Each dot represents
250 acres

Map 9-18. Hazelnuts

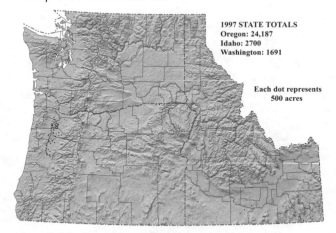

1997 STATE TOTALS
Oregon: 24,187
Idaho: 2700
Washington: 1691

Each dot represents
500 acres

Map 9-19. Snap Beans (Bush and Pole)

region's acreage of barley, oil seeds, hay, and alfalfa crops.

Newly emerging and expanding agricultural areas were identified in the 1999-2000 State and County agricultural reports. These areas include irrigated cropland expansion in Morrow, Crook, and Lake counties in Oregon; Benewah, Custer, and Cassia counties in Idaho; and Chelan, Walla Walla, and Kitsap counties in Washington.

The series of dot density maps (maps 9-12 through 9-30) are based on statistics from the 1997 Agricultural Census. They illustrate the unique geographic patterns of crop and livestock production found throughout the region.

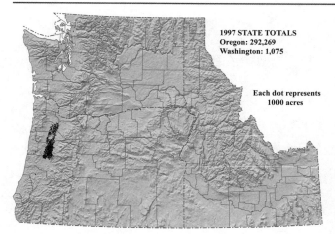

1997 STATE TOTALS
Oregon: 292,269
Washington: 1,075

Each dot represents
1000 acres

Map 9-20. Ryegrass

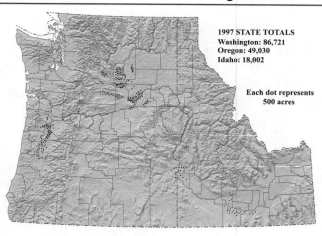

1997 STATE TOTALS
Washington: 86,721
Oregon: 49,030
Idaho: 18,002

Each dot represents
500 acres

Map 9-21. Sweet Corn

1997 STATE TOTALS
Washington: 204,674
Oregon: 10,254
Idaho: 7,201

Each dot represents
500 acres

Map 9-22. Apples

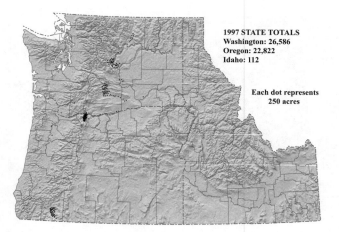

1997 STATE TOTALS
Washington: 26,586
Oregon: 22,822
Idaho: 112

Each dot represents
250 acres

Map 9-23. Pears

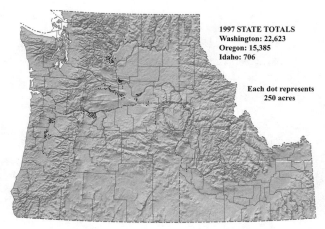

1997 STATE TOTALS
Washington: 22,623
Oregon: 15,385
Idaho: 706

Each dot represents
250 acres

Map 9-24. Cherries (Tart and Sweet)

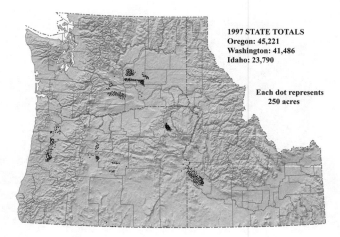

1997 STATE TOTALS
Oregon: 45,221
Washington: 41,486
Idaho: 23,790

Each dot represents
250 acres

Map 9-25. Mint

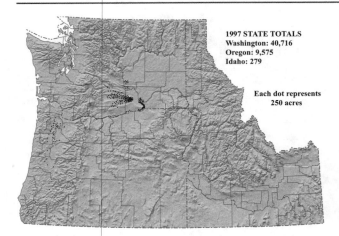

1997 STATE TOTALS
Washington: 40,716
Oregon: 9,575
Idaho: 279

Each dot represents
250 acres

Map 9-26. Grapes

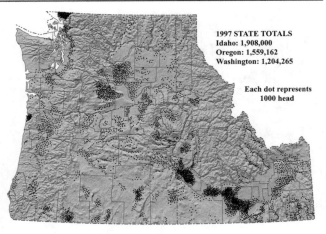

1997 STATE TOTALS
Idaho: 1,908,000
Oregon: 1,559,162
Washington: 1,204,265

Each dot represents
1000 head

Map 9-27. Cattle and Calves

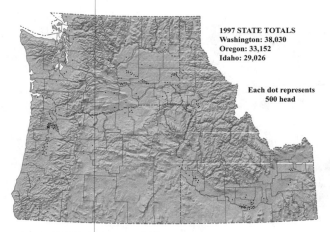

1997 STATE TOTALS
Washington: 38,030
Oregon: 33,152
Idaho: 29,026

Each dot represents
500 head

Map 9-28. Hogs and Pigs

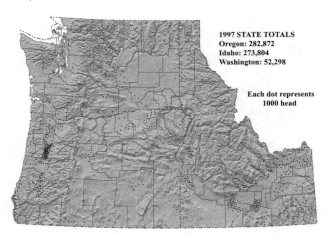

1997 STATE TOTALS
Oregon: 282,872
Idaho: 273,804
Washington: 52,298

Each dot represents
1000 head

Map 9-29. Sheep and Lambs

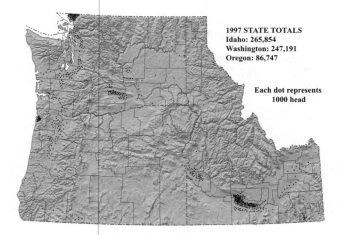

1997 STATE TOTALS
Idaho: 265,854
Washington: 247,191
Oregon: 86,747

Each dot represents
1000 head

Map 9-30. Milk Cows

Sources

Census of Agriculture 1997, 1992, 1987. USDA. National
  Agricultural Statistics Service, State and County Data.
  Volume 1: Geographic Area Series, Volume 2: Subject
  Series.
Economic Research Service, 1999-2000. County Reports.
  USDA. Oregon State University Extension Service.
Idaho Agricultural Statistics Service. 1999. Idaho Department
  of Agriculture. http://www.nass.usda.gov/id/
Washington Agricultural Statistics Service. 1999. Washington
  Department of Agriculture. http://www.nass.usda.gov/wa/

Chapter 10
Forest Resources, Ownership, and Harvest
J. Douglas Brodie

The Pacific Northwest is generously endowed with forest lands, including some of the world's most productive growing areas. The best temperate timber production sites are located west of the Cascade Mountains where Douglas-fir and hemlock-spruce types are found. In the interior, pine, spruce, and fir are highly productive when compared with other North American timber types. In total, 46 percent of the three-state area supports some degree of forest cover, and 75 percent of this is classified as commercial forest land capable of producing 20 cubic feet per acre per year (map 10-1). Much of the land has a productive rate five to eight times more than this minimum level. Parks, wilderness areas, wildlife, recreation and scenic preserves are classified as reserved, and as such are not rated for productivity (see figure 10-1). Federal lands constitute 53 percent of the forest lands in the Pacific Northwest and a comparable proportion of growing stock (maps 10-2 and 10-3). Current political sentiment favors management emphasis other than timber, however there is room for production levels higher than at present.

Annual harvest of timber in the Pacific Northwest supports a major basic segment of the economy, but over the past two decades a pair of major trends have converged to reduce employment. First, technological changes in harvesting and manufacturing have reduced the manpower necessary to process a given volume of timber by more than half. Second, the Federal Government which accounted for about half of the harvest prior to 1990, has retreated to harvest levels that are well below 10 percent (map13.2). These trends are discussed in greater detail in the chapter on Manufacturing and Service Industries. In very recent years forest technology has moved in the direction of resource-saving techniques as the potential for labor-saving techniques have been largely realized.

Timberland Ownership

Ownership of commercial forest land has significant consequences for timber management, timber harvest and the regional economy. Forest industry ownerships are generally located in the region's more productive forest lands and are managed to support the owner's processing mills. In contrast, public ownerships include lands of lower productivity as well as lands appropriated for production of non-market recreation, scenic and fish and wildlife goods and services. All forests, whether public or private,

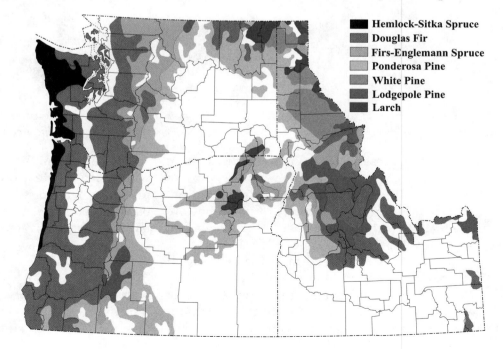

Map 10-1. Generalized Commercial Forest Types

- Hemlock-Sitka Spruce
- Douglas Fir
- Firs-Englemann Spruce
- Ponderosa Pine
- White Pine
- Lodgepole Pine
- Larch

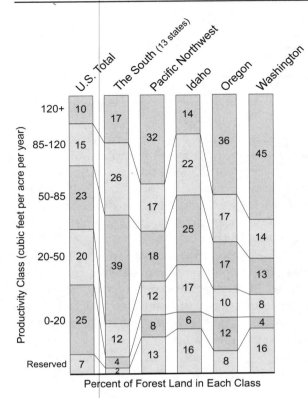

Figure 10-1. Timberland Productivity: Pacific Northwest in the National Context, 1997 base

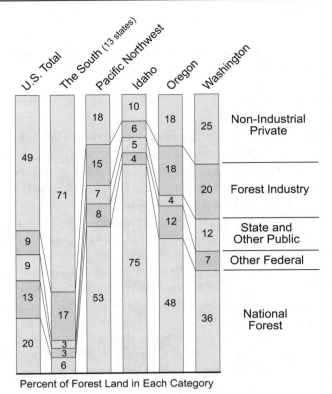

Figure 10-2. Forest Land Ownership: Pacific Northwest in the National Context, 1997 base

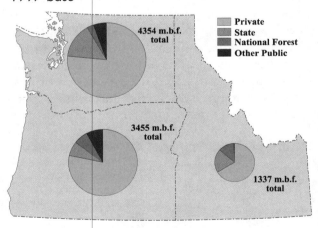

Map 10-2. Timber Harvest by Ownership (in million board feet), 1999

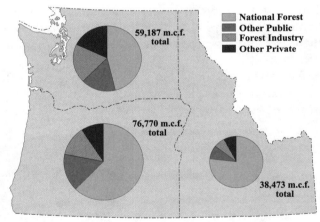

Map 10-3. Volume of Softwood Growing Stock on Timberland (in million cubic feet), 1997

harvested or preserved, provide a wide range of societal benefits such as aesthetic values, erosion control, wildlife habitat and outdoor recreation. Public lands can be dedicated to uses that are incompatible with intensive harvest management, such as roadless recreation and wilderness.

For the Pacific Northwest more than 60 percent of the region's timberlands are in public ownership. Over half is in federal ownership through the Forest Service (46 percent) and the Bureau of Land Management (5 percent).This is in contrast to the

situation in the Southern Forests of the United States, with 9 percent federal ownership and 3 percent other public ownership (see figure 10-2). On a national basis, in recent years, more than 90 percent of the harvest is from privately managed forests.

Major Forest Types

For purposes of timber supply the region can be divided into two zones: Oregon-Washington west of the Cascade Mountain summit and Eastern Oregon-

Washington-Idaho. The Cascade-Coastal zone is characterized by abundant rainfall from fall to spring (see details in the chapter on Climate). Major timber species here are Douglas-fir, western hemlock, western red-cedar, true firs (*Abies* sp.) and Sitka spruce. There is limited utilization of hardwood species dominated by red alder, with very limited use of Oregon white oak and big-leaf maple.

East-side and Idaho forests occur at the higher elevations which intercept sufficient rain and snowfall to support tree growth. Major species are ponderosa pine, Douglas-fir, lodgepole pine, Engelmann spruce, western larch, western white pine and true firs (*Abies* sp.).

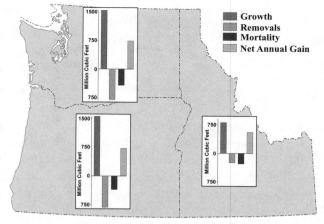

Map 10-4. Softwood Growth, Removals, and Mortality, 1996

Productivity, Harvest, Growth and Mortality

Productivity is compared in table 13-1 across the three states, nationally and in the Southern United States. The basis of comparison is cubic feet per acre per year growth potential. Twenty cubic feet per acre per year—about a quarter of a cord—is the lowest class defining the lower limit of commercial use. One hundred and twenty cubic feet plus defines the upper class—about 1.6 cords. However, the very best lands in the Pacific Northwest exceed this level severalfold. Note the high level of Oregon and Washington lands in the highest classes relative to the United States and the South. Idaho also has lower productivity, similar to the east sides of Oregon and Washington.

Timber harvest by ownership and amount is illustrated on map13-2. Historically (prior to 1991) harvest in Oregon was about double that in Washington; however this is no longer the case, with Oregon's harvest significantly lower. This is due to Oregon's greater reliance on Federal lands for historic harvests. Idaho has an even higher proportion of federal lands, but is not impacted to the same extent by endangered species curbs. Map 13-2 indicates that at present, forest harvest in the Pacific Northwest, as in the United States, is predominantly private.

Map 13-3 shows the volume of live standing timber (growing stock) by state. Oregon contains 44 percent of the timber but supports only 37 percent of the harvest. This contrasts with Washington, which has 34 percent of the growing stock and 48 percent of the harvest. Note the respective proportions of federal growing stock that have recently contributed little to harvest.

When forest growth exceeds the combination of mortality and removals by harvest, there is a net annual gain in growing stock. Map 10-4 shows that each state is experiencing substantial gain in growing stock. This comprises a large excess of growth over harvest on public lands and a closer balance on private. Such a situation cannot prevail throughout the century-long forest production cycle. Growth drops as forests age and either mortality or harvest must rise to provide a long-term zero balance.

The accumulation of growing stock shown on map13.4 has prevailed for about a decade, a small proportion of the forest production cycle. Politically, federal land management may move towards a balance of commodity and non-market preservation services, probably at a lower commodity level than in past decades, or it can continue at current levels of little significant federal harvest. The Pacific Northwest's forest industry will continue at its current levels or show modest growth depending on the resolution.

Sources

RPA (Resources Planning Act) July 2000. Final Statistics USDA Forest Service.

W. Brad Smith, John S. Vissage, David Darr and Raymond Sheffield. 2001. *Forest Resources of the United States, 1977.* Gen. Tech. Rept. GTR-NC-219. St. Paul, Minnesota: USDA Forest Service, North Central Research Station.

Warren, Debra. June 2001. Production Prices, Employment and Trade in Northwest Forest Industries. Data for all quarters 1999. USDA Forest Service Resource Bulletin PNW-RB235 P. 171 (Source for 1999 Timber Harvest by Ownership, map 13.2).

Chapter 11

Soils

Julia A. Jones

Differences among soils result from the interaction of several major soil-forming factors: 1) geology—the parent material from which the soil developed; 2) the climate during soils development, especially soil temperature and moisture regimes; 3) the nature of the organic materials in the soil, reflecting the influence of the biota, particularly vegetation; 4) the relief, reflecting local physiography; and 5) the time over which the soil developed.

Soil Taxonomy

Soils may be differentiated and classified in many ways; the two major approaches in recent years have been by soil genesis or development (inferential classification) and by diagnostic soils properties (taxonomy). The taxonomy classification system presented here depends largely on soil properties that can be observed in the field or laboratory. It is commonly referred to as the Soil Taxonomy system and has been adopted by the U.S.D.A. Soil Conservation Service. Table 11-1 facilitates comparison between the two systems.

Soil orders. Of the ten soil orders which have worldwide distribution, seven, comprising a total of twelve dominant suborders, are shown on map 11-2. Soil orders, the highest taxonomic category, are generalized by common properties, including horizon development and pattern, color, soil moisture, and degree of oxidation. Hence, the distinguishing characteristics selected for the orders tend to give a broad climatic grouping of soils. Soil orders have the suffix –*sol*. The formative element of the order name is usually descriptive, e.g., *Aridisols* are soils developed in areas with little moisture.

Suborders. Each order is subdivided into suborders primarily on the basis of characteristics which produce classes with the greatest genetic homogeneity. These characteristics include moisture regime, temperature, mineralogy, color, texture, and horizon properties. Altogether, forty-seven suborders have been identified; the twelve dominant suborders in the Pacific Northwest are described in the legend. Suborder nomenclature employs a prefix for that characteristic which is important in defining the suborders and a suffix derived from the appropriate order name, e.g., *Argids* are soils in the Aridisol order with argillic or clay horizons.

Great groups. The great group level attempts to consider the soil assemblage (similarity of diagnostic horizons), together with similarity of soil moisture

Table 11-1. Soil orders in the soil taxonomy compared with examples of great soil groups in the 1938 genetic system.		
Formative Element of Soil Taxonomy Groups in the 1938 Genetic System	Derivation of Formative Element	Examples of Great Soil
Alfisols	Nonsense syllable from "pedalfer"	Gray-Brown Podzolic soils, Noncalcic Brown soils, and Planosols
Aridisols	Latin *aridus*, "dry"	Desert, Sierozem, Solonchak, Brown soils, and Reddish Brown soils
Entisols	Nonsense syllable from "recent"	Azonal soils
Histisols	Greek *histos*, "tissues"	Bog soils
Inceptisols	Latin *inceptum*, "beginning"	Sol Brun Acide, Ando, Brown Forest, and Jumic Grey soils
Mollisols	Latin *mollis*, "soft"	Chernozem, Chestnut, Brunizem, and Brown Forest soils
Oxisols	French *oxide*, "oxide"	Laterite soils and Latosols
Spodosols	Greek *spodos*, "wood ash"	Podzols and Brown Podzolic soils
Ultisols	Latin *ultimus*, "last"	Red-Yellow Podzolic soils and Reddish-brown Lateritic soils
Vertisols	Latin *verto*, "to turn"	Grumosols

Source: Soil Conservation Service, *Soil Classification, A Comprehensive System*, 1960.

and temperature regimes. It is the highest category evaluating the whole soil. The Soil Conservation Service recognizes 203 great groups, and these are named by affixing a prefix of one or more formative elements to the suborder name. Therefore a great group will have a name, e.g., Dur*argid* for an indurate, clay-layered Aridisol.

Families and series. Soil families are differentiated on the basis of properties important for utilization, especially for plant growth; soil series comprise a collection of soil individuals with essentially uniform differentiating characteristics. Soil series are given place names suggesting the fusion of the hierarchical soil taxonomy outlined above with real soils observed as soil individuals. Soil series are mapped and described in considerable detail, and provide the resource manager with important information. It should be noted, however, that mapped soil series represent dominant groupings of soil individuals, while the actual region mapped will almost certainly include a minority of other soil individuals.

Type and phase. The comprehensive soil taxonomy also identifies soil type, which represents a lower category based on texture of the plow layer, and soil phase, of which texture is just one significant property distinguishing a variety of soil species.

The U.S.D.A. Soil Taxonomy has undergone several important modifications since this atlas was first published but, since these modifications have not been incorporated in revisions to soil surveys, they are not reflected in the map of soil orders. The two most notable modifications, which are likely to affect the mapping of soils in the Pacific Northwest in two important ways, are: 1) the addition of a kandic subsurface horizon and the kandi- and knaphli- great groups, and 2) the addition of a new soil order, Andisols.

A kandic horizon is similar to an argillic horizon except that it contains low-activity clays and high amounts of exchangeable aluminum, reflecting long periods of intense weathering. Because extreme weathering of clay may occur in some portions of the Coast Range and the foothills of the Cascades, it is conceivable that some soils previously classified as Haplohumults in these areas might now have the designation Kandihumults or Knaphlohumults.

More importantly, most of the soils mapped as Cryandepts and perhaps other soil great groups in the Pacific Northwest may well be reclassified in the

new order Andisols. Andisols are soils which have andic soil properties throughout a depth of 14 inches or more in subhorizons which may be buried but are within 24 inches of the soil surface. Andic soil properites are low bulk density, high aluminum and iron oxide content, and high phosphate retention, characteristic of volcanic ash and the weathering products of other volcanic materials. Since many of the soils of the Cascades, Coast Range, and mountains of Idaho are dominated by volcanic materials, many soils in these areas may eventually be remapped as Andisols.

Soil Survey Status

Map 11-1 shows the status of soil surveys in the Pacific Northwest as of 2000. Soil surveys for agricultural, engineering, and planning purposes are made cooperatively by federal and state government personnel, usually with the U.S.D.A. Soil Conservation Service in charge and the agricultural experiment stations attached to land-grant universities as chief contributors. Other agencies, including Bureau of Land Management, Bureau of Indian Affairs, Bureau of Reclamation (irrigation suitability studies), Forest Service, and state forest departments, may enter into cooperative agreements. This joint effort, initiated in 1899, is referred to as the National Cooperative Soil Survey.

Modern soil surveys are extensive documents describing the geography of the region's soils, normally on a county basis, initiated on a priority basis depending on the presence of productive agricultural lands. Soil maps on a scale of 1:20,000 based on air photos and soils series descriptions are qualified by pedological notes. The surveys include sections on use and management of soils for a variety of purposes.

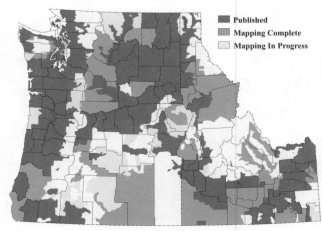

Map 11-1. Soil Survey Status, 2000

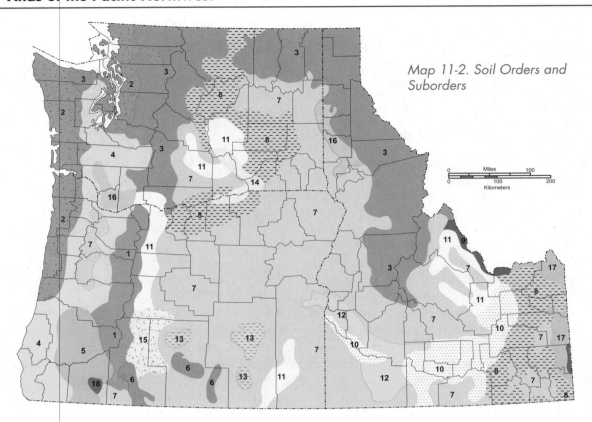

Map 11-2. Soil Orders and Suborders

Inceptisols

Inceptisols are soils with weakly differentiated horizons exhibiting some alteration of the parent material, but sill containing weatherable materials. The B horizon typically has little clay accumulation. In the Pacific Northwest, these soils generally occur under cool summer climate where parent materials are of late of post-Pleistocene origin and do not show translocation of clay. The order is present in the Puget Lowland, Coast Range, Cascades, and Idaho mountains. Two suborders are shown:

Umbrepts are soils with surface horizons darkened by high contents of organic matter, having crystalline clay minerals, with relatively high capacity to hold exchangeable cations but with acidic reaction, and are freely drained. They develop in areas of high winter precipitation and moderate winter temperatures in the Coast Range, Oregon Cascades, and Puget Lowland where coniferous forest is the prevailing vegetation.

1 Cryumbrepts—in cold regions.

2 Haplumbrepts—in temperate to warm regions.

Andepts are soils with high contents of volcanic ash and are therefore of low bulk density. They are of recent development, occurring in mountainous areas in Idaho and in the North Cascades under cool summer conditions.

3 Cryandepts—in cold regions.

Ultisols

Strong weathering and leaching and a warm (mean annual temperature 46° F), moist (40-120 inches mean annual precipitation), and a summer-dry climate help produce Ultisols. These soils have a clay-rich horizon low in bases. Ultisols develop in a variety of parent materials and usually exhibit considerable stability. This order is found in the low hilly regions between the Cascades and Coast Range, where they generally support coniferous forest growth, have good drainage, and display increasing acidity and decreasing base saturation with depth. Vegetative nutrient cycling is a key factor in the formation of these soils. Many are reddish. Two suborders are distinguished:

Humults are highly organic Ultisols developing under moist, cool to cold winters, and warm to hot dry summers. Humults show good drainage and are mostly dark colored. They develop on steep slopes, are easily eroded, and are found in southwester Oregon and the foothills of the Cascades and Coast Range.

4 Haplohumults—with subsurface horizon of clay and/or weatherable minerals; in temperate climates.

Xerults are freely drained Ultisols in areas of Mediterranean climate with little organic material in the upper horizons and are seldom saturated with water. They are confined to the hilly regions in the middle portions of the Rogue and Umpqua drainages and support a mixed coniferous-broadleaved evergreen vegetation with xeric elements.

5 Haploxerults—with a surface clay-rich horizon either having weatherable minerals or a decreasing clay content with depth, or both.

Mollisols

Soils that have dark-colored friable, organic-rich surface horizons and which are high in bases, occurring in areas having a cold subhumid and semiarid climate. Mollisols are widespread in the region, especially in areas of steppe and shrub-steppe vegetation. These soils may have clay-enriched horizons, calcic horizons, sodium-rich horizons, or indurate horizons. Most soils are well drained, but wet soils may have soluble salts of high exchangeable sodium or both. Three suborders are shown:

Aquolls are Mollisols that are seasonally wet with a thick, nearly black surface horizon and gray subsurface horizon. In south-central Oregon in the Warner Valley and Klamath Lake area, horizons have been altered, but no accumulation of calcium or clay has taken place.

 Haplaquolls—with horizons in which some materials have been altered or removed, but still may contain some calcium carbonate or gypsum.

Xerolls are Mollisols in winter-moist, summer-dry climates. Such soils are continually dry for long periods of time. With irrigation and when adequate natural soil moisture is available, these soils are important for grain and forage. These are the prevailing soils in the steppe and shrub-steppe areas of the region.

 Argixerolls—with subsurface clay horizon, either thin or brownish.

 Haploxerolls—with subsurface horizon high in bases, but with little clay, calcium carbonate, or gypsum.

Borolls are Mollisols of cool and cold regions exhibiting black surface horizons. In the Pacific Northwest they are confined to the extreme eastern portion of Idaho.

Argiborolls—with subsurface clay horizon, in cool regions.

Aridisols

As suggested by the name, this order occurs in dry areas where the soils are never moist for periods of more than three consecutive months. The soils are low in organic content and the horizons are light in color and have a soft consistency when dry. These soils are found in the rainshadow area of the Cascades and in extensive areas in southern Idaho. Two suborders are shown:

Orthids are Aridisols that display accumulation of calcium carbonate and other salts but do not have clay accumulations in horizons. Such soils are found in scattered localities in the drier areas of the Pacific Northwest.

Calciorthids—with a horizon containing much calcium carbonate or gypsum.

Camborthids—with horizons from which some materials have been removed or altered, but still contain calcium carbonate or gypsum.

Argids are Aridisols distinguished by a horizon in which clay has accumulated. These are mostly found in the Snake River Plain to the south of Boise.

 Haplargids—with loamy horizon of clay, without sodium (alkali) accumulation, but may have calcium accumulation below the argillic horizon.

Natragids—with a clay accumulation horizon and alkali (sodium) accumulation.

Entisols

Soils in this order exhibit little or no horizon development. In the Pacific Northwest these soils develop in sandy parent material and are of very recent origin on gently sloping terrain. They continue to receive parent material. They occur east of the Cascade Range. One suborder in shown on the map:

Psamments are Entisols with loamy fine sand to coarser sand texture developing in areas of shifting to stabilized sand dunes. Sand origin is largely fluvial but with local redeposition by wind.

Torripsamments—moist for less than three consecutive months and developing under cool to warm soil temperatures promoting soluble salt accumulation.

Xeropsamments—freely drained soils developing from weatherable materials under moist-winter, dry-summer climates.

Alfisols

Soils in this order are differentiated by clay-enriched horizons, moderate organic matter accumulation, and a gray to brown color. They are usually leached an are acidic occurring where at lease three months of growing season are cool and moist. Three areas are dominated by Alfisols: The hilly region north of Portland; the area northeast of Moscow; and the mountains near the eastern boundary of Idaho. Two suborders are shown:

Udalfs are Alfisols with a mesic or warm temperature regime and are almost always moist despite periods of summer dryness. These soils are brownish or reddish. The area north of Portland in which Udalfs prevail has a complex of other soils as well. The Udalf area in Idaho occurs in steep mountainous terrain.

Hapludalfs—with subsurface clay horizon below a thin eluvial horizon. These are good farming soils.

Boralfs are found in cool and cold regions and may be water-saturated in winter. A bleached eluvial horizon often grades into a horizon containing clay or alkali. They occur in the mountains of eastern Idaho.

 Cryoboralfs—in cold regions; with sandy upper layers, grayish color, and subsurface clay horizon.

Vertisols

Relegated to this order are clayey soils that have wide, deep cracks which form during the dry season. They occur in areas with marked dry-wet periods. One suborder is present:

Xererts are Vertisols that have wide, deep cracks that open and close once a year, remaining open for more than two months in summer and closing for more than two months in winter. In the Pacific Northwest, one area in the vicinity of Medford is characterized by this suborder.

Chromoxererts—with a brownish surface horizon.

Chapter 12
Water Resources
Keith W. Muckleston

The Pacific Northwest, considered as a whole, appears to be richly endowed with water. The volume of runoff from the region exceeds that of any other major water resources region in the conterminous United States, surpassing most regions manyfold. Moreover, in terms of per capita runoff, the relative position of the region is even more favorable. The utility of the resource is diminished, however, by marked variations in spatial and temporal patterns of supply.

Supply

The most significant source of fresh water within the Pacific Northwest is the Columbia River system. Rising in the Rocky Mountains of the United States and Canada, this system provides drainage for approximately 75 percent of the region and accounts for about 55 percent of the total runoff. When runoff from Canada is included, the Columbia system discharges approximately 65 percent of the total.

East of the Cascade Range, the Columbia Basin is divided into seven sub-basins (see map 12-1). Much of the land is subhumid to arid, and traversed by rivers that originate in various mountain ranges lying both within and to the north and northeast of the region. The Rocky Mountains are the source of much of the flow.

Three additional sub-basins east of the Cascade Range are not part of the Columbia System. A number of streams in Oregon with internal drainage are designated as the Oregon Closed Basin, and portions of the Klamath and Bear rivers also drain small parts of the region. The Klamath rises in Oregon, flows through northern California, and discharges into the Pacific Ocean. Waters of the Bear River rise in Utah and Wyoming before crossing southeastern Idaho, and finally discharge into Utah's Great Salt Lake.

Of the four humid sub-basins west of the Cascade Range, two—the Willamette and Lower Columbia—are part of the Columbia River system, while the

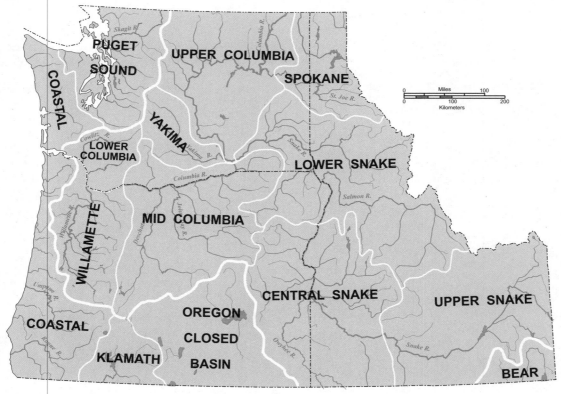

Map 12-1. Drainage Basins and Sub-basins

streams of the Coastal and Puget Sound sub-basins discharge into waters of the Pacific Ocean.

The relative discharge of some regional rivers is shown in table 12-1. The runoff value for an area is derived by subtracting evapotranspiration and deep percolation from the amount of precipitation received. The values on map 12-2 refer to the mean annual depths in inches of water entering streams and rivers from locations within the various shaded areas. Each inch of runoff per square mile contributes 17.4 million gallons of water to surface flow. The depths of runoff from areas within a shaded area may be inferred.

The Pacific Northwest may be divided into two subregions based on runoff characteristics. West of the Cascade Mountains, runoff is generally high, reflecting relatively heavy precipitation and moderate levels of evapotranspiration. Indeed, the yield of runoff west of the Cascades is unrivaled in the conterminous United States. Yields of more than 80 inches are common in the Coast and Cascade ranges, while some of the windward slopes of the Olympic Mountains contribute more than 160 inches. Streams

west of the Cascades produce about two-thirds of the total runoff from the Pacific Northwest although they drain less than one-fourth of the region.

By contrast, the much larger subregion east of the Cascade Range generates markedly lower levels of runoff per unit area. Much of it contributes less than 10 inches per square mile, and most of the surface water originates in relatively small mountainous areas. The position of mountains can be identified on the map by locating areas of relatively high runoff (20 inches or more). For example, the Blue Mountains in northeastern Oregon and southeastern Washington, the Wallowa Mountains in northeastern Oregon, and the Bitterroot and Coeur d'Alene mountains along the northeastern border of Idaho stand out as islands of relatively high runoff.

Map 12-3 indicates that about one-half of the Pacific Northwest is underlain by aquifers with moderate to large potential yields of groundwater. The value of this source is great because it generally coincides with areas of heavy water use. At present, aquifers in the Snake River Plain account for most of the groundwater use in the region, although extensive withdrawals are

Table 12-1. Discharge (in millions of acre-feet/year) of selected rivers in the Pacific Northwest

Columbia	180.1
Columbia (at The Dalles)	133.7
Snake	36.8
Willamette	23.8
Rogue	8.2
Skagit (at Concrete)	10.3

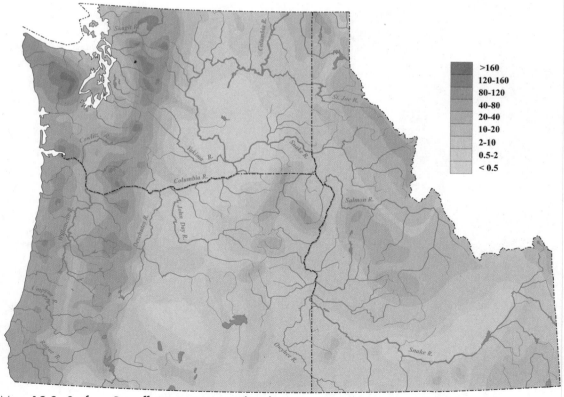

Map 12-2. Surface Runoff, in mean annual inches

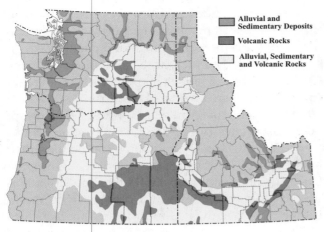

Map 12-3. Major Aquifers

also made in some parts of the Puget Sound and Willamette sub-basins.

Map 12-4 illustrates that the patterns of temporal distribution of surface runoff vary considerably within the region. The hydrographs show average monthly discharges as a percentage of the yearly average. If the runoff remained constant throughout the year, 8.33 percent would be discharged each month.

Through much of the region's history the temporal patterns of runoff largely reflected natural phenomena within a river basin, including: its location in either marine or continental subregions of the Pacific Northwest; the type and extent of natural vegetation within the drainage basin; and the structure of aquifer units underlying the basin. Although the combined effects of natural phenomena remain dominant in most rivers basins within the region, anthropogenic influences have become more important in some basins through increasingly intensive water use. Principal anthropogenic influences include stream flow depletions from extensive irrigation withdrawals and the construction and operation of large dams and storage reservoirs, the major purpose of which is to reduce temporal variations of runoff.

Columbia River. The hydrograph of the Columbia River at The Dalles, Oregon, reflects average discharge conditions for a 120-year period from 1879-1999. It shows that a disproportionately high percentage takes place during the late spring and early summer. This pattern results because most of the precipitation above The Dalles falls on the various ranges of the

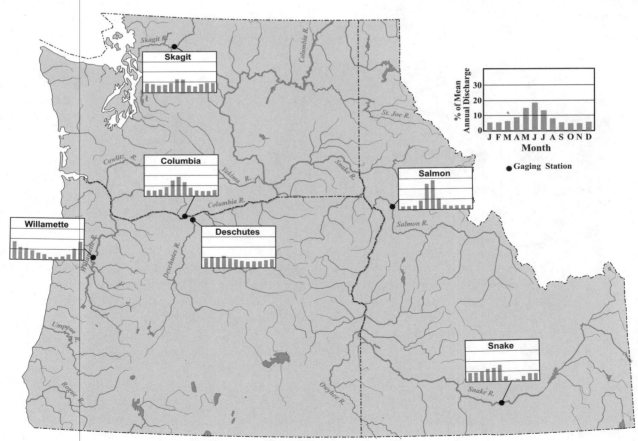

Map 12-4. Surface Water Yearly Flow Cycle

Rocky Mountains stretching from northwestern Wyoming through Idaho and western Montana and far into British Columbia. Although most of the precipitation takes place in the late autumn and winter, it is retained in the mountainous headwater areas of the Columbia in the form of snow and ice, being released months later as melt water.

In the latter half of the twentieth century the natural runoff pattern was modified by the provision of large volumes of upstream storage. Thus the main flows of May, June, and July, although still noticeably higher than those of other months, are reduced while, conversely, the mean discharge levels in the late fall and winter are increased by the release of stored water.

Salmon River. The hydrograph for the Salmon River illustrates the mean monthly discharge for a fifty-five year period of record from 1910 to 1965. In this case the combined discharge of May and June constitutes approximately one-half of the yearly total. The July discharge as a percentage of the total is somewhat less than that of the Columbia River because the more southerly location of the Salmon drainage basin results in an earlier period of maximum runoff. Very little storage or irrigation development in the Salmon River Basin means that the present monthly pattern of discharge remains essentially unchanged.

Snake River. The hydrograph of the Snake River at Milner, Idaho, reflects the headwater conditions in the Middle Rockies as well as anthropogenic modifications. The relatively heavy spring runoff is characteristic of a snowmelt regime, but occurs earlier than those in the Salmon and Columbia river drainage because of a more southerly location. Heavy irrigation use above Milner further reduces the already modest summer flows.

Deschutes River. The unusually moderate temporal variation of runoff in the Deschutes Basin reflects the fact that much of it is underlain with porous basalts. These basaltic and andesitic volcanic rocks of Quaternary and late Tertiary age absorb potentially high runoff and later release it when discharge would otherwise fall to much lower levels. Provision of storage and irrigation development have not notably altered the hydrograph at its confluence with the Columbia, but significant modifications are present in some other reaches of the system.

Willamette River. The temporal flow regime of the Willamette River is representative of many rivers west of the Cascades in both Washington and Oregon. Runoff reflects the temporal distribution of precipitation because relatively little is retained as ice and snow. The Willamette hydrograph is compiled from a thirty-year period of record (1960-1999). The temporal distribution of present flows has been modified somewhat by the completion of many flood-control reservoirs since the end of World War II. While the high mean flows of the mid winter months have remained practically unchanged, those of February through April have been reduced somewhat when reservoirs are refilled. The low mean flows of July, August and September have been increased appreciably by releases from upstream storage.

Skagit River. This hydrograph is atypical of rivers west of the Cascades. Relatively higher mean flows occur in June and July because much of the runoff originates from snowmelt at high elevations in the North Cascades of Washington and British Columbia. Since completion of Ross Dam by Seattle City Light in 1949, considerable reservoir storage space reduces summer high flows while increasing flows during the winter when energy demands are highest.

Water Use

Water uses may be divided into two major categories: instream uses, which utilize water within stream banks, and offstream uses, which divert water out of its channel before use.

Instream Uses include generation of hydroelectric energy, navigation, fish and wildlife habitat, waste carriage and assimilation, recreation, preservation of wild and scenic rivers, and maintenance of riverine ecosystems. Unlike other regions of the western United States, water utilization in the Pacific Northwest is characterized by heavy dependence on instream uses, especially for the generation of hydroelectric energy. The Pacific Northwest is the nation's unrivaled leader in the production of hydropower, utilizing a volume of water that is several times the total regional discharge. This results because the same water is used repeatedly at successive dams and powerhouses along several large rivers. For example, in the United States the mainstem of the Columbia River includes eleven monumental dams with very large hydroelectric generating facilities. For more detail on hydroelectric

Bonneville Dam and lock. (Photo courtesy of U.S. Corps of Engineers, Portland District)

generation, see the following chapter on energy resources.

Navigation is another major instream use. Large expenditures by the federal government have been made to enhance inland water navigation on the Columbia System. From Portland to the Pacific a 40-foot channel is maintained. In addition, from the Bonneville Locks at river mile 145 to the Port of Lewiston in Idaho, a chain of eight reservoirs stretches 320 miles, which not only allows slack water navigational conditions for inland water carriers but also guarantees a navigation channel of 14 feet depth. Spacious navigation locks at the eight dams lift barge tows from 8 feet above mean sea level at the Bonneville lock to 738 feet on the reservoir reaching Lewiston, Idaho.

Early efforts to promote navigation have altered hydrologic conditions even though navigation is no longer significant on some rivers. The situation on the Willamette is a case in point. Although there is no longer commercial navigation on the river above Willamette Falls, near Portland, summer releases of water from flood control reservoirs continue to be made in accordance with a 1938 Act which directs that releases be adequate to maintain a flow of 6,000 cubic feet per second for navigation at Salem. During the normal low water months of July-September these releases coincidentally contribute significantly to improved water quality in the Willamette.

Two proposals related to navigation continue to fuel sharp disagreement: The first would deepen the channel between Portland and the Pacific to facilitate the passage of very large ships used increasingly in modern maritime commerce; the second would breach the four federal dams on the Lower Snake River in order to improve migration for salmon.

Channel dredging is vigorously opposed by environmental and fishing interests, while dam removal is staunchly resisted by organizations representing navigation, agriculture, energy, and economic development.

Another significant flow use is the maintenance of fish and wildlife habitat. Water resource developments in the region have affected aquatic life markedly. Although enhancement of habitat sometimes results, the consequences have more frequently been negative. Inadequate consideration of biological factors during project design and/or operation have resulted in severe losses. Animal communities, especially fur bearers, have in general been negatively impacted by the development of water resources. On the other hand, one very large irrigation project (the Columbia Basin Project) has greatly enhanced the habitat for migratory waterfowl by creating many lakes and extensive marshes in a semiarid area.

Valuable anadromous fisheries (salmon and steelhead) have been adversely affected by the development of water resources. This is particularly evident in the Columbia-Snake system. The once bountiful natural runs that were thought to be inexhaustible have declined sharply and some have even disappeared. How to preserve and enhance remaining runs continues to be the focus of controversy among various interests.

Hatchery programs may have mitigated some of the losses. Indeed, hatchery fish now far outnumber wild stocks. These programs are less successful above the confluence of the Columbia and Snake rivers, however, because of the cumulative effects of losses at dams below the hatcheries. Despite the apparent success of hatcheries, many fishery biologists are becoming increasingly concerned about potential threats to wild runs posed by hatchery fish.

Some runs of anadromous salmonoids have been listed under the Endangered Species Act and approximately 40,000 miles of streams and rivers are now reserved for anadromous fish habitat. If anadromous fisheries are to be substantially increased over the present low levels, some reduction in the future output of hydropower, irrigated agriculture, water transport, and perhaps other water-related goods and services probably will be necessary.

Another instream use of water is by recreationists. Many outdoor recreational activities are water-oriented. The region has a disproportionately large per capita supply of surface waters suitable for outdoor recreation, and all types of recreational uses of water in the Pacific Northwest have grown rapidly over the last half century.

The Pacific Northwest has a disproportionately large number of rivers designated under the Wild and Scenic Rivers Act. As shown in the chapter covering recreation, many of the wild and scenic rivers are in rugged and remote parts of the region— locations ideal for upstream storage. Implementation of the Wild and Scenic Rivers Program requires tradeoffs. Superior aesthetic/leisure-time experiences, white-water recreation, and scientific benefits are gained at the expense of such traditional benefits as slack-water recreation, hydroelectric generation, and provision of upstream storage. For example, over twenty million acre-feet of potential storage is foregone at major potential storage sites in existing and study river areas.

One of the principal instream uses of water is to carry away, dilute, and assimilate wastes. When the ratio of wastes to the volume of receiving waters is small, assimilation of organic wastes and adequate dilution of many other waste products takes place. In such instances, water quality is not seriously impaired, and this was the case in the early settlement period of the region. During the twentieth century, however, the rapid growth of population and economic productivity in the Pacific Northwest caused the volume and variety of wastes deposited in the region's waters to increase markedly. This overtaxed the capacity of some of the receiving waters to assimilate and/or dilute wastes, resulting in the present poor water quality (pollution) in some of the region's surface waters. In addition, in some tributaries of the Columbia-Snake system east of the Cascades, heavy irrigation withdrawals and con-

sumptive use also reduce the assimilative capacity of the streams.

Improved treatment by industries—especially in chemical recovery—has been chiefly responsible for decreased levels of biochemical oxygen demand in the region, thus freeing up oxygen for fish and other aquatic life. However, there is an apparent widespread increase in the presence of organic and inorganic toxins from non-point sources of pollution, including over twenty million acre-feet of irrigation return flows. In addition, water quality problems exist downstream from densely populated areas, including excessive counts of coliform bacteria and low levels of dissolved oxygen. Although the region has relatively few problems associated with siltation, erosion of the loess-mantled Palouse Hills creates undesirable levels of turbidity and turbine scour at some of the generating plans on the lower Snake River.

Thermal pollution is considered a serious problem in some river reaches because anadromous salmonoids have a low tolerance to temperatures exceeding 68 degrees Fahrenheit. Such temperatures are periodically encountered, for example, in reaches of the lower Snake River and in the Yakima sub-basin.

Despite considerable flood storage, levee construction, and channel improvements, much riverine land remains susceptible to inundation. Unregulated flows on some tributaries of the Columbia and in the Puget Sound and Coastal sub-basins contribute to continued property damage. Another contributing factor is the continued conversion of flood-prone lands to more intensive uses, which may be encouraged by a false sense of security following structural flood protection measures.

Offstream Uses include: irrigation; livestock watering; public supply (which usually furnishes municipal, residential/domestic, commercial, and light industrial needs); self-supplied industrial; mining; and thermoelectric cooling.

Irrigation is clearly the dominant offstream use in the region, accounting for more than four times the total withdrawals by all other uses combined. Irrigators in Idaho withdraw slightly more than half the regional total while those in Washington and Oregon each withdraw almost one-quarter. East of the Cascades irrigation is the dominant use in each of the ten sub-basins. Agricultural water use even represents an important part of the total withdrawals in two of the sub-basins—the Willamette and the Coastal—in the relatively humid western part of the

Pacific Northwest. This reflects the normally dry summers which require agriculturists to irrigate many of the crops.

An important aspect of irrigation is its large consumptive use, which can adversely effect other water users. Consumptive use refers to the part of the water withdrawn that is evaporated, transpired, or incorporated into the product. Therefore it is not returned to streams or economically accessible groundwater for subsequent uses. In the Pacific Northwest approximately 40 percent of the water withdrawn for irrigation is used consumptively, which represents almost 96 percent of total water consumption in the region. Finally, much of the irrigation water that does return to surface and groundwater contains undesirably high levels of silt, salts, and agricultural chemicals, reducing its value for reuse.

Public supply withdraws the second largest volume of water in the region, although it is only 7 percent as much as irrigation. The relative amounts withdrawn by state are roughly proportional to their populations. The leading sub-basins in declining order of use are Puget Sound, Willamette, and Spokane. The region's two leading municipal systems—operated by Seattle and Portland—rely heavily on surface waters from the Cascades, while Tacoma and Spokane depend on groundwater. In Idaho groundwater provides over 90 percent of the public supply, reflecting the widespread availability of subsurface sources. Public water supply in Oregon derives over 80 percent of its water from surface waters, owing to the state's population concentrations in the Willamette Valley. In Washington sources of public supply are about evenly divided between surface and groundwaters.

Self-supplied industrial withdrawals in the Lower Columbia sub-basin comprise approximately 80 percent of the total. The distribution of industrial withdrawals reflects in large measure the location of the pulp and paper industry, which is concentrated in the Lower Columbia, Puget Sound, and Coastal sub-basins. Food processing is usually the most significant industrial use of water east of the Cascades, but primary metals are significant in the Clark Fork-Kootenai-Spokane and Mid-Columbia sub-basins.

In the Pacific Northwest relatively little water is withdrawn to cool thermoelectric plants, reflecting the continued dominance of hydroelectric generation. This is in sharp contrast to most other major U.S. water resource regions where such withdrawals rank either first or second among offstream uses. In the Pacific Northwest thermoelectric withdrawals are concentrated in the Hanford Nuclear Reservation and in southwestern Washington to serve large coal-fired plants near Centralia.

Transboundary Water Management

Transboundary water management in the Pacific Northwest is significant because rivers cross jurisdictional boundaries at many points in the region, potentially carrying negative and/or positive attributes with them. Actions by water users upstream may significantly alter the quantity, quality, and/or timing of runoff in the rivers of a down-stream jurisdiction. Conversely, water management downstream may affect those upstream through creation of impoundments that encroach into the upstream area or by limiting access of migratory fish or barge traffic to upstream areas. Water-related externalities such as these involve both national and subnational jurisdictions in the region.

International Water Management. The Columbia River system is shared by seven U.S. states and the Canadian province of British Columbia. The Columbia's drainage area in Canada comprises 15.4 percent of the total watershed but contributes 30.6 percent of the total runoff. British Columbia contributes about as much runoff to the Columbia-Snake system as the combined input from Idaho, Montana, Wyoming, Nevada, and Utah.

Cooperative management by the United States and Canada results from a treaty finalized in 1964, under the terms of which the two countries agree to the principle of sharing downstream benefits. Canada provides storage capacity and in return receives one-half of the value of the resulting benefits accruing to the United States. Canada received a lump-sum payment of $254 million as its share of anticipated increased hydroelectric generation in the United States over a thirty-year period after completion of the treaty dams. In addition, the United States paid Canada $64 million for sixty years of reduced flood damages which would result from Canadian storage. Since the thirty-year period has elapsed, Canada's share of increased generation in the United States is returned to the border.

Interests associated with electrical energy and/or more intensive development of riverine lands benefit from the cooperative development of the Columbia River system. It has markedly increased hydroelectric output, while also decreasing flood damage in both countries. This was achieved for the

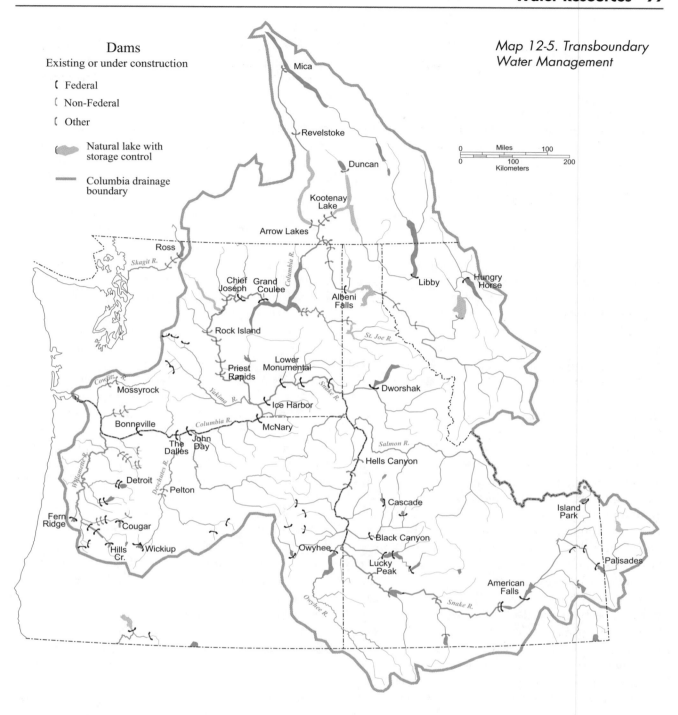

Dams

Existing or under construction

(Federal

(Non-Federal

(Other

Natural lake with storage control

Columbia drainage boundary

Map 12-5. Transboundary Water Management

Mica

Revelstoke

Duncan

Kootenay Lake

Arrow Lakes

Ross

Skagit R.

Chief Joseph

Grand Coulee

Albeni Falls

Libby

Hungry Horse

Columbia R.

St. Joe R.

Rock Island

Lower Monumental

Priest Rapids

Dworshak

Yakima R.

Snake R.

Ice Harbor

Cowlitz R.

Mossyrock

Bonneville

Columbia R.

McNary

John Day

The Dalles

Deschutes R.

Detroit

Pelton

Salmon R.

Hells Canyon

Willamette R.

Fern Ridge

Cougar

Hills Cr.

Wickiup

Owyhee

Cascade

Black Canyon

Lucky Peak

Island Park

Palisades

American Falls

Owyhee R.

Snake R.

most part through provision of large storage reservoirs at Libby, Mica, Arrow Lakes, and Duncan (see map 12-5) which reduce high flows from snowmelt in the late spring and early summer and increase flows from the start of October through March, when the regional demand for electrical energy is high. The graph of the Columbia River's annual flow cycle is shown on map 12-4.

Both Canadian storage and contribution to total runoff are very important to hydroelectric output in the Pacific Northwest. Most of the region's total hydroelectric generating capacity is installed on the mainstem of the Columbia River at eleven dams from Grand Coulee to Bonneville Dam (see map 10.5 of electric generating facilities). On this 725-mile reach of the Columbia, 19,000 Mw of generating capacity have been installed, much of it since the treaty to take advantage of increased flows from storage releases during the autumn and winter seasons. Canada contributes significantly to the total volume of water flowing in this major power-producing reach of the Columbia River: approximately three-quarters of the flow at Grand Coulee decreasing to two-fifths of the total river flow at Bonneville Dam.

Cooperative development of the Columbia River also creates important flood damage reduction benefits in both countries. The major benefits in the United States are in the Portland-Vancouver area. Here total storage in the system—much of it in Canada—is projected to reduce record flow by 45 percent. In Canada, the principal benefits are along a major tributary, the Kootenay (Kootenai in the United States), which rises in Canada and then swings through Montana and northeastern Idaho before returning to Canada. Libby Dam in Montana provides flood control and hydropower benefits downstream in Canada. The dam also backs water across the U.S.-Canadian border and many miles into British Columbia, which Canada agreed to under the terms of the treaty. It is noteworthy that Libby Dam also provides flood crest reduction benefits on the United States side of the border, as well as increasing hydropower output in the autumn-winter period at downstream power plants in Canada and the Pacific Northwest. Downstream benefits accruing in Canada from storage at Libby are not shared with the United States

The results of the 1964 treaty are not all positive. Treaty implementation has been harmful to anadromous salmonoids by altering the annual flow cycle and stimulating the installation of additional generating capacity along the Columbia between Grand Coulee and Bonneville Dams. The interests of salmon fishers—tribal, commercial, and sports—received little attention during treaty negotiation.

The Ross Dam agreement is another example of innovative cooperation. Seattle City Light wanted to increase the output of hydroelectric generation from its Skagit River plants by increasing the height of Ross Dam. But doing this would have caused the existing reservoir to further encroach onto Canadian territory, which was strongly resisted by British Columbia. A solution was reached when the provincial utility, BC Hydro, agreed to supply Seattle City Light with the electrical energy that increasing the height of the dam would have provided. This energy is supplied in return for payment to BC Hydro of the funds Seattle would have expended in the construction and operation of the higher dam.

The United States and Canada have made considerable progress on cooperative transboundary water management, but challenges remain. For example, how can provisions of the U.S. Endangered Species Act be met in transboundary waters, when doing so may have negative effects in Canada, which does not have similar legislation? This problem became apparent when United States efforts to increase numbers of white sturgeon in the Kootenai and salmon in the Columbia affected the timing of discharge from storage reservoirs.

Intraregional Water Management. There is also need for increased transboundary water management within the Pacific Northwest, particularly between upstream and downstream states. Idaho, Montana, Utah, and Wyoming are usually considered to be the upstream states, while Washington and Oregon are downstream entities. Water management in one part of the region can have repercussions on water uses in other parts. For example, if new large-scale irrigation developments are undertaken in Idaho's Snake River Plain, the quantity of water available for hydropower and other uses is diminished in the downstream states of Washington and Oregon. Conversely, salmon harvest in reaches of the Columbia system in Washington and Oregon adversely affect fishing interests in Idaho. Over the last several decades, sporadic attempts by states in the Pacific Northwest to allocate waters of the Columbia-Snake system between them have been unsuccessful. Only piecemeal progress has been made: Idaho and Wyoming have concluded an interstate compact on division of the Snake River, while Oregon and California have done the same for the Klamath River.

Since 1980 a four-state organization—the Northwest Power Planning Council—has attempted to influence the planning and management of energy production and fish and wildlife in the region. It has had some modest success but in recent years strains between upstream and downstream states have resurfaced. Discord stems from desires by downstream states to aid salmon migration through releases of water from reservoirs in upstream states. Upstream states benefit relatively little if at all from improved salmon migration and prefer that the reservoir waters in question be used for resident fish and recreation.

Sources

Columbia River Water Management Group. *Columbia River Water Management Report—Water Year 1998.* Portland, Oregon, 1999.

Hubbard, L. E., et al. *Water Resources Data Oregon—Water Year 1999.* Water Data Report OR-99-1. Portland, Oregon, 2000.

Chapter 13
Energy Resources and Distribution
Steven R. Kale

During the 1990s, demand for energy in the Pacific Northwest continued to increase roughly in proportion to growth in population and economic activity. Entering the twenty-first century, the region was hard hit by an imbalance between energy demand and supply, especially for electricity. Wholesale prices rose dramatically from $30 or less per megawatt-hour to a general range of $200 to $300 per megawatt-hour and to more than $1,000 per megawatt-hour on occasion.

Many observers attributed high prices at least in part to a 1996 law deregulating the electricity market in California. The reasoning behind deregulation was that it would result in a more competitive market and lower prices. Instead, for a variety of reasons, supplies of electricity were not available to meet demand. Higher prices contributed to a renewed emphasis on conservation and new generation, which in turn led to a better balance between demand and supply of electricity. By 2002, prices had fallen closer in line to those suggested by historical trends.

Most of the region's electricity is generated from hydro sources. Compared to other states, the Northwest is considerably more dependent on hydroelectricity. Environmental concerns such as hydro's impact on anadromous fish migration suggest that relatively little of the region's future electricity needs will be tapped from new hydro sources.

Natural gas is accounting for an increasingly larger share of the region's energy consumption, especially for electricity generation and space heating. Increasing demand has been accompanied by higher prices, which in the Northwest are slightly above or below the national average. Gasoline prices are higher in the Northwest than in much of the rest of the United States. Insufficient competition among the region's major distributors is among the reasons cited for high prices. The contribution of coal and nuclear to the region's energy supply and consumption is small and is not likely to increase much if at all in the near future (see figure 13-1).

Conservation is a significant contributor to the Northwest's energy needs. Its contribution, however, ebbs when prices are low and increases when prices

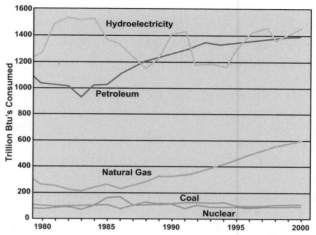

Figure 13-1. Pacific Northwest Annual Energy Consumption, 1980-2000

are high. To promote greater conservation, regional utilities and governments have established a number of non-profit organizations such as the Northwest Energy Efficiency Alliance (see figure 13-2).

The Northwest has vast supplies of renewable energy but, except for hydro, they are not utilized at anywhere near their potential level. Biomass has long been the region's second most important source of renewable energy. Usage of wood-based biomass fuels is declining along with declines in timber production and with concerns about wood burning's impacts on air quality, especially particulate emissions. The production of biogas from waste materials is increasing but is a small portion of the region's total energy supply. Geothermal and solar energy production are important in selected locations but contribute little overall to regional space heating or electricity generation. Wind-based electricity generation has grown substantially and currently is the most promising candidate for future additional development. To expand usage of renewables, regional entities have created "green power" options for consumers to purchase all or a portion of their electricity from renewable sources.

Hydroelectricity

Hydroelectricity accounts for about 40 percent of the energy consumed in the Pacific Northwest, and for about 83 percent of the electricity generated. While just over 3 percent of the nation's population lives in the region, 50 percent of the nation's generation of hydroelectricity occurs there. More than a third of the total hydroelectric capability in the United States is located in the Columbia River Basin. Correspondingly, the three states account for about a third of the nation's renewably generated electricity.

On June 3, 1889, the region's and nation's first long-distance commercial transmission of electricity from hydropower flowed 14 miles between Oregon City and Portland, Oregon. Two waterwheels at Willamette Falls generated electricity which was used primarily for lights and later became important for streetcars.

As the importance of electricity increased, dams were built to harness water power. Much of the region's hydroelectricity now comes from generating facilities at Columbia Basin dams built by the U.S. Bureau of Reclamation, the Army Corps of Engineers, and others (see map 13-1). Of the 11 dams and generating facilities on the main stem of the Columbia, the largest is Grand Coulee in north-

eastern Washington. Generating capability at Grand Coulee is about 7,000 megawatts, which exceeds the total capability in seventeen states and is over six times the capability of the Columbia Generating Station nuclear facility near Richland, Washington. Hydro facilities also are located on streams outside the Columbia River system in western Oregon, western Washington, and southeastern Idaho.

The Bonneville Power Administration, a sub-agency of the U.S. Department of Energy, markets electricity generated at federal system dams. The BPA accounts for about 45 percent of the region's electricity consumption, and markets electricity to utility districts and cooperatives, investor-owned utilities, and selected industrial customers, the largest of which are companies operating ten aluminum smelters.

Under federal law, power from the BPA must be sold first to publicly owned utilities in the Northwest. If surplus power exists, it is sold to private utilities in the region and to public and private utilities outside the region, primarily California. This "preference" law occasionally comes under attack from producers and consumers in high-cost areas

Map 13-1. Electric Generating Facilities, 2001

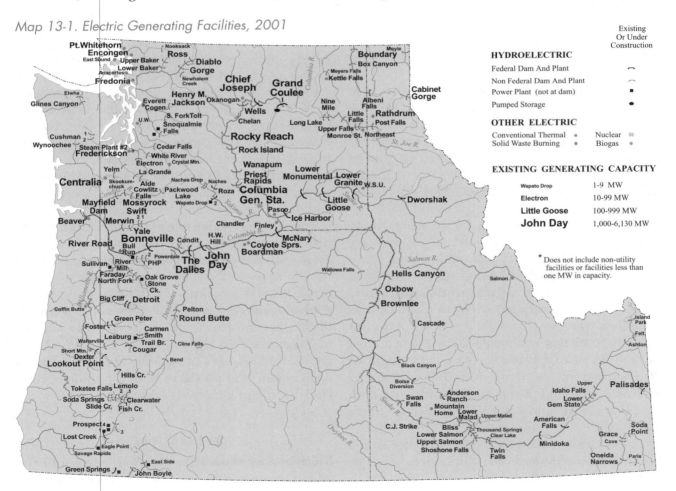

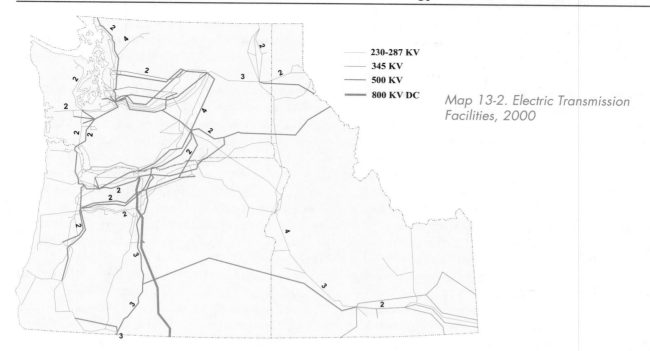

230-287 KV
345 KV
500 KV
800 KV DC

Map 13-2. Electric Transmission Facilities, 2000

who would like to acquire low-cost Northwest power or force the BPA to sell at market rates rather than at cost. Pressures to scrap the preference provision have contributed to calls for regional interests to buy or otherwise acquire the BPA.

Due to higher-than-expected costs of electricity associated with deregulation in California, insufficient investment in new power plants and conservation, contractual obligations to sell more electricity than available from federal sources, and other factors, the BPA worked with the region's aluminum industry in 2001 to curtail operations and free-up about 1,000 megawatts of lower-priced electricity from the smelters. About five thousand workers lost their jobs, although at most facilities, they were financially compensated during the shutdown. For a number of reasons including foreign competition, increasing costs, and uncertain supplies, some observers wonder how economically viable the region's aluminum industry will be in the future.

Transmission lines move hydro and non-hydro electricity from production facilities to regional and national markets. The transmission line network is most developed between generating facilities and major population centers (see map 13-2). The BPA owns and operates about 80 percent of the region's bulk transmission capability. Other utilities own the rest.

Growing demand, greater generating capability, and little transmission construction since 1987 have contributed to constraints in regional transmission

capability. Constraints are reported to be greatest between Montana and states to the west, between the John Day Dam and locations to the north, and across the Cascade Mountains in Oregon and Washington. The BPA and other groups are addressing constraints and meeting increased demand for capacity by employing more efficient technologies and proposing to build new lines. Where feasible, the lines would be built along existing power line corridors to minimize environmental impacts and costs.

To improve operating efficiency, increase system reliability, and eliminate discrimination in system usage, the Federal Energy Regulatory Commission (FERC) in 1999 issued an order calling for the nation's electric utilities to form regional transmission organizations. In response to the FERC's order, the BPA and a number of major utilities in eight western states and British Columbia have begun to form a regional transmission organization whose proposed name is RTO West. Due to complexities of reaching consensus among the region's utilities, RTO West has been slow to form and is not targeted to become operational until at least 2005.

Historically, the Pacific Northwest and Pacific Southwest have exchanged electricity seasonally: the Northwest exports power in the spring and early summer and imports it in the winter. A large portion of the exchanged electricity moves between the Los Angeles area and Columbia River dams and transmission facilities via a direct current intertie with a northern end near The Dalles Dam, and an alternating current intertie with a northern end near the John Day Dam.

The Celilo Converter Station, which began operating in 1970, is the northern end of an 846-mile direct-current intertie between The Dalles, Oregon, and Los Angeles. This direct-current intertie can carry up to 3,100 megawatts of electricity southward. Converters at Celilo are near the end of their useful lives and are expected to be replaced by the end of 2003. Although the alternating-current lines are more expensive to operate and lose more power than the direct-current lines during transmission, they can be operated more flexibly and hooked up with generating facilities along the line. When operating at full capacity, the direct-current and alternating-current lines can transmit nearly enough power to serve the entire Los Angeles area.

The seasonal exchange of electricity breaks down in low-streamflow years when the Northwest does not have enough power to meet its needs. Seasonal exchanges are further reduced by the need to send water through spillways to enhance downstream migration of salmon smolts. In the 2001 low water year, it was estimated that sending water through spillways for salmon migration rather than through generators may have reduced the amount of electricity generated by about 10 percent of the total marketed by the BPA.

Most, if not all, of the region's sites for large hydroelectric facilities have been developed. Because the development of new small-scale hydro systems is restricted by concerns about protection of habitat for fish and wildlife, most future additions to capacity likely will occur through increased efficiency of existing facilities.

Making streams more fish-friendly is a major consideration in relicensing of operations at electricity-generating and other dams, and in some cases, for dam removal. In all three Northwest states, the FERC has authority for licensing and relicensing dam operations, and state agencies have varying levels of oversight and review authority. Nationally, about four hundred dams will be up for FERC renewal in the next ten to fifteen years; this includes twenty-seven in Oregon and twenty-eight in Washington.

Several dams already have been slated for removal. In 1992, for example, President George H. W. Bush signed the Elwha River Restoration Act calling for the removal of the Elwha and Glines Canyon dams and generation facilities, to enhance salmon migration in the Elwha River on Washington's Olympic Peninsula. Continuing controversy delayed appropriating funds for removal; however, in February 2000, the federal government bought the two dams. Removal of the Elwha Dam is targeted for 2004.

Other electricity-generating dams scheduled or being considered for removal include the Condit Dam on the White Salmon River in Washington, and several dams in Oregon's Sandy River drainage. Breaching four dams on the lower Snake River in

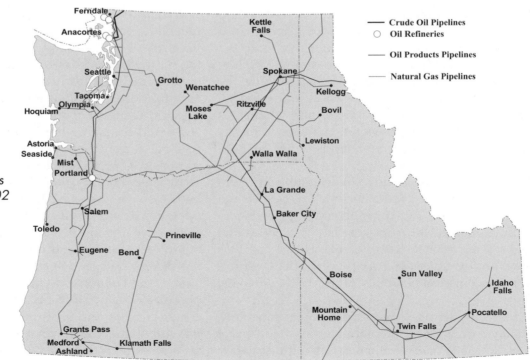

Map 13-3. Pipelines and Refineries, 2002

Washington is among the region's most controversial environmental issues. Breaching the four dams would enhance fish migration but would eliminate more than 1,100 average megawatts of electricity generation and end commercial navigation on the lower Snake.

A portion of the region's electricity comes from the Columbia River system in Canada. The Columbia River Treaty, signed by the U.S. and Canada in 1961 and ratified in 1964, stipulates conditions for coordinating operation of the river system. Half of the Columbia River system's eight major storage dams were built as a result of the treaty. For the first thirty years of the treaty, Canada sold its share of the generation, about 500 average megawatts, to the United States. Under terms of the renegotiated agreements, Canada will continue selling its Columbia system power to the United States.

Petroleum

Petroleum accounts for about 40 percent of the Pacific Northwest's energy consumption. During the 1990s, petroleum consumption exceeded hydro consumption in four of ten years. The transportation sector uses about 75 percent of the region's consumption of petroleum; most of the remaining consumption is attributable to the industrial sector.

No petroleum is produced in the Pacific Northwest, and no regional production is expected in the foreseeable future. Regional crude oil supplies are obtained via the Trans-Mountain Pipeline from Canada, and ocean tankers, primarily from Alaska. Four refineries in Whatcom and Skagit counties in Washington process the crude oil into gasoline and other products. Pipelines, ships, barges, or trucks move oil from refineries in Washington and California to regional markets (see map 13-3).

The Olympic Pipe Line Company operates a 300-mile pipeline between Puget Sound refineries and Portland; the pipeline moves the equivalent of 1,800 tanker trucks of petroleum products daily. Altogether, the Olympic system pipelines move about 4.9 billion gallons of fuel annually. A smaller pipeline operated by Kinder Morgan Energy Partners moves petroleum products between Portland and Eugene, Oregon. Ships traveling via the Columbia River provide about 10 to 20 percent of Portland's petroleum products.

The region also imports petroleum products by pipeline from Montana, Utah, and Wyoming. Chevron Pipe Line Company operates a pipeline from Salt Lake City to Spokane by way of Pasco, Washington. Yellowstone Pipeline runs from Billings, Montana to Moses Lake, Washington. Petroleum products are transported away from pipelines primarily by trucks and by barge from Portland to terminals further up the Columbia River, primarily to Pasco.

In the mid-1990s, the Olympic Pipe Line Company proposed building a 230-mile pipeline between the Puget Sound and Pasco. The Cross-Cascades pipeline would have carried 45,000 barrels of petroleum products daily and reduced the need for barge and truck movements to and from Pasco. In 1999, the company withdrew its Cross-Cascades proposal after fumes and fire from a pipeline leak killed three people in Bellingham, Washington.

Liquefied petroleum gas, commonly known as propane, is used for heating and cooking in parts of the Pacific Northwest, mostly in rural areas and cities without natural gas service. A small amount of propane is used to fuel motor vehicles.

Retail gasoline prices often are higher in parts of the Pacific Northwest than in other states. For example, in 1999, Oregon had the nation's second highest gasoline prices, Washington ranked fifth highest, and Idaho ranked seventeenth. Among the reasons cited for higher prices in the Pacific Northwest are insufficient competition, absence of production, and relatively few pipelines.

Natural Gas

Natural gas accounts for about 15 percent of the Pacific Northwest's energy consumption, up from less than 10 percent of the regional share at the beginning of the 1990s. The industrial sector uses about 50 percent, the residential sector uses 20 to 25 percent, and the commercial sector uses 15 to 20 percent. Transportation and electric utilities represent small but growing markets for natural gas.

Increasing demand for natural gas has resulted in higher prices. Depending on location within the region, prices in the Northwest are below or slightly above the national average, which in 1999 was $4.26 per million Btu. By comparison, state averages and ranking nationally were as follows for the Northwest: Idaho—$4.02 (fortieth), Oregon—$4.39 (twenty-eighth), and Washington—$3.91(forty-first).

Williams Gas Pipeline–West operates the Northwest Pipeline transmission system and serves all regional investor-owned gas utilities. PG&E National Energy Group's Gas Transmission Northwest, which primarily serves California, also provides natural gas to Northwest customers. Duke Energy Gas Trans-

Coyote Springs Generating Plant in Boardman, Oregon, generates power with a combined cycle cogeneration (gas/oil) unit. (Photo by Steven R. Kale)

mission is a Canadian company whose pipelines connect with Williams gas lines at Sumas, Washington, and Huntington, British Columbia. Avista Utilities, Cascade Natural Gas Corporation, Intermountain Gas Company, NW Natural, and Puget Sound Energy distribute gas from the transmission companies to the region's residential and non-residential customers.

About 80 percent of the region's natural gas comes from Canada; most of the remainder comes from Colorado, New Mexico, Utah, and Wyoming. Nearly all new gas supplies come from Canada. The region's only producing gas field is near the small community of Mist, Oregon, northwest of Portland. This field, which began producing in 1979, supplies a small amount of the region's natural gas consumption. In Washington, gas previously was produced at several locations, including the Bellingham Gas Field east of Ferndale, the Rattlesnake Hills Gas Field north of Richland, and the Ocean City Gas and Oil Field west of Hoquiam, which ended production in 1962.

NW Natural, formerly Northwest Natural Gas, uses the Mist field to help supply gas to its customers in northwestern Oregon and southwestern Washington. After gas is extracted, the underground reservoirs are used as gas storage facilities. In 2002, the reservoirs had the capacity to store 10.5 billion cubic feet of gas, the equivalent of fifty-six days' worth of supply for the entire NW Natural customer base. Gas also is stored underground at Jackson Prairie south of Chehalis, Washington. Approximately 15 billion cubic feet of gas, enough to heat one million homes for a month in winter, can be stored at the Jackson Prairie site. Above-ground storage facilities for liquefied natural gas are located in Nampa, Idaho; Newport and Portland, Oregon; and Plymouth, Washington.

Deregulation of natural gas prices, higher electricity costs, and concerns about heating with oil or wood have encouraged many consumers in the Pacific Northwest to choose natural gas for heating. About one-third of residences in Idaho, Oregon, and Washington heat with natural gas. New homes rely heavily on gas heating where available.

For utilities and private generating companies, natural gas is the fuel of choice for new electricity-generating plants. In several locations, the new facilities co-generate steam for generation and for industrial uses such as the processing of food or timber products. Pulp and paper mills are major co-generation producers and consumers.

In most communities where natural gas generating facilities are proposed, residents tend to be supportive as a result of the new jobs and increased property taxes and other payments that the new facilities will bring. Some observers, however, question using gas to generate electricity because the process is less efficient than using gas directly for heating. Opposition also has arisen out of concerns that much of the gas-generated electricity is marketed outside the Pacific Northwest, emissions from burning fossil fuels contribute to global warming, and construction and operation of new facilities could have adverse impacts on water quality and supplies, air quality, land uses, and view sheds obscured by new buildings and power lines. The State of Oregon, for example, has established mitigation standards for carbon dioxide emissions when licensing new power plants.

Increased natural gas usage has led to the need for additional capacity in transmission and local distribution lines. Much of the additional capacity is being built to serve new electricity generating plants. Williams Gas Pipeline, for example, is planning to build a 49-mile line to serve a new 600-megawatt generating facility schedule for completion in 2003 at Satsop, Washington. Other examples of new pipeline capacity are proposals to build a 60-mile line between NW Natural's storage fields at Mist and a distribution line at Mollala, Oregon, and a 60-mile natural gas line from the I-5 corridor to the Coos Bay area on the Oregon coast.

Landfill sites and sewage-treatment plants produce biogas, which is more dilute than natural gas and typically must be processed before it can be used. Landfill biogas is used directly to power lime kilns at the Ash Grove Cement plant in Portland, and to generate electricity at the Coffin Butte Resource Project near Corvallis, Oregon; Short Mountain Project near Eugene, Oregon; Northside Landfill in Spokane, Washington; Roosevelt Landfill in Klickitat County, Washington; and Tacoma Landfill in Tacoma, Washington. A number of the region's cities have sewage-treatment plants that use biogas for heating or generating electricity.

As natural gas prices increase, interest grows in finding new supplies. Seeps along fault lines, gas in water wells, and geological formations suggest small but potentially commercially promising gas supplies in several areas of the Northwest. Many parts of the Puget Sound and the Columbia River Basin in Washington have the potential for natural gas production. Methane from coal-bed deposits in western Washington may someday become feasible to develop commercially. Besides the Mist area in Oregon, the Southern Tyee Basin in Coos, Curry, Douglas, and Lane Counties are underlain by geological formations that may have the potential for gas development.

Additionally, the U.S. Department of Energy and private companies are exploring the possibility of tapping gas supplies found in methane hydrates, which are ice-like substances found in the Arctic permafrost and deep ocean sediments. The Hydrate Ridge off the Oregon coast is one of the areas being considered for further exploration.

Coal

Coal provides 3 to 4 percent of the Pacific Northwest's energy. About 90 percent of the region's consumption of coal is used to generate electricity; another 5 to 10 percent is used in the industrial sector.

Coal was mined near Coos Bay, Oregon, in the 1850s primarily for export to California. Coal later was mined east of Seattle and Tacoma and near

Ellensburg, Washington. Currently, the only regional production of coal occurs near Centralia, Washington, where the TransAlta Corporation owns and operates a 1340-megawatt electricity generation facility fueled by nearby coal deposits. Due to concerns about air pollution, the company is investing $200 million to install scrubber technologies to reduce emissions. TransAlta also is building a 248-megawatt gas-fired generating facility at the Centralia location.

Portland General Electric operates a 530-megawatt coal-fired plant near Boardman, Oregon; coal for this plant is shipped by rail from Wyoming. The Pacific Northwest also imports electricity from coal-fired facilities outside the region, primarily in Montana and Wyoming.

Nuclear Energy

Nuclear fuels, used to generate electricity, account for about 2 percent of the Pacific Northwest's energy consumption. In 1951, the world's first useable quantities of nuclear power were generated near Atomic City, Idaho, at the Idaho National Engineering and Environmental Laboratory's Experimental Breeder Reactor-1 which is now a National Historic Monument.

The region's only nuclear electricity-generating facility is located on the Hanford Nuclear Reservation near Richland, Washington. The 1170-megawatt Columbia Generating Station, formerly known as Washington Nuclear Plant-2, began operating in 1984. It is one of five nuclear facilities that the Washington Public Power Supply System, known as Energy Northwest since 1998, started in the 1970s near Richland and Satsop, Washington. Due to enormously high cost overruns and the regional oversupply of electricity, construction of four facilities was terminated in the 1980s.

The Satsop nuclear site has become the home of the Satsop Development Park, a business and technology park with 440 acres of developable land and several businesses. Future plans call for a natural-gas electricity-generating facility and possibly the world's second tallest climbing wall at one of the fifty-story nuclear cooling towers.

From 1976 to late 1992, Portland General Electric operated the 1100-megawatt Trojan Nuclear Plant near Rainier, Oregon. Trojan faced considerable opposition in the 1980s and early 1990s, including several ballot measures calling for its closure. In January 1993, PGE decided to close Trojan permanently in response to the high costs of replacing defective generators and the ready availability of replacement power. PGE expects to complete decommissioning of the plant in 2005.

A third nuclear plant, the N-Reactor at the Hanford Nuclear Reservation, was operated by the U.S. Department of Energy from 1963 to 1987 to produce plutonium and steam for the 800-megawatt Hanford Generating Project. The N-Reactor was deactivated in 1998, after which the facility was closed off entirely for fifteen years until safe storage work can begin.

Conservation

Conservation is an energy resource because it reduces the need to obtain new energy supplies. Conservation is often defined as increased efficiency in using energy, and is a significant contributor to the Pacific Northwest's energy needs. Between 1978 and 2000, the region acquired more than 1,300 average megawatts of savings through conservation and energy efficiency improvements (see figure 13-2).

The Bonneville Power Administration and the Northwest Power Planning Council are major players in the region's acquisition of energy savings through conservation. The BPA has been involved with more than half of the region's energy savings from conservation through its support of efforts such as weatherization programs, the Super Good Cents residential program, adoption of energy-efficient building codes and model conservation standards, and programs to wrap water heaters, install low-flow shower heads, and increase insulation standards in manufactured homes. Since their inception, programs of the BPA and the region's private and public utilities have contributed to the weatherization of more than 400,000 homes and over 80,000 new energy-efficient homes.

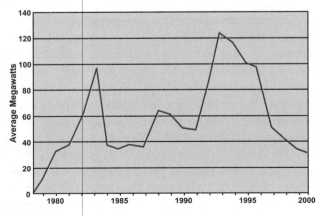

Figure 13-2. Northwest Conservation Savings, 1978-2000

Created after the U.S. Congress passed the Pacific Northwest Power Planning and Conservation Act of 1980, the Northwest Power Planning Council is charged with adopting program measures to protect, mitigate, and enhance fish and wildlife while assuring the Pacific Northwest an adequate, efficient, economical, and reliable power supply. The council has presented its programs in a series of power plans, the most recent of which was in 1998, and expects to complete the region's fifth edition of the power plan in 2003.

The plans identify conservation as the cheapest way to meet the region's energy needs for electricity. The 1998 plan, for example, identified approximately 1,535 average megawatts of conservation that could be cost effective to develop over a twenty-year period. About 60 percent of the savings would be acquired in the industrial and commercial sectors through replacement of lighting, improvements in heating and cooling systems, repair of equipment, and similar actions.

The rate of acquiring energy savings through conservation depends on a variety of factors, including power prices. When prices are high, the incentive to conserve increases; when prices are low, implementation of conservation measures wanes. Relatively low prices in the latter half of the 1990s contributed to a decline in the implementation of conservation measures compared to the latter part of the 1980s and early 1990s. Interest in conservation rebounded with price spikes in 2000 and 2001.

Conservation supporters remain challenged to develop policies and programs to support a steady rate of investments in conservation independent of changes, especially declines, in wholesale prices. To renew the focus on conservation and energy efficiency, the region's utilities and governments have established new entities to promote market transformation activities wherein consumers have more choices for purchasing energy-efficient products. The Northwest Energy Efficiency Alliance, established in 1996, is one of several regional organizations facilitating market transformation through its programs to promote compact fluorescent lights, resource-efficient washing machines, energy-efficient residential windows, and a variety of initiatives for commercial and industrial energy efficiency.

Renewable Energy Sources

Hydroelectricity, biomass, solar, wind, and geothermal are the main types of renewable energy sources in the Pacific Northwest. The three states of the Northwest are more dependent on renewable energy for electricity generation than any other states in the United States. In Idaho, 97 percent of electricity in 1998 was generated from renewable sources; figures for Oregon and Washington were 79 and 80 percent, respectively. Hydro sources account for most of the region's renewably generated electricity.

Federal data for renewable energy are sketchier than data for non-renewable sources. Thus identifying renewables' contribution to the Northwest's total energy demand and supply is challenging. Much of the following discussion is based on regionally generated information.

Biomass. After hydroelectricity, biomass is the second-most used source of renewable energy in the Pacific Northwest. About four percent of the region's total energy consumption is attributable to wood and waste. Industrial uses account for 75 to 80 percent of wood and waste consumption; residential uses account for 15 to 20 percent.

In Oregon, industrial facilities generated about 120 average megawatts of electricity from biomass in 2001. Six of the state's paper mills used pulping liquor to produce steam and recover chemicals; two of the mills co-generated steam and electricity. Additionally, sixty-six industrial facilities used biomass boilers to supply heating or process steam; eight of the sixty-six industrial facilities co-generated steam and electricity.

Historically, wood has been a major source of the region's home heating. In Oregon, about 20 percent of all households use wood for primary or back-up heating. In 1983 Oregon became the first state in the nation to pass a law requiring wood stoves to meet emissions limits for particulates. A similar law was passed in Washington in 1987. Subsequent state and federal legislation further identified measures to improve air quality in non-attainment areas for particulates. To help meet air-quality standards and promote the usage of other fuels, utilities and other groups developed programs to replace older wood stoves with weatherization and either new clean-burning wood stoves or other types of heating systems.

Garbage or sewage is used for heating or generating electricity at several locations in the Pacific Northwest. As noted in the discussion of natural gas, the St. Johns Landfill in Portland helps to power lime kilns at an Ash Grove Cement plant, and landfills in or near Corvallis and Eugene in Oregon and Klickitat County, Spokane, and Tacoma in Washington supply biogas for heating and electricity. In addition, biogas was formerly produced at the Rossman Landfill near Oregon City, Oregon, where it was cleaned and fed directly into pipelines, and for heating adjacent county shop facilities.

The Short Mountain Landfill Gas Project near Eugene, Oregon, and the Coffin Butte Landfill near Corvallis, Oregon, are among the older landfills producing biogas. The Short Mountain Landfill Gas Project began operating in 1992. Methane is extracted, collected, cleaned, and injected into combustion engines where it turns crankshafts which then turn generators. The project generates about twenty million kilowatt-hours annually, enough to power about 1,400 homes. The Coffin Butte landfill site near Corvallis began operating in 1995, is used to power generators with a capability of 2.5 megawatts, and produces enough electricity for two thousand households annually.

A number of the region's cities use biogas from sewage; thirty sewage treatment plants in Oregon alone have anaerobic digesters that produce biogas. One of the better-known projects is the City of Portland's Columbia Boulevard Wastewater Treatment Plant, which began using methane gas from sewage in 1999 to generate 1.4 million kilowatt-hours of electricity annually, enough to save more than $60,000 in energy costs. A fuel cell is used to extract hydrogen from the gas; the gas is then combined with oxygen to create a chemical reaction that produces electricity. The Portland project is only the third commercial fuel cell of its kind in the nation.

Biomass and other solid wastes such as garbage are burned in incinerators to generate electricity. The largest solid-waste incinerator in the region is at Lewiston, Idaho, where a 59-megawatt plant uses biomass and fossil fuels to power a co-generation facility. Other co-generation facilities using biomass and fossil fuels include a 47-megawatt plant at Camas, Washington; a 43-megawatt plant at Everett, Washington; and a 36-megawatt plant near Wauna, Oregon. Incinerators fueled with solid-waste only include a 23-megawatt plant at Spokane, Washington; a 11-megawatt plant near Brooks, Oregon; a 2-megawatt plant in Skagit County, Washington; and a 1-megawatt plant at Bellingham, Washington. A 50-megawatt incinerator at Tacoma, Washington, burns garbage, wood wastes, and coal.

Several dairy operations produce electricity from methane gas resulting from decomposition of cow manure. Craven Farms operated a facility in Tillamook County, Oregon, from 1997 to 1999 when the farm was sold as a result of financial problems. The Cal-Gon dairy farm near Salem, Oregon, converts 35 to 40 tons of manure daily to methane gas, which is used to generate 100 average kilowatts of electricity, enough for about sixty-five homes. In 2004, a dairy operation in eastern Oregon near Boardman is expected to begin producing methane gas to generate about 4 average megawatts of electricity. Similar operations have been considered elsewhere, including near Myrtle Point, Oregon.

Other types of biomass fuels in the Pacific Northwest include agricultural residues and ethanol. Agricultural residues continue to receive increased attention as grass seed growers in Oregon's Willamette Valley and elsewhere seek ways to use straw for fuel or other products rather than burning it in the field.

Ethanol is mixed with gasoline to create an oxygenated fuel sold in gasoline stations in urban areas that do not meet standards for carbon monoxide emissions. In the year 2000, Oregon and Washington consumers used 43 million gallons of ethanol in various gasohol blends; this represented 2.9 percent of the nation's total usage of alcohol used in gasohol. Oregon's and Washington's share of the nation's ethanol-usage total was slightly more than their share of the nation's vehicle miles traveled. Federal statistics do not show any usage of ethanol-based fuels in Idaho in 2000. Northwest consumption of ethanol-based fuels dropped substantially when Oregon in 1993 and Washington in 1995 eliminated state tax exemptions for gasohol.

Most of the region's ethanol is imported from the Midwest where it is produced from grain, primarily corn. The J. R. Simplot Company operates the only production facilities in the Northwest at Caldwell and Burley, Idaho, where ethanol is produced from potato wastes. New ethanol facilities have been proposed in Oregon at Clatskanie and Island City, and in Washington at Longview and Moses Lake.

Solar Energy. Active and passive space and water heating are the main uses of solar energy in the Pacific Northwest. The amount of solar radiation east of the Cascade Mountains is almost as much as is available in the southwestern United States The contribution of solar to the region's energy needs, however, is greater west of the Cascades where most of the region's population resides. Cloudy parts of the Northwest receive almost half as much solar energy as the deserts of Arizona and California. Total potential supply of solar energy in the Northwest is estimated at more than 200,000 average megawatts (See map 13-4).

The installation of solar collectors nationally dropped dramatically with the expiration of federal solar tax credits at the end of 1985. State incentives continue to support solar development, and in Oregon, an estimated 16,000 water-heating systems and 1,600 space-heating systems have been installed.

In the 1980s, about three dozen cities and counties in the Pacific Northwest implemented solar access ordinances to ensure that access to sunlight is protected from shading by vegetation or buildings. Field investigations have shown that protection from shading and proper orientation of houses can result in energy savings of 10 to 20 percent without the installation of solar equipment. By the early twenty-first century, most jurisdictions in the Northwest had either eliminated the ordinances or were not aggressively enforcing them for a variety of reasons, including low energy prices, reduced sales of solar collectors, opposition by developers, and a focus on housing density which sometimes precludes good solar access.

Sunlight also can be converted to electricity via solar thermal facilities such as concentrating collectors or salt ponds, and via photovoltaic collectors. No solar-thermal power plants or salt ponds are presently in the region. Small-scale photovoltaic collectors are located at demonstration facilities, remote locations, and sites not easily served by the power grid throughout the Pacific Northwest. These include collectors installed on rooftops of buildings, highway signs and billboards, translator sites for radio stations, signaling devices, lights, water pumping facilities, and restrooms at public

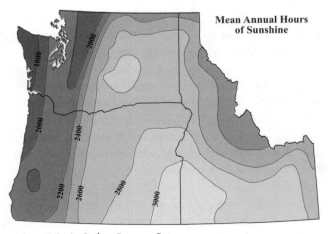

Map 13-4. Solar Power Resources

recreation areas. Oregon's and Washington's net metering laws, which allow customers to sell excess electricity from solar panels or other renewable sources to a utility, have facilitated the installation of photovoltaic collectors in a few locations.

The region's largest photovoltaic installation is a 40-kilowatt facility at the site of the terminated WNP-1 nuclear plant on the Hanford reservation in Washington. This facility, which is estimated to provide enough power for fifty homes, was financed in part through the U.S. Department of Energy's Brightfields Program which provides funding for the installation of solar equipment on abandoned or contaminated industrial properties, sometimes termed brownfields. Such properties are believed to be well suited for photovoltaic arrays because they are sited directly on the ground and do not penetrate the surface or disturb underlying materials.

On April 22 (Earth Day), 2002, Oregon became the only state in the United States to have a photovoltaic system installed on its capitol building. About one-third of the electricity generated by the sixty solar panels is used to light the building's Oregon Pioneer statue. The remaining two-thirds is fed into the regional transmission system. Proceeds from Portland General Electric's "Clean Wind" customers paid for the solar panels, engineering, and the information kiosk in the capitol.

In Ashland, Oregon, the City of Ashland and the Bonneville Environmental Foundation have funded installation of roof-mounted photovoltaic systems on four buildings: the Oregon Shakespeare Festival's administration building, Southern Oregon University's library, and Ashland's police station and city council chambers. Together, the four systems supply 30 kilowatts of generating capability.

All three Northwest states are participating in the State and Local Partnerships program of the national Million Solar Roofs initiative started in June 1997. The goal of the initiative is the installation of one million photovoltaic and solar water- or space-heating collectors nationwide by 2010. Partners in the program are committed to installing at least five hundred collectors by 2010. Activities in Idaho, Oregon, and Washington focus largely on outreach and fostering education and awareness.

Wind. The potential for generating electricity from wind machines is greatest in the Columbia River Gorge, along the coast, and in selected mountainous parts of the region (see map 13-5). The Pacific Northwest's wind energy potential is estimated at 16,900 megawatts; among states nationally, Idaho

ranks thirteenth, Oregon ranks twenty-second, and Washington ranks twenty-third in wind energy potential.

Improved technology, higher energy prices, government incentives, and better mitigation for environmental impacts have contributed to the recent competitiveness of wind energy. In recent years, new wind energy facilities have begun operating at several locations in Oregon and Washington. The first of these was the Vansycle Ridge Wind Farm in Umatilla County, where in November 1998, thirty-eight wind machines began operating with a generating capability of 25 megawatts.

In 2001, generation began at the Stateline Wind Power Project in 2001 near Touchet, Washington, with a generating capability of 263 megawatts from 273 wind machines in WA and 127 machines in Oregon. The Stateline project is the second largest wind farm in the United States, and generates enough electricity to power sixty thousand homes. Also in December 2001, forty-one turbines began operating at the Condon Wind Project near Condon, Oregon. With the completion of forty-two additional turbines in 2002, the project has a 50-megawatt capability and produces about 13 average mega-watts. Other projects include the Nine Canyon Wind Farm near Kennewick, Washington, and the Klondike facility near Wasco, Oregon.

With continuation of federal tax credits and other incentives, further wind energy development is expected. A 2001 BPA solicitation for wind energy projects led to twenty-five proposals which, if all were built, would add 2,600 megawatts of generating capability. Ten proposals were for Oregon sites, eight were for Washington sites, and the rest were for sites in other western states and Canada. Only a few of the proposals are expected to lead to actual projects

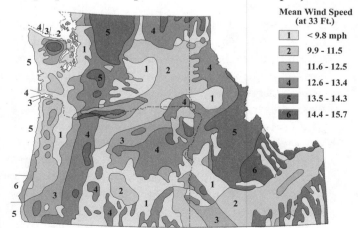

Mean Wind Speed (at 33 Ft.)	
1	< 9.8 mph
2	9.9 - 11.5
3	11.6 - 12.5
4	12.6 - 13.4
5	13.5 - 14.3
6	14.4 - 15.7

Map 13-5. Annual Average Wind Speed

Stateline Wind Power Project, Washington and Oregon. (Photo by Steven R. Kale)

in the near term. Utilities in the region also buy electricity generated by wind turbines in other states such as Wyoming.

Geothermal Resources. Known and potential geothermal resources underlie much of the Pacific Northwest (see map 13-6). Geothermal's direct use applications in the region include heating buildings, swimming pools, hot tubs, and baths at commercial resorts, heating and cooling water to raise plants and fish, and heating and cooling facilities for industrial purposes. In a few locations, buildings are meeting their heating and cooling needs with heat exchangers using water from low-temperature geothermal wells.

According to the Geo-Heat Center at the Oregon Institute of Technology, Idaho leads the region in the number of sites with direct use applications (sixty-eight), while Oregon has fifty-two and Washington has six. About half of these sites are for resorts and spas.

The first large-scale use of geothermal energy in the region began with construction of the Warm Springs Heating District in Boise, Idaho, in the 1890s. In 1982, water from the newly developed Capitol Mall Geothermal System began heating buildings in downtown Boise. With declining water levels in the geothermal aquifer, the Idaho Department of Water Resources in 1988 imposed a cap on the amount of water that could be withdrawn from the aquifer. This was followed by successful efforts to return reused geothermal water to the aquifer via an injection well. The downtown geothermal heating district now serves about fifty buildings covering more than two million square feet of floor space. In addition, about four hundred homes are heated geothermally in the Boise area.

In Klamath Falls, Oregon, about 550 homes, businesses, schools, and other buildings use geothermal heat. In 1981, the City of Klamath Falls developed a district heating system to serve fourteen buildings in the downtown area. Since its initial development, a number of other downtown-area buildings have been added to the system. Geothermal heat in Klamath Falls also is used to melt snow on sidewalks, ramps for handicapped persons, highways, and the nation's only geothermally heated bus stop and passenger transfer area. A high-tech plant nursery is one of the latest users of the area's geothermal resources.

Idaho, Oregon, Washington, and western Montana have the potential to generate up to 11,000 megawatts of electricity from geothermal power. The Northwest Power Planning Council has identified eleven specific areas where there may be about 2,000 megawatts developable, enough power to serve more than 1.3 million homes. As of spring 2003, however, no electricity generating geothermal facilities were operating in the Pacific Northwest.

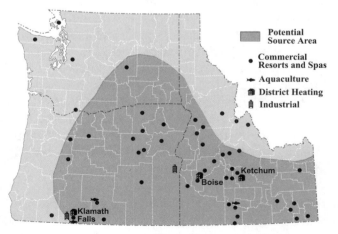

Map 13-6. Geothermal Resources and Facilities.
In addition to the locations of facilities shown on the map are a number of locations where geothermal resources heat greenhouses, residences, and other buildings.

Table 13-1. Number of Sites with Direct Use Geothermal Applications			
	Idaho	Oregon	Washington
Aquaculture	2	2	0
District Heating	5	2	0
Greenhouses	14	4	0
Industrial	0	3	0
National Labs	1	0	0
Power Plants	0	1	0
Resorts and Spas	36	18	6
Space Heating	10	22	0

Concerns about resource availability, high costs, low electricity prices, land-use and cultural conflicts, and environmental impacts are among the factors that have worked against the development of the region's geothermal resources for generating electricity.

During the early 1980s, experiments to generate electricity using geothermal water began at Raft River, Idaho. After disappointing results, the efforts were discontinued. In the early 1990s, the Northwest Power Planning Council, the Bonneville Power Administration, and others explored the feasibility of pilot geothermal projects near Vale, Oregon; the Newberry Volcano about 35 miles south of Bend, Oregon; and Glass Mountain in northeastern California, about 25 miles south of the Oregon border. In 1993, following preliminary exploration, the developer of the proposed Vale project found that the resource was not cost-effective to develop. After completing environmental documentation and well-testing, work on the Newberry project was suspended in 1996. Although test-hole drilling found temperatures of 600 degrees Fahrenheit, the hottest in North America, the tests did not find sufficient high-temperature water at a shallow-enough depth to make a plant economically feasible.

Spikes in electricity prices and energy policies contribute to ongoing interest in geothermal research and demonstration. Proposals periodically emerge for development at the Newberry site and other sites such as the Alvord Desert south of Burns, Oregon, and Glass Mountain just south of the Oregon border in California. The BPA, for example, continues to work with various groups exploring the feasibility of geothermal development in northern California, and in 2001, signed a Record of Decision to acquire more than 49 megawatts of electricity from the proposed Fourmile Hill geothermal facility in Siskiyou County. If developed, the project would be the BPA's first geothermal resource.

Future Consumption and Supply of Energy

Among the most important forces influencing the future supply and consumption of energy in the region are population and economic growth, and fish and wildlife concerns. Growth is resulting in pressure to use more fossil fuels, especially natural gas. Rapid growth could lead to renewed pressure for nuclear, coal, or coal-gasification facilities; such development would be highly controversial as a result of concerns about costs and environmental impacts.

Restructuring of the electric utility industry is one of the more significant issues facing the region in the future. Supporters of deregulation believe that it will result in a more competitive energy market and lower prices, and use the deregulation of natural gas prices and transmission as an example of successful restructuring. Opponents fear that restructuring could lead to market manipulation and higher prices, and point to the effect deregulation in California had on the Northwest.

By early 2003, Oregon had become the only Northwest state where the legislature and governor had approved a bill restructuring the electric utility market. Originally scheduled to begin on October 1, 2001, the bill's debut was delayed until March 1, 2002 because of high prices and negative backlash from deregulation in California.

Oregon's legislation allows, but does not require, large industrial and commercial consumers to buy electricity competitively from wholesalers. Unlike California's legislation, Oregon's does not require investor-owned utilities to sell generating plants, does not prohibit them from purchasing energy on long-term contracts, and does not put a cap on retail rates.

Under Oregon's legislation, residential consumers continue buying price-controlled electricity from their publicly or privately owned utility, and have the choice of paying the cost-of-service rate or a "green" rate which is based on renewable energy's proportion of the consumer's total bill. Additionally, for 10 years after the legislation becomes operative, 3 percent of revenues from power sales will be set aside for public purposes in the following proportions: 10 percent—schools, 53 percent—other conservation, 19 percent—renewables, 13 percent—low-income weatherization, and 5 percent—low-income housing energy efficiency. At least 80 percent of the conservation funds must be spent in the service territory where the funds are collected and cannot be spent on region-wide market transformation strategies.

Neither Washington nor Idaho has passed deregulation legislation, in part due to concerns that since their electricity prices already are lower than elsewhere, few benefits would accrue from deregulation. Both states, however, have developed pilot programs that allow for different rate options, for example, rates that vary by peak and non-peak usage or for renewable energy purchases.

Partly as a result of the establishment of energy efficiency and "green power" programs, conservation and renewable energy will receive more attention. This attention will increase even more if energy prices rise rapidly. Lower prices could mean reduced or slowly implemented conservation in the absence of public sector incentives and support. Without sufficient mechanisms in place to reduce the burden to stockholders and ratepayers, the possibility of stranded costs will work against implementation of higher-priced conservation technologies.

Non-utility companies will increase their share of the region's energy production, most noticeably for electricity. Few utilities will build new generating facilities, in part because of the uncertainty of the energy market. Much of the power from independent producers will be sold to large utilities or to the Bonneville Power Administration.

Concerns about wildlife and fish, especially anadromous species, will continue to receive much attention. More water for salmon runs could mean less water for the generation of hydroelectricity. Removal or breaching of dams to enhance salmon migration will mean more of the region's power will come from higher-priced sources such as natural gas. While the proposed breaching of the four lower Snake River dams would enhance salmon migration, it could negatively affect other sectors of the economy such as transportation and agriculture.

In the 1990s, global warming became an increasingly important issue. A warmer climate in the Pacific Northwest would probably result in less water for hydroelectricity and other uses. Greater usage of fossil fuels could accelerate the build-up of carbon dioxide and other gases that appear to cause the greenhouse effect and global warming. While the seriousness of this issue is subject to changing political priorities, it remains a long-term concern, both globally and to the long-run energy future of the region.

Selected Sources

American Wind Energy Association, *Inventory of State Incentives for Wind Energy in the U.S.,* March 2001.

Brown, Brian, "Klamath Falls Geothermal District Heating Systems," *Geo-Heat Center Bulletin,* March 1999, pp. 5-9.

Elliot, D. L., C. G. Holladay, W. R. Barchet, H. P. Foote, and W. F. Sandusky, *Wind Energy Resource Atlas of the United States.* Richland, Washington: Pacific Northwest Laboratory.

Kale, Steven R., "Solar Access Protection in the Pacific Northwest," *Northwest Environmental Journal,* Vol. 5, No. 2 (1989), 241-69.

Northwest Gas Association, "Natural Gas Supply, Storage, and Price" and "Natural Gas and the Pacific Northwest." Northwest Power Planning Council, "Power Plants in the Pacific Northwest," February 4, 2002.

Oregon Department of Geology and Mineral Industries, "The Oil, Gas and Geothermal Regulatory and Reclamation Program at DOGAMI."

Oregon Institute of Technology, "U.S. Geothermal Projects and Resource Areas," Geo-Heat Center, January 31, 2003. http://geoheat.oit.edu/dusys.htm.

Oregon Office of Energy, "Recent Renewable Power Projects," August 14, 2000.

U.S. Department of Energy, *Electric Power Annual 2000,* Volume 1, DOE/EIA-0348(2000)/1, August 2001.

U.S. Department of Energy, *Historical Natural Gas Annual— 1930 Through 2000,* DOE/EIA-E-0110(00), December 2001.

U.S. Department of Energy, *Renewable Energy Annual 2000 with Data for 1999,* DOE/EIA-0603(2000), March 2001.

White, John, *2001 Oregon Biomass Energy Book.* Salem: Oregon Office of Energy, July 2001.

Chapter 14
Ocean Resources

James W. Good

The ocean off the Pacific Northwest coast is rich in natural resources. Abundant salmon, crab, shrimp, groundfish, and other species contribute to important commercial fisheries that provide high-quality protein for domestic consumption and export. Ocean sport fishers vie for many of the same species. Offshore deposits of minerals and oil and gas are as yet unexploited. Maritime commerce is a dominant industry in the region. Large and small ships and barges transport oil, other bulk cargo, containers, agricultural products, and logs to and from Pacific Northwest ports. Through trade, they link the northwest with many nations on the Pacific Rim and beyond.

Human use of marine resources is not without its environmental and economic costs. Domestic and industrial pollution threaten coastal and deepwater habitats and marine life, periodic oil spills foul beaches, marine mammals, and seabirds, and the viability of the fishing industry is threatened by over-harvest of fisheries and competition for waterfront space.

This chapter describes ocean resources in the Pacific Northwest and how these resources are used and managed for public and private benefit. The growing number of conflicts in marine resource use are also described, as are attempts to resolve them.

Living on the "Ring of Fire"

Located on the Pacific Rim's "ring of fire," the northwest is a tectonically active region. Not far offshore is the Juan de Fuca-Gorda Ridge mid-ocean spreading center complex, which forms the boundary between the small Juan de Fuca plate and the massive Pacific plate to the west (see map 14-1). Even closer to shore is yet another plate boundary, the Cascadia Sub-duction Zone (CSZ). The CSZ is the junction between the westward-moving North American continental plate and the eastward-moving Juan de Fuca oceanic plate. At the CSZ boundary, the oceanic plate dives under the continental plate. Although there have been no major earthquakes along this giant fault since Euro-American settlement, geologic and other evidence suggests that this plate boundary is seismically active, yielding very large (magnitude 8-9+) earthquakes approximately every five hundred years (+/- two hundred years). The most recent event was on January 26, 1700, meaning that we are entering the window for the next great earthquake on this fault.

The Continental Margin

The continental margin is composed of sedimentary and volcanic rocks covered with mud and sand. Its major structural features landward of the CSZ are the continental slope and shelf (see map 14-2)

The continental shelf underlies shallow coastal waters out to about 650 feet (200 meters) in depth and ranges in width from about 12 nautical miles (nm) at Cape Blanco to nearly 50 nm off Grays Harbor. Numerous nearshore rocks and islands host large populations of breeding seabirds and marine mammals. Prominent submarine banks near the outer edge of the shelf provide important habitats for many forms of marine life.

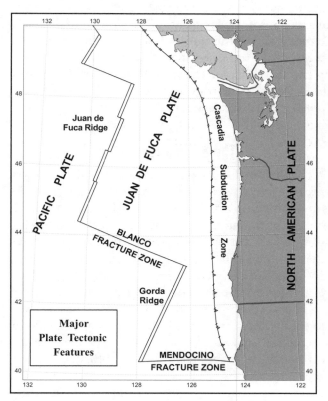

Map 14-1. Major Plate Tectonic Features

At the edge of the shelf, the continental slope plunges 2,000 meters or more than a mile to the seafloor. The slope is dissected by seven steep submarine canyons, such as the prominent Astoria Canyon at the mouth of the Columbia River. These canyons serve as channels for movement of sediments across the slope into the deep ocean abyss.

Sand and mud cover most of the continental margin, although there are significant rock outcroppings. Movement of sediments is greatest close to shore, where they are transported by nearshore littoral currents. Offshore currents also move sediments, albeit more slowly, and large storms stir up bottom sediments all along the shelf.

Major oceanic currents affecting the natural processes and resources in the summer include the southward-flowing California surface current and the northward-flowing California undercurrent (see maps 14-3 and 14-4). These summer currents, reinforced by strong north and northwest winds and the coreolis effect, result in an offshore flow of nearshore waters, with a corresponding upwelling of cold, nutrient-rich waters from the deep. In the winter, south and southwest winds dominate, resulting in the northward-flowing Davidson current and downwelling of surface waters. Periodically, this "normal" summer-winter cycle is upset by global weather phenomena, such as the strong El Niños that occur on average every eight to nine years. Warmer water conditions, higher sea levels, and reduced biological productivity result, often persisting for many months. Longer-term climate phenomena, such as the recently described Pacific Decadal Oscillation, also play important roles in offshore productivity and fisheries.

The Marine Ecosystem

Pacific Northwest coastal waters are among the most productive in the world, fueled largely by the upwelling described above. Upwelled, nutrient-rich waters stimulate large "blooms" of phytoplankton throughout spring and summer. These tiny plants, in turn, provide food for marine "grazers" like copepods and euphausiids that then serve as food for larger crustaceans and fish, and other marine life.

The waters of the Pacific Northwest are ecologically significant for another reason. They are an "ecotone"—a boundary region between the subarctic ecosystem to the north and the Californian current ecosystem to the south. Populations at the edges of their ranges tend to be more variable and sensitive to changes in environmental conditions. Coho

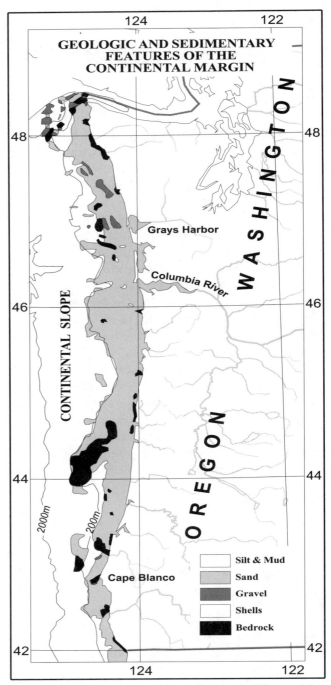

Map 14-2. Geologic and Sedimentary Features of the Continental Margin

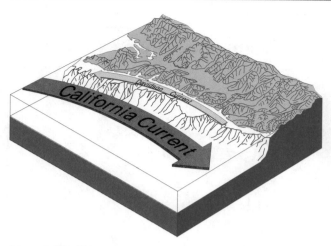

Map 14-3. Winter Ocean Currrents

Map 14-4. Summer Ocean Currents and Upwelling

salmon, more attuned to the subarctic, are an example of such vulnerable species.

This rich oceanic ecosystem is home to large populations of valuable fishery resources, thousands of breeding and feeding seabirds, and diverse marine mammal populations. Ocean commercial fisheries include salmon, shrimp, crab, tuna, whiting, and diverse groundfish species, including rockfish, sablefish, ling cod, halibut, and sole. These fish, together with hundreds of other species, comprise a complex oceanic food web. The health of some of these fisheries is threatened by a combination of natural variations in ocean food availability, land-based development and habitat alteration, and overfishing.

More than a dozen species of marine birds breed along the Pacific Northwest coast, including cormorants, auklets, petrels, gulls, murres, oyster-catchers, and tufted puffins. Others are regular visitors or migrants, including loons, grebes, albatrosses, shearwaters, pelicans, and numerous ducks and shorebirds. Pollution, human disturbance, and loss of habitat are major concerns.

A variety of whales, dolphins, porpoises, seals, and sea lions are also found in coastal waters of the Pacific Northwest. Common to the nearshore are California gray whales, who migrate south from summer feeding areas in the Arctic to winter calving areas in Baja California, retracing the journey northward in the spring. Many other whale species frequent offshore waters during their migrations. Harbor seals and California sea lions are also common along the Pacific Northwest coast, hauling out on beaches and rocky shores and islands; the endangered Steller's sea lion breeds along the southern Oregon coast. Sea otters, once common throughout the Pacific Northwest coast, are now

found only along the rugged Olympic coast of Washington.

Offshore Ownership and Jurisdiction

On March 10, 1983, President Reagan signed a proclamation that established the Exclusive Economic Zone (EEZ), a resource zone that is contiguous to the territorial sea of the United States and its territories (see map 14-5). The EEZ extends 200 nm from the coastal low-water baseline from which the territorial sea is measured. Within 3 nm, Oregon and Washington own and manage natural resources, whereas federal territorial sea jurisdiction extends to 12 nm for control of navigation, commerce, and pollution. EEZ resources in the 3 to 200 nm zone are under exclusive federal ownership and jurisdiction, although federal resource managers must consult with adjacent states and take their concerns into consideration when setting fishing regulations, leasing areas for oil and gas, permitting pollution discharges, or allowing other uses and activities. Beyond EEZ lies the high seas and international seabed, an area governed by international customs and conventions. The most important of these is the United Nations Law of the Sea Treaty of 1982, which the United States complies with, but has yet to ratify.

Commercial and Recreational Fisheries

Commercial and recreational fisheries in the Pacific Northwest are an important regional industry, whether measured in pounds of fish caught, dollar value for commercial catches at the dock, or in personal income generated in fishing communities. The bulk of the fish caught and value generated in the industry are from the commercial fisheries in the

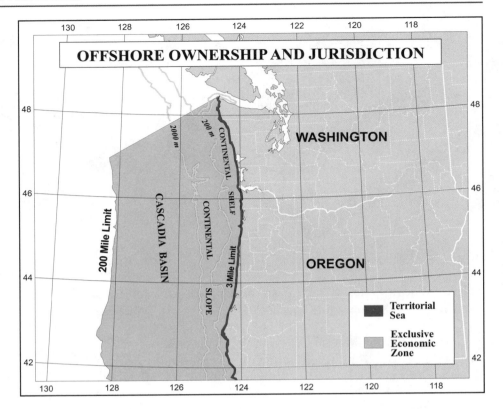

Map 14-5. Offshore Ownership and Jurisdiction

ocean off Washington and Oregon, and in Puget Sound. But the Washington-Oregon distant water fleet, fishing in a number of important Alaskan fisheries, also contributes substantially to the regional economy.

Diverse Fisheries. The fishery resources harvested commercially in local waters by non-Indians are diverse in terms of the numbers of species harvested, areas fished, and the type of gear used. Species fished include five salmonid species (chinook, coho, sockeye, chum, and pink), albacore tuna, groundfish (rockfishes, snapper, halibut, ling cod, sablefish, flounders and soles), crab, shrimp, whiting and a variety of other species (sharks, clams, sea urchins, shad, and others). Indian treaty rights fisheries for salmon and steelhead are also important commercial and ceremonial fisheries. Aquaculture contributes to the "landings" as well, with salmon and oysters making up most of the harvest. Some of the ocean fisheries are in very deep water (e.g., albacore, some groundfish), others are nearshore (e.g., crab), while still others are inshore, bay, or river fisheries (see maps 14-6 and 14-7). The size of boats and the type of gear varies with the fishery as well. Trawlers are large and use nets to catch groundfish, mid-water schooling fish, and shrimp. Pots are used to fish for crab all along the coast, and are also an alternative method to catch sablefish. Trollers fish with hooks

and lines for salmon and albacore, and longliners go after halibut and sablefish.

Commercial Fish Landings and Value. Landings of food fishes at Washington and Oregon ports by non-Indian fishers have averaged 329 million pounds (150 million kilograms) annually from 1975 to 2000 (see figures 14-1 and 14-2), although there have been significant year to year fluctuations. In 2000, landings were 378 million pounds (830 million kilograms) with a dockside value of nearly $215 million (see figures 14-3 and 14-4). This was 4.1 percent of the nation's total by poundage and 5.9 percent by value. Oregon accounted for 69 percent of 2000 landings by weight, but only 38 percent by value, the difference attributed to the much larger proportion of low-value Pacific whiting in the Oregon harvest, and the greater proportion of high-value crab and salmon in the Washington harvest. Major fishing ports include Bellingham, Westport, and Seattle in Washington and Astoria-Warrenton, Newport, and Charleston in Oregon. Based on licenses issued, commercial fishers numbered about 3,150 in Washington, and about 3,175 in Oregon in 2000. These license numbers are significantly lower than in 1990 (52 percent less for Washington and 48 percent less for Oregon), and are indicators of the decreasing economic viability of fishing as a profession in these difficult times of declining stocks

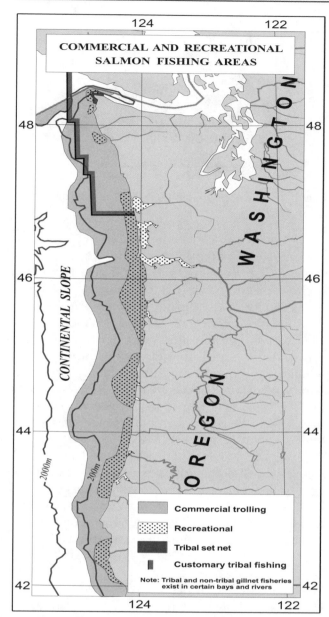

Map 14-6 Commercial and Recreational
Salmon Fishing Areas

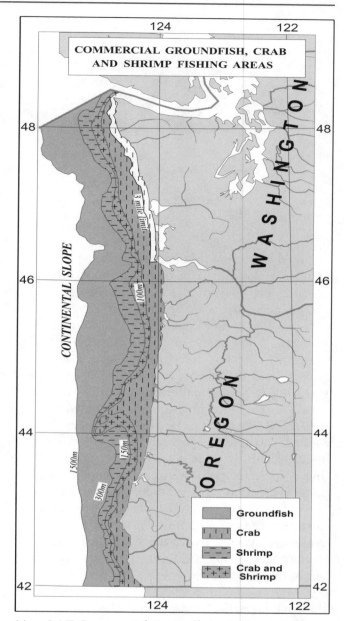

Map 14-7 Commercial Groundfish, Crab, and Shrimp
Fishing Areas

and more restrictive management. Fish handling and processing seasonally employ an additional 6,000 to 7,000 in the two states, a slight increase over 1990.

Recreational fisheries. Recreational fisheries from private boats and passenger-carrying charter boats are also a significant contributor to the region's economy. The recreational fleet included more than 350 licensed charter boats in 2000 and many more small private craft, fishing mostly in nearshore ocean waters and in Puget Sound. Important ocean recreational fishing ports in Washington include Westport, Ilwaco, Neah Bay, and La Push. In Oregon, Newport, Charleston, Astoria-Warrenton-Hammond, Winchester Bay,

Brookings, and other smaller ports support important recreational fisheries. Salmon, principally coho and to a lesser extent chinook, are the prime recreational fishing target, mostly in nearshore waters (see map 14-6). However, season and area closures in recent years have led to increased emphasis on recreational groundfishing in nearshore and deeper waters, with rockfishes, ling cod, and halibut the new species of interest.

Increasing Problems in Fisheries. Although commercial fisheries are an important sector of the economy, they have experienced a number of serious problems in recent years, some environmental and some human-

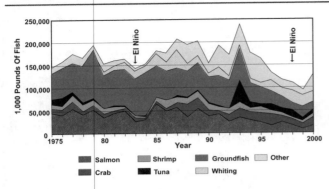

Figure 14-1. Washington Commercial Fisheries Landings, 1975-2000

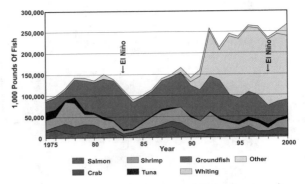

Figure 14-2. Oregon Commercial Fisheries Landings, 1975-2000

induced. During and after El Niños, for example, changed ocean environmental conditions result in significant declines in the productivity of certain fish species, such as salmon (see figures 14-1 and 14-2). Longer-term shifts in ocean environmental conditions—the Pacific Decadal Oscillation or PDO—also affect ocean and fisheries productivity. For example, since the 1997-98 El Niño, we appear to have shifted to a cooler, wetter phase of the PDO, signaling the return of improved ocean productivity for the region. Other problems that beset the industry include declining stocks and catches, too many fishing boats, excessive "bycatch" of non-target species, habitat damage, and competition from lower-priced farmed fish. Allocation conflicts are also on the increase among commercial gear-type groups, between commercial and recreational fishers, and between Indian and non-Indian fishers. These problems and conflicts have increasingly politicized the fisheries management process and driven many out of the fishing business.

Fisheries Conservation and Management. Responsibility for management varies with the fishery. Inshore fisheries, such as Dungeness crab, that are primarily within the three-mile territorial seas are managed by the respective states. Most marine fisheries, however, are under the jurisdiction of the Pacific Fisheries Management Council (PFMC), which includes representatives from Washington, Oregon, California, and Idaho, as well as public and industry members. The PFMC (and other regional councils in other areas) was established under the Magnuson Fisheries Conservation and Management Act of 1976. The overall goals of the act are to promote the sustainable harvest of species in the 200-mile Fisheries Conservation (now the EEZ) and "Americanize" fisheries in the zone which at the time were largely foreign. The PFMC writes fishery management plans for individual fisheries, such as

salmon and groundfish, considering scientific information available on stocks, reproductive capacity, fishing-fleet capacity and gear types, and socioeconomic concerns. The halibut fishery is managed by the International Pacific Halibut Commission. A variety of management measures are used to regulate the different fisheries, including selective time and area closures, limited entry schemes, and quotas and other rationing systems. The 1996 Sustainable Fisheries Act, which amended the 1976 fisheries law, includes a variety of provisions designed to help depleted stocks recover, to limit bycatch, and to protect "essential fish habitat." Among the most controversial of these stock recovery options are proposals to establish no-fishing areas called marine reserves. Marine reserves would be designed to protect the spawning and rearing areas of depleted fish stocks, eventually contributing fish to fishable areas outside the reserve.

Oil and Gas Resources

The offshore geology of the Pacific Northwest is extremely complex. While available geologic information indicates that there are several sedimentary basins where oil and gas may be trapped (see map 14-8), these basins are poorly defined. Following a federal offshore oil and gas lease sale off Washington and Oregon in 1964, twelve wells were drilled at promising offshore sites and numerous others just inland. However, most wells were dry holes, and while there were "shows" of both oil and gas at a few sites, no "recoverable" deposits of oil and gas were discovered.

Interest in offshore leasing for oil and gas exploration surfaced again in the 1980s. In 1989, both Washington and Oregon state legislatures placed a moratorium on oil and gas leasing in state waters (0-3 nm). Oregon made the moratorium permanent in 1994 with adoption of the Territorial Sea Man-

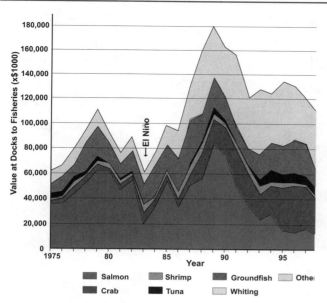

Figure 14-3. Landed Value of Washington
Commercial Fisheries, 1975-2000

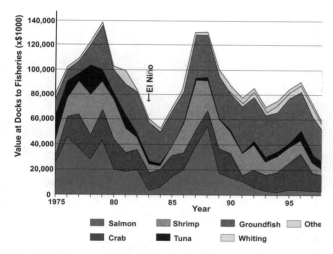

Figure 14-4. Landed Value of Oregon
Commercial Fisheries, 1975-2000

agement Plan. In federal waters (3-200 nm), a 1990 moratorium called a halt to oil and gas leasing until the year 2000; it was then extended until 2012. Reasons for these moratoria include insufficient scientific information, concern about potential risks and impacts to economically-valuable fisheries and other marine resources, general public opposition because of these risks, and the assessment by industry and federal resource managers that there is very little recoverable oil and gas in the area.

Marine Minerals

There are a number of potentially valuable marine mineral resources in the Pacific Northwest, including polymetallic sulfides, placers, and sand and gravel. As with other seabed resources, exploitation of marine minerals is under state jurisdiction inside 3 nm and under federal control in the remainder of the 200-nm EEZ.

Polymetallic sulfides are massive deposits of ore that contain iron, zinc, copper, and other metals. They are deposited in areas of hydrothermal vents along mid-ocean spreading centers. The seafloor off the Pacific Northwest is unique in that two such "mid-ocean" spreading centers are within the 200-mile EEZ boundary—the entire Gorda Ridge and a portion of the Juan de Fuca Ridge. The federal government attempted to lease the Gorda Ridge for mineral exploration in the early 1980s, but the proposal was canceled because of public outcry and a lack of industry interest.

Placers are concentrated deposits of heavy mineral-bearing sands. Placers found off the Oregon and Washington coasts contain magnetite (iron), chromite (a source for chromium), ilmenite (a source of titanium), zircon, garnet, gold, platinum, and other potentially valuable minerals. Historically, gold was mined from beach placers in southern Oregon. In the late 1980s, there was considerable interest by industry and government in exploring for chromite-rich placer deposits offshore. The federal government and Oregon and California formed a technical task force to gather more complete data on the deposits known to occur there. While the research was inconclusive as to economic recoverability, the 1991 Oregon legislature passed a law banning offshore mineral exploration because of potential threat to habitat for fisheries and other living resources. Placer sands off northern Oregon and Washington are mostly iron oxides, the least valuable placer mineral, and one unlikely to be exploited.

Offshore gravel deposits are estimated to be 1.9-9.8 billion cubic yards offshore the Washington coast and 130-650 million cubic yards offshore Oregon. Gravel is thus the most abundant marine mineral resource. While it is unlikely to be mined soon, offshore gravel may be considered in the future to supplement dwindling onshore supplies of high quality construction aggregate.

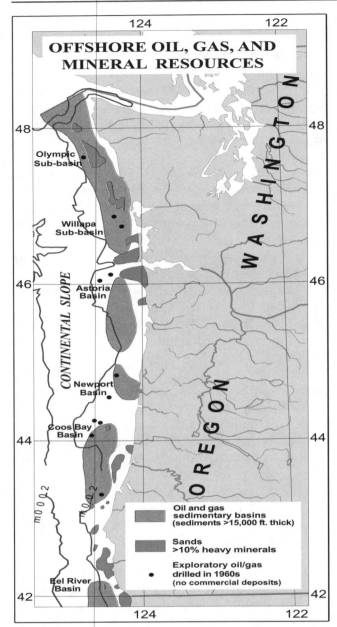

Map 14-8 Offshore Oil, Gas, and Mineral Resource Potential

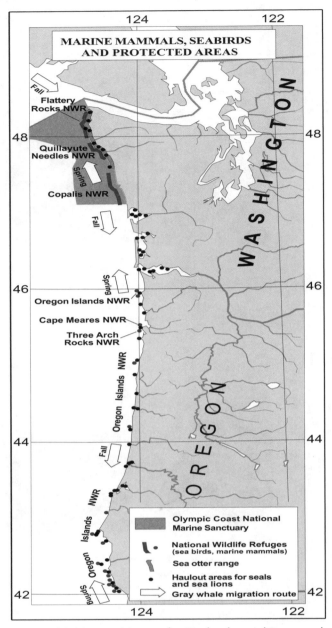

Map 14-9 Marine Mammals, Seabirds, and Protected Areas

Marine Resource Protection

Over the past thirty years, marine conservation has focused primarily on protecting marine birds and rebuilding depleted stocks of marine mammals, including harbor seals, sea lions, and whales (see map 14-9). Many critical nesting, resting, and migration sites for seabirds and coastal waterfowl are protected along the Oregon and Washington coasts as part of a system of national wildlife refuges. Many of these are offshore rocks and islands that are part of the Oregon Islands National Wildlife Refuge and the Flattery Rocks, Quillayute, and

Copalis National Wildlife Refuges off the Washington coast.

Populations of marine mammals, protected under the federal Marine Mammal Protection Act of 1972, have rebounded dramatically in the last thirty years. Harbor seals in Oregon, for example, increased from 2,500 to 10,000 since 1972. As a consequence, marine mammal conflicts with human uses and activities have also increased, especially regarding commercial and recreational fisheries. Whales, including the coastal migrant gray whale, are also common inhabitants of Pacific Northwest waters. They and other whales are protected under federal law and international agreements and managed by the International Whaling Commission.

In 1992, the Olympic Coast National Marine Sanctuary was established, including all EEZ waters north of Grays Harbor, Washington. While many traditional uses are permitted, oil and gas development is prohibited. Proposals for other federal sanctuaries in Washington and Oregon have been made, but none have been designated. Most recently, the marine protection debate has shifted to the need to protect essential fish habitat for spawning and rearing of depleted stocks such as rockfish.

Differing degrees of marine resource protection are also provided at national seashores, recreation areas, marine intertidal gardens, estuarine research reserves, and other coastal wildlife refuges. Particular attention is being given to protecting rocky intertidal areas from overuse.

Toward a More Integrated Ocean Management

One of the frequent long-time criticisms of marine resource management is that the United States does not have a coherent "national ocean policy." Critics charge that management of ocean resources at both the state and federal levels is too resource- or use-specific and poorly integrated. The result is increasing conflict among resource users and other interest groups, with no efficient, equitable means for resolution. At the national level, the Oceans Act of 2000 established the U.S. Commission on Ocean Policy, the first of its kind since 1966. Numerous proposals for improved ocean governance, sustainable fisheries, and marine research and development are being examined by the commission. For example, regional commissions have been proposed that would provide for overall coordination of ocean uses and space, as well as for dispute resolution. Meanwhile, at the state level, actual experiments in integrated ocean management have been undertaken, including innovative ocean planning efforts in Oregon and Washington. In 1990, Oregon produced the nation's first state "ocean management plan," followed by a territorial sea management plan in 1994, which has served as the basis for resolving a variety of disputes.

Further Reading

Strickland, R. and D. J. Chasen. 1989. *Coastal Washington: A synthesis of information.* WSG 89-1. Seattle: Washington Sea Grant.

Parmenter, L. and R. Bailey. 1985. *The Oregon Ocean Book.* Salem: Department of Land Conservation and Development.

Oregon Ocean Resources Management Task Force. 1990. *The Oregon Ocean Plan.* Salem, Oregon.

Oregon Ocean Policy Advisory Council. 1994. *Oregon Territorial Sea Management Plan.* Salem, Oregon.

Good, J. W. 2000. *Summary and Current Status and Health of Oregon's Marine Ecosystems.* Chapter 3, Section 2, pages 21-32, Oregon State of the Environment Report. Salem: Oregon Progress Board.

Chapter 15
Minerals and Mining
Peter Wampler

Production from the minerals and mining industries is vital to a variety of sectors of the Pacific Northwest economy. The demand for natural aggregate rock alone has increased in importance as the Northwest construction industry surges ahead. While aggregate mining and production may not bring forth the romantic vision of grizzled prospectors panning stream deposits, or blasting mine shafts looking for gold and silver, the sheer volume of production is most important and impressive. It is estimated that, on average, the per capita use of natural aggregate in the Pacific Northwest amounts to about 10 tons per year. This is roughly equivalent to each person stopping by the local hardware store to pick up a fifty-pound bag of rock every day, three hundred and sixty-five days a year!

Many of the valuable metals mining districts in the Pacific Northwest were mined out many years ago and are now nothing more than tourist attractions or a wide spot on a dusty road. Historically productive metal mines have been shut down or mothballed in response to current low metal prices and high production costs and/or environmental concerns. The overall value of minerals produced in the United States continues to increase annually, but the importance of metal mining has decreased markedly (see figure 15-1).The decrease in metals production has been largely replaced by increased production of industrial minerals and construction aggregates.

Mineral Production

The total average annual nonfuel mineral production in the United States has increased 69.7 percent over the last two decades, from $23,351 million in 1980-82 to $39,633 million in 1998-2000. The increase in total nonfuel mineral production for the Pacific Northwest was slightly higher than the U.S. average, increasing 84.8 percent, from $710 million in 1980-82 to $1,388 million in 1998-2000.

Idaho ranked thirty-third among the states in overall mineral production for the year 2000, and accounted for 0.91 percent of the total U.S. nonfuel mineral production. Phosphate rock, silver, construction sand

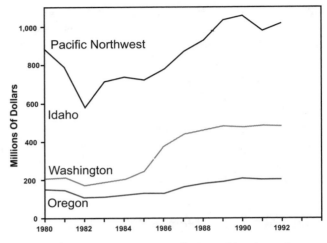

Figure 15-1. Value of Mineral Production (in millions of dollars)

and gravel, molybdenum, and lead were, by value, Idaho's leading nonfuel minerals. Average annual mineral production has recently declined slightly in Idaho (-0.80 percent) to roughly 1980 levels. In 2000, molybdenum concentrates and construction sand and gravel values (listed in descending order of change) increased by about $5 million each, and those of Portland cement and zinc about $2 million each. Smaller increases also occurred in copper and industrial garnet. But gold production in 2000 decreased by more than $15 million, phosphate rock by $2 million, and smaller yet significant decreases in industrial sand and gravel, lead, and crushed stone offset overall production gains, resulting in a small net decrease in value for the year.

In 2000, Idaho's only remaining large gold mine, Meridian Gold Company's Beartrack Mine in Lemhi County, was closed, and the Sunshine Mining Company, owners of the legendary Sunshine Mine in Shoshone County, filed for bankruptcy. The Sunshine Mine has produced more than 10,900 metric tons (t) since its discovery in 1884, making it one of the world's largest silver mines. Several closed precious-metal mines were undergoing reclamation or cleanup during 2000.

Oregon ranked thirty-sixth among the states in minerals production for the year 2000, and accounted for 0.76 percent of the total U.S. nonfuel mineral production. Industrial minerals accounted for virtually all of Oregon's nonfuel mineral production in 2000. Based on the value of minerals produced, crushed stone and construction aggregates remained Oregon's two leading nonfuel mineral commodities, followed by Portland cement, diatomite, and lime. The nickel smelter at Riddle, Oregon, was shut down March 31, 1998 after several years of processing nickel ore imported from New Caledonia. Cleanup at Formosa Resources Corporation's Silver Butte Mine, which ceased operation in 1993, was ongoing until the late 1990s.

Washington ranked twenty-fourth among the states in the year 2000, and accounted for 1.54 percent of the total U.S. nonfuel mineral production. In 2000, four of Washington's mineral commodities, construction sand and gravel, crushed stone, Portland cement, and gypsum, accounted for more than 72 percent of the state's nonfuel mineral value.

Major metal-mining activities included gold mining and exploration at the Lamefoot and K-2 gold deposits, and development work to reopen the Pend Oreille lead-zinc mine. The Crown Jewel gold deposit is in the appeals process concerning water rights. Major non-metal production in 2000 includes Olivine Corporation, which mined 36,000 tons of refractory-grade olivine from its Swen Larsen quarry in Whatcom County, and two companies in Okanogan and Stevens Counties which mine dolomite (calcium magnesium carbonate) and limestone (calcium carbonate) for use as a feed lime and soil conditioner.

Environmental Issues, Reclamation, and Future Trends

Environmental regulations, labor and production costs, and low metal prices have forced many mining companies to explore for metals outside U.S. borders. Mining occurs in developing countries where environmental regulations and enforcement are weaker, consequent environmental impacts are greater, and lack of labor practices laws often result in exploitation of workers.

Oregon, Washington, and Idaho all have laws that require reclamation of mining sites to a beneficial use after mining. Post-mining beneficial uses include agriculture, fish and wildlife habitat, industrial sites, forestry, and wetlands. Bonds are posted by mining companies to insure that reclamation is completed according to an approved plan. Aggregate sites require mining permits and must adhere to land use

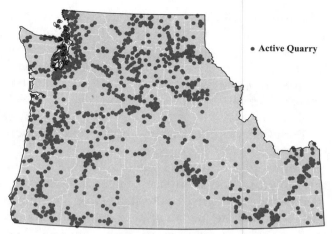

Map 15-1. Active Sand and Gravel Production Sites

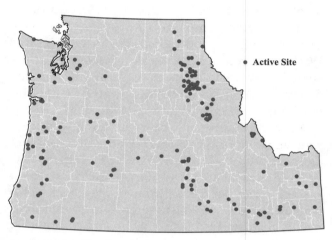

Map 15-2. Clay Production Sites

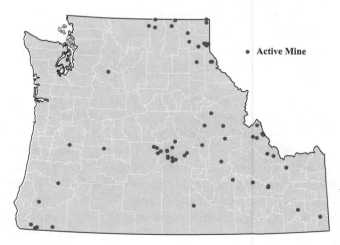

Map 15-3. Active Metal Mines

planning regulations. Local and state land use regulations may result in several years of negotiations prior to approval, all of which increase start-up expenses. The development of large regional aggregate extraction sites with more extensive disturbance has largely replaced small local quarries and gravel pits.

Both Oregon and Washington have reclamation award programs to recognize mining operators who perform outstanding reclamation. In 1996 Oregon and Washington jointly produced a best management practices manual to share effective mining practices with aggregate mining operators around both states. These mining practices were also taken on the road in the form of workshops and training session around both states. An on-line version of the manual can be found at http://www.wa.gov/dnr/htdocs/ger/pdf/bmp.pdf.

Catastrophic flooding in 1996 in Oregon and Washington resulted in river avulsion into river side gravel pits. Some of the most dramatic impacts occurred near Yakima, Washington; Chehalis, Washington; Barton, Oregon; and Medford, Oregon. In some cases entire river courses were altered when rivers flowed into gravel excavations. Impacts such as these, combined with listed endangered fish species present in many northwest rivers, have caused many floodplain mining sites to be either banned, as in some Washington counties, or more strictly regulated as in most of Oregon, Washington, and Idaho.

An increasing emphasis is being placed on reclaiming river sites to mimic natural river landforms so that off-site impacts will not be increased by the presence of the mining site during a flood. Efforts are also under way to convert gravel ponds to off-channel habitat that may actually benefit juvenile salmonids and other anadromous fish.

Recycling of concrete and asphalt has become increasingly important in the northwest. According to the National Asphalt Pavement Association, 80 percent of asphalt is recycled nationwide, and forty-four states use recycled concrete as road base. Recycling has three main benefits: 1) reduced waste in landfills; 2) reduced transportation costs; 3) decreased need for mining new aggregate resources.

Sources

Site locations derive from digital databases obtained from the Washington State Department of Natural Resources (DNR) SURFMINES database, the Oregon Department of Geology and Mineral Industries Mined Land Reclamation Program (DOGAMI-MLR) database of mining sites, and the Bureau of Land Management (BLM) mine site database.

Minerals production statistics were largely collected from the minerals yearbook, mineral commodity summaries, and annual summaries by the Idaho Geological Survey, the Oregon Department of Geology and Minerals Industries, and the Washington Department of Natural Resources.

Chapter 16
Manufacturing and Service Industries
William B. Beyers

Almost 6.5 million people were employed in the Pacific Northwest in 2000. Figure 16-1 indicates the industrial distribution of this employment, while Table 16-1 describes in more detail the composition of employment at the state level, and rates of change in employment over the 1987-1997 decade. As figure 16.1 indicates, the largest share of employment was in various service industries, which accounted for 63 percent of total employment. Government employed another 14 percent, while manufacturing accounted for 11 percent of regional employment. Primary sectors (farming, forestry, fishing, and mining) accounted for 5 percent, and construction accounted for 6 percent of total employment. The Northwest gained over 1.4 million jobs between 1990 and 2000, an increase of 28 percent. This growth rate was well above the national average (20 percent) for the same time period. However, this growth rate has been uneven, both among industries and geographically. The bulk of this employment gain was in the various service industries, while manufacturing employment grew slowly. Idaho had much stronger growth in manufacturing than Oregon, while Washington manufacturing employment has fallen iin the last few years largely because of downturns in the aerospace sector. The growth of manufacturing in the Northwest contrasts with the United States as a whole, which experienced a slight decline in manufacturing employment over the same time period.

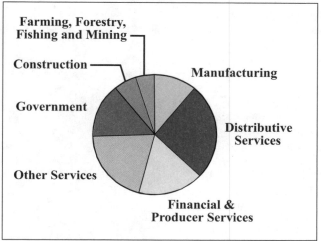

Figure 16-1. Employment Shares in the Pacific Northwest, 2000

Map 16-1 shows the distribution of employment at the county level. It clearly indicates the concentration of employment in the major metropolitan areas of the Pacific Northwest. Most county economies in the Northwest are small, with fewer than twenty thousand employees. Map 16-2 shows the percentage change in employment by county between 1990 and 2000. While the absolute growth in employment was concentrated in the metropolitan areas of the region, this figure also shows that many smaller rural counties experienced rapid growth. Rapid suburban growth is evident near Portland, Seattle, Spokane, and Boise. Over the 1990-2000 time

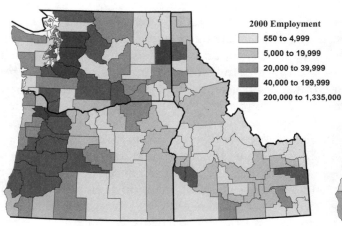

Map 16-1. Total Private Non-agricultural Employment, 2000

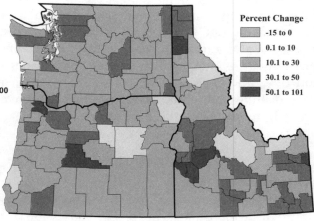

Map 16-2. Change in Employment, 1990-2000

Table 16-1 Employment by Industry

	1997 Employment (1000s)				Change	Percent Change			
	ID	OR	WA	Region	1987-97	ID	OR	WA	Region
Total	715.0	2000.9	3363.3	6079.2	1639.4	45.9	36.7	35.3	36.9
Farm	34.1	64.4	80.5	179.0	6.1	-12.7	7.9	8.6	3.5
Ag. Services, forestry, fishing	19.0	38.3	61.5	118.8	39.3	70.4	47.0	45.4	49.4
Mining	3.8	3.1	5.2	12.2	0.7	15.8	7.4	0.2	6.5
Construction	51.0	115.0	189.0	355.0	146.2	105.6	99.4	49.6	70.0
Manufacturing total	81.5	262.9	394.5	739.0	126.1	39.8	19.8	17.8	20.6
Food Products	16.4	22.6	37.2	76.2	14.2	12.8	15.9	32.8	22.8
Wood Products	12.3	47.8	32.2	92.3	-20.3	9.7	-27.0	-10.4	-18.1
Printing & Publishing	5.1	15.9	23.8	44.8	8.7	46.8	18.8	23.4	24.0
Nonelectrical Machinery	8.8	27.7	25.3	61.9	24.2	101.2	78.5	42.3	64.1
Electrical Machinery	19.6	18.5	17.3	55.4	21.4	438.7	60.6	-8.1	63.0
Transportation Equipment	2.1	15.1	85.6	102.8	14.0	96.0	53.2	9.9	15.7
Instruments	0.8	11.4	29.2	41.4	20.7	52.7	-7.3	266.4	99.3
Other Manufacturing	16.3	104.1	143.9	264.2	43.4	-16.1	44.3	11.3	19.7
Trade & Services total	418.5	1264.4	2103.7	3786.6	1175.0	56.1	44.2	43.5	45.0
Transp., Commun. & utilities	31.2	89.9	155.2	276.4	73.3	39.9	30.3	38.9	36.1
Wholesale Trade	32.6	101.4	163.1	297.0	77.8	43.4	35.0	34.3	35.5
Retail Trade	129.4	353.8	572.2	1055.5	314.1	60.5	41.0	39.6	42.4
Eating & Drinking	33.3	105.8	167.2	306.3	86.8	52.7	42.9	35.2	39.5
Other Retail	96.2	248.0	405.0	749.2	227.3	63.4	40.3	41.5	43.6
Finance, Insurance, real estate	38.4	132.3	246.7	417.4	85.8	16.9	24.5	28.2	25.9
Producer Services	35.1	133.7	208.0	376.8	184.6	88.3	120.0	84.4	96.0
Health Services	41.6	118.8	211.2	371.6	146.2	127.7	51.2	64.3	64.8
Other Services	110.2	334.6	547.2	992.0	293.3	51.7	41.4	40.5	42.0
Federal - Civilian	12.7	29.9	66.7	109.3	-2.4	6.7	-0.5	-4.4	-2.2
Federal - Military	10.0	13.4	77.8	101.2	-8.2	-21.9	-14.1	-3.9	-7.5
State government	26.0	58.2	126.3	210.4	33.9	31.6	1.5	27.0	19.2
Local government	58.4	151.1	258.1	467.6	122.7	42.5	28.1	38.8	35.6

Source: U.S. Regional Economic Information System and U.S. County Business Patterns

period, nonmetropolitan counties in the Northwest had employment gains of 25.9 percent, slightly below the 28.5 percent gain of metropolitan counties. However, many "amenity" counties such as Blaine, ID, Deschutes OR, or San Juan, WA have had very rapid rates of employment growth linked to in-migration of retirees, wealthy second-home owners, tourism, and footloose entrepreneurs. Slow-growth rural counties tend to be associated with extensive agriculture and timber production.

Manufacturing

The structure of manufacturing employment varies among the Northwest states, as shown in figure 16-2. This figure, and the data used in the balance of this chapter, are based on the SIC classification system, which after 1997 was replaced by the non-comparable NAICS classification system. The SIC system was used in this chapter and therefore data refer to the period ending in 1997. Washington's manufacturing sector is larger than those of Oregon and Idaho taken together, but in the late 1990s it has experienced declining employment. Washington's manufacturing sector continues to be led by transportation equipment manufacturing, which in turn is dominated by the Boeing Company, which has shed tens of thousands of jobs over the past few years. Wood and forest products are important in all three states, but wood products employment has suffered a decline of 18 percent regionally between 1987 and 1997, while food products employment has grown across the region. The wood products downturn has been particularly sharp in Oregon, where lumber is no longer king, having been overtaken by hi-tech employment. Table 16-1

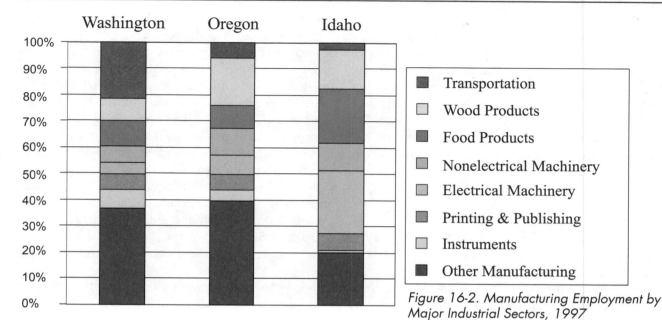

Figure 16-2. Manufacturing Employment by Major Industrial Sectors, 1997

Legend:
- Transportation
- Wood Products
- Food Products
- Nonelectrical Machinery
- Electrical Machinery
- Printing & Publishing
- Instruments
- Other Manufacturing

indicates the importance of nonelectrical and electrical machinery and instruments in the growth of manufacturing employment across the Northwest.

Manufacturing employment is most heavily concentrated in the major metropolitan areas of the region, as shown on Map 16-3. Figure 16-3 shows the composition of this employment for the Metropolitan Statistical Areas, which accounted for 72 percent of total manufacturing employment in the Pacific Northwest in 1997. It is evident that there are major structural differences in Northwest metropolitan area economies. Manufacturing employment in the Seattle PMSA is dominated by the transportation equipment sector; no other metropolitan area in the region exhibits such a concentration in this sector. The Boise economy has a very strong concentration in electrical and nonelectrical machinery, while the economies of Portland-Vancouver and Tacoma are more diverse in their industrial structure. These four metropolitan areas accounted for almost 80 percent of total metropolitan manufacturing employment in 1997.

Smaller metropolitan areas tend to have concentrations of employment in particular manufacturing industries. Although wood products have diminished in importance, they still remain a relatively strong component in the Eugene-Springfield, Salem, Medford, Yakima, Bellingham, and Corvallis economies. Corvallis shows an exceptionally high concentration of nonelectrical machinery employment, while food products are a significant component in the Salem, Yakima, and Bellingham economies. Strong dependence upon primary metals is evident in Spokane and Bellingham.

While manufacturing employment as measured in absolute numbers is highest in the large metropolitan areas, it is nevertheless important to the economies of many smaller places in the Northwest. Map 16-3 shows some manufacturing employment in almost all counties in the Northwest. Map 16-4 shows the leading manufacturing sector by county. The metropolitan areas whose structure is described in figure 16.4 tend to have relatively diversified manufacturing employment structures, with no particular sector dominating total employment. In contrast, most smaller rural counties tend to have one industry that accounts for a majority of manufacturing employment, as indicated on map 16-4. This map documents the continuing importance of forest products manufacturing across much of the rural Pacific Northwest. Food products manufacturing is a leading sector over much of the rural Snake River Plain counties in southern Idaho, in Columbia

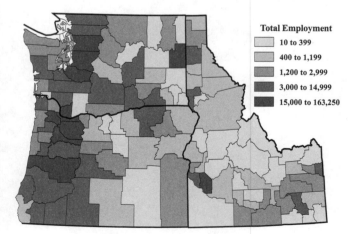

Total Employment
- 10 to 399
- 400 to 1,199
- 1,200 to 2,999
- 3,000 to 14,999
- 15,000 to 163,250

Map 16-3. Manufacturing Employment, 1997

Basin counties in Eastern Washington, and in eastern Oregon. It should also be noted that the absolute number of jobs in many of these counties is small, as indicated on map 16-3. While food and forest products are the mainstays of the manufacturing sector for most rural counties in the Northwest, there are cases of other specialties, such as the wooden furniture sector in Teton County, Idaho, or the sporting goods manufacturers in Hood River Oregon.

Food Products

Food products manufacturing is important in most of the metropolitan area economies and is also found in many nonmetropolitan areas, as shown on map 16-5. Major food products sectors include meat and dairy products, canning and freezing of fruits and vegetables, baking, beet sugar processing, beverage production, and miscellaneous food products including fish and seafood, roasted coffee, potato and corn chips, and pasta. Production is oriented to both local and export markets in the United States and abroad. Meat and dairy products production tends to be located near to the region's major metropolitan areas, although specialty dairy products processing establishments are found in some rural counties. Canning and freezing plants are located near major

agricultural areas in southern Idaho, the Willamette Valley, eastern Washington, and northern Puget Sound. Small bakeries are found in towns as well as in city neighborhoods throughout the region, but most employment is associated with large commercial baking establishments in the region's major metropolitan areas. Breweries and soft-drink operations are primarily located in the major metropolitan areas of the region, while wineries have proliferated in Western Oregon, in the Yakima, Columbia, and Walla Walla valleys in Washington, and in Southern Idaho. A considerable portion of the Eastern Washington wine grape crop is vinified in suburban Seattle locations. Miscellaneous food products employment is concentrated in major metropolitan areas.

Food products manufacturing industries are part of a larger industrial complex which includes the region's agriculture sector, and the channels of distribution that move agricultural commodities to food products manufacturers and to consumers. This system includes transportation services, wholesaling, agricultural services, and retailers selling Northwest food products to household consumers. It also includes producers of packaging materials such as paper, glass, and plastics, and manufacturers of machinery and equipment used in farming and in the food products processing sectors.

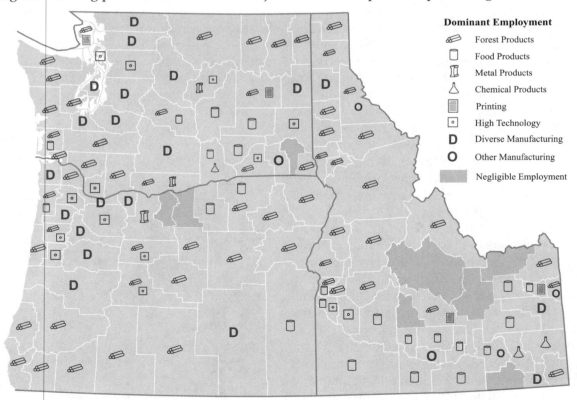

Map 16-4. Manufacturing Employment Structure, 1997

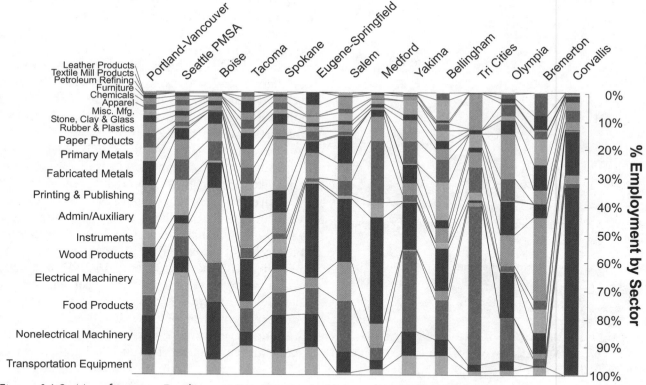

Figure 16-3. Manufacturing Employment Percentages in Metropolitan Statistical Areas

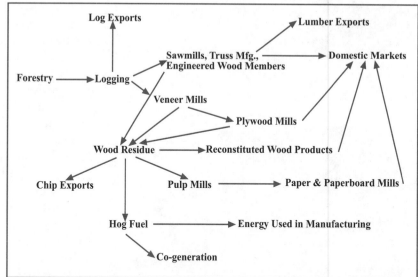

Figure 16-4. Forest Products Industrial Complex

Forest Products

The forest products industry has historically been the largest manufacturing sector in the Pacific Northwest, as measured by jobs. However, as a result of a combination of reductions in timber supply levels (especially from federal forest lands) and improvements in labor productivity levels, employment in forest products manufacturing declined to about 118,000 in 1997 which was 16 percent of total manufacturing employment. This sector is composed of a number of integrated subsectors, which range from the growing of timber (forestry) to harvesting timber (logging) and processing it into semifinished or finished products (see figure 16-4). Important manufacturing sectors include logging, sawmills, truss manufacturers, producers of engineered wood members, veneer and plywood production, reconstituted wood products mills, and pulp and paper mills. Wood residue from these industries is

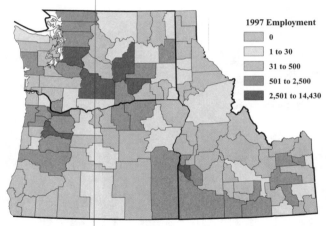

Map 16-5. *Food Products Manufacturing Employment,*
1997

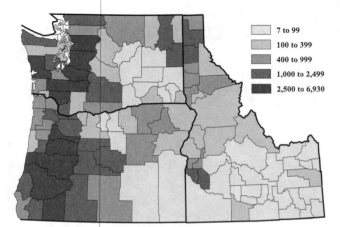

Map 16-6. *Wood Products Manufacturing*
Employment, 1997

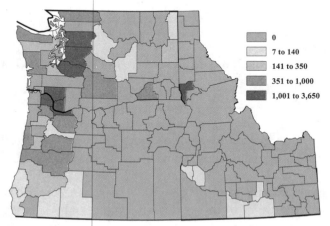

Map 16-7. *Pulp and Paper Manufacturing Employment,*
1997

fully utilized, either as inputs to the production of pulp and paper products or reconstituted wood products (such as oriented-strandboard), or it is exported to foreign countries or used as hog fuel to produce energy utilized in the forest products manufacturing process, or to produce electricity sold in the regional energy grid. There are other smaller market linkages not shown in figure 16-5. Map 16-6 identifies the distribution of employment in the wood products sector, while map 16-7 shows the location of employment in the pulp and paper manufacturing sector. Map 16-4 documented the widespread importance of forest products production in rural counties in the Pacific Northwest. Map 16-6 shows that the wood products component of the industry is much more broadly dispersed than the pulp and paper sector (map 16-7). While wood products employment is important east of the Cascades in all three Pacific Northwest states, the largest concentration of jobs is in westside counties. The wood products sector includes many small establishments in subsectors such as logging, as well as large integrated complexes such as found in Longview, Washington. In contrast, the pulp and paper sector is composed primarily of a few large-scale establishments, each of which employs hundreds or thousands of workers. A single pulp mill is frequently supplied by many sources of residual materials, and is located where there is an ample supply of water for use in manufacturing processes.

Figure 16-4 indicates that the markets of the various forest products sectors are located predominantly outside the Pacific Northwest. This market is split between foreign (largely Far Eastern) markets and the domestic construction or paper markets. In recent years about 13 percent of Washington's and about 11 percent of Oregon's timber harvest has been sold in the log export market, a much smaller share than over the previous decade. The majority of these shipments have been to Japan and South Korea. Sawmills, truss mills, engineered wood member mills, and veneer and plywood mills consume the bulk of the rest of the timber harvest. While most of the mills' product is sold in domestic construction markets, foreign markets have grown in importance in recent years.

Printing and Publishing

Printing and publishing manufacturing employment is widely distributed throughout the Pacific Northwest, as indicated on map 16-8. Newspaper printing and

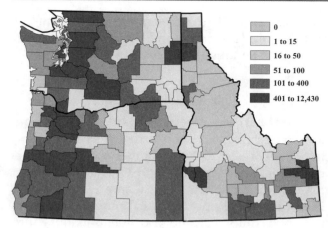

Map 16-8. Printing and Publishing Industry
Employment, 1997

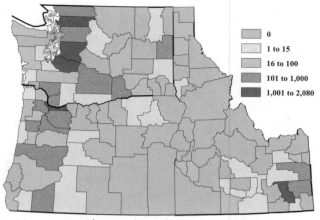

Map 16-9. Chemicals and Petroleum Refining
Employment, 1997

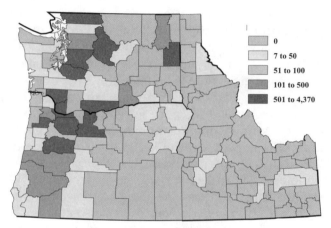

Map 16-10. Primary Metals Manufacturing
Employment, 1997

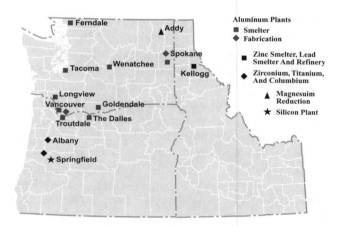

Map 16-11. Nonferrous Metals Plants

commercial printing are the two most important constituents of this industry, and are found even in relatively small rural counties. In some smaller counties printing is among the most important manufacturing industries, as indicated on map 16.4. Most establishments in this industry are small, and map 16.8 shows that the total level of employment in most counties is small. The largest concentrations of printing employment are found in the metropolitan areas where the major daily newspapers are printed.

Chemicals and Petroleum Refining

Chemicals and petroleum refining employment is highly concentrated in the Pacific Northwest. As map 16-9 indicates, most counties have no employment in these sectors. Petroleum refining primarily occurs in four refineries in Skagit and Whatcom counties, utilizing crude oil imported by tanker from Alaska and the Far East. Asphalt products plants are also found in this sector, with the largest employment located in the major metropolitan centers. Chemicals manufacturing activity is diverse. West of the Cascades it is supportive of the forest products industry, providing chlorine and adhesives. In major agricultural areas it again plays a supportive role, with modest employment levels. Phosphatic fertilizer and inorganic chemicals are important in southeast Idaho. Most employment in Benton County related to the historic production of plutonium has now been classified with waste management services.

Primary Metals

Primary metals is a relatively small industry, employing only 24,000 people, and accounting for only 3 percent of manufacturing employment in 1997. It is very unevenly distributed, with many counties having no employment, or only a few jobs, as map 16-10 illustrates. However, it is an important industry in

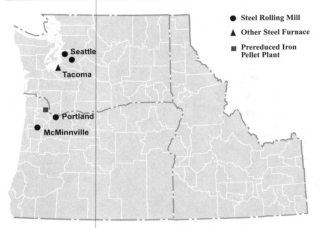

Map 16-12. Steel and Ferroalloy Plants

the particular localities (mostly rural) where large-scale mills are found, and it has consumed a large share of the electrical power produced at the hydropower dams found in the Pacific Northwest.

Aluminum reduction mills dominate the primary metals industry in the Pacific Northwest (see map 16-11). These mills account for about 40 percent of the domestic smelting capacity for primary aluminum. Plants are located in Spokane, Ferndale, Wenatchee, Tacoma, Goldendale, The Dalles, Longview, Vancouver, and Troutdale. Alumina, which is used to make aluminum metal, is imported primarily from Australia in bulk carriers, and transported by rail or barge to interior mills. These mills were located in the Northwest from the 1930s into the 1960s following the availability of cheap federal hydropower from Columbia and Snake River dams, and because of public policies that encouraged their construction through the offering of long-term low-cost power contracts. Today their energy cost has risen, but aluminum plants traditionally have made use of large supplies of interruptible secondary power that has frequently been sold at lower costs than firm power on a long-run contractual basis. In 2003, market conditions have led to the closure of most aluminum smelters, and it is uncertain whether production will resume at these facilities. Major aluminum fabrication facilities are located in Spokane, Vancouver, Longview, and Troutdale. Millersburg, in Linn County, Oregon, is a major producer of titanium, columbium, and zirconium metals and metal alloys, as well as of silicon metal products. A major ferrosilicon plant is located near Riddle, Oregon, while a large magnesium facility is located in Addy, Washington.

Ferrous metals production in the Northwest is based on scrap iron and steel. Primarily located in Portland and Seattle/Tacoma, these plants use electrical furnaces to melt scrap, which is primarily used to produce rebar and other shapes for the construction industry (see map 16-12).

High-technology Sectors

The Northwest has developed a substantial high-technology manufacturing sector, which is primarily located in or near to the major metropolitan areas of the region, as shown on map 16-13. High-technology manufacturing is defined as the sum of employment in nonelectrical and electrical machinery, transportation equipment, and instruments manufacture. There are varying definitions of high-technology manufacturing. Some of these definitions include just these four manufacturing industries, some include other industries (such as parts of chemicals or petroleum refining, biotechnology, computer services, and research), and some exclude parts of these four sectors. Figure 16.4 shows the composition of employment in the MSAs of the Northwest. Across the region as a whole, the four industries regarded as high-technology account for 44 percent of total manufacturing employment in MSAs. In the Seattle PMSA the aerospace sector led by Boeing dominates the high-technology sector, but truck assembly, nonelectrical and electrical machinery, and instruments manufacture are also of importance. The region from Eugene to Vancouver also contains a major concentration of high-technology industry, but with a very different character from that found in the Puget Sound area. Often dubbed the Silicon Forest, this complex is strongly tied to electronic equipment, computing equipment, instruments, and the manufacture of electronic components. Boise and Spokane have smaller but rapidly growing high-technology sectors. Boise's high-technology sector

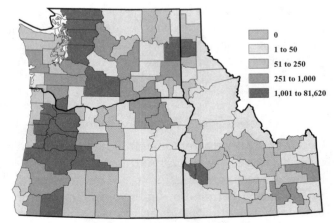

Map 16-13. High-technology Manufacturing Employment, 1997

is concentrated in semiconductors and computer equipment and components. Spokane's high-technology employment is primarily in transportation equipment and nonelectrical machinery. Not shown on map 16.13 is the major concentration of Navy shipbuilding workers in Bremerton, or the sonar-related workforce at Keyport in Kitsap County. Both are classified with government employment. High-technology sectors typically have a large share of nonproduction workers, and a substantial commitment to research and development. The Washington aerospace industry provides a good example of the occupational profile of high technology manufacturers. In 1995, 37 percent of the aerospace sector's labor force were engaged in blue-collar occupations, while the balance (63 percent) are engaged in managerial, professional and technical, sales, clerical, and service occupations, most of which require high educational and skill levels. Strong ties with regional colleges and universities for research and labor force training are common for high-technology manufacturers. While the Northwest has a combination of indigenous high-technology firms and branch plants of domestic and foreign corporations, entrepreneurs in these firms have often been the source of innovative ideas for new, spin-off high-technology businesses. The region has recently felt the impact of business cycles in high-technology industries in the form of job reductions and high unemployment rates.

Other Manufacturing

The manufacturing industries described above account for over three-fourths of total manufacturing employment. Smaller industrial groups include fabricated metals, plastics, stone-clay and glass, furniture, and apparel manufacture.

Services

Service industry employment in the Northwest is the largest component of the regional economy today. As shown in figure 16.2, service industries have also been the source of most new jobs in the region in recent years, and this trend is expected to continue over the next decade. In contrast to many lines of manufacturing, where producers are drawn to the location of resources such as timber or relatively inexpensive electricity, most service industries are located in proximity to their markets. Thus, the overall pattern of service industry employment mirrors the overall distribution of population in the

Northwest. However, there are systematic variations in the structure of service industries as we move from small towns to major metropolitan areas or from neighborhood shopping centers in cities to major retail malls in suburban centers. While household consumer markets are of primary importance for many service industries, this is not the case for all services. Some of the most rapidly growing service industries are primarily dependent upon businesses or governments as their clients, not households. It is therefore necessary to differentiate between consumer-oriented and business-oriented services.

Consumer-oriented Services

Household consumers are the most important markets for retailing, health services, basic financial, insurance, real estate services, entertainment, social and educational services, and some repair services. Services such as legal and banking services have mixed business and household markets. Demand for these services is based on people's residential and work locations, and their spatial distribution is related to the size of the market needed for a service firm to compete successfully. Services in frequent demand (such as groceries) rely on localized trade areas for their clients, while services that are demanded only occasionally (such as writing-pen repair) rely on much larger trade areas for their clients. This results in the development of a hierarchy of trade centers, showing clusters of service firms with similar trade areas. In some cases, agglomerations of offices providing specialized services arise, as in the case of specialized health-care services in cities such as Spokane and Seattle, while in other cases diverse sellers cluster in town centers or suburban shopping districts such as Southcenter near Seattle, and Lloyd Center near Portland. For people living in the parts of the Northwest with a low population density, these service functions are clustered at the lowest levels of this hierarchy in nearby small towns, while the demand for more specialized service functions is satisfied in nearby medium-sized centers, and the most specialized functions are supplied by businesses located in the region's major metropolitan areas. Within major metropolitan areas, a similar spatial differentiation is found, but because of higher densities of settlement the spacing of suppliers is closer than is the case in the more sparsely populated parts of the region.

The overall distribution of retail employment, which is shown on map 16-14, exhibits a distribution that is suggestive of a regional trade center hierarchy.

At the top of this hierarchy are the central business districts of Seattle and Portland plus suburban centers located in King and Multnomah counties. Metro fringe counties such as Snohomish, Washington, and Clackamas, Oregon, and supra-regional trade centers such as Boise, Idaho, or Eugene, Oregon, are the next level down this hierarchy, followed by regional trade centers such as Idaho Falls, Idaho, or Bend, Oregon. Subregional trade centers form the next level down the hierarchy, being focussed on towns such as Wenatchee, Washington, or Klamath Falls, Oregon. The lowest order in this hierarchy are small rural trade centers, such as Bonners Ferry, Idaho, Burns, Oregon, or South Bend, Washington.

The distribution of retail employment in 1997 shows a pattern very similar to the overall distribution of employment (map 16-1). This distribution reflects the geography of demand for services tightly linked to localized household markets, such as groceries, drugs store items, and clothing. Some retail activities are linked to nonlocal consumer demands, such as from tourists. The eating and drinking employment distribution reflects this tendency, as shown on map 16-15. This map shows the relative distribution of employment in this sector in 1997, through the use of location quotients, which show the share of employment in this industry in a given county relative to the share in the United States as a whole in 1997. The patterns on this map show a number of counties with an employment concentration more than 40 percent higher than the national average. Strong concentrations in counties along the Pacific Ocean coastline and in Blaine, Idaho, reflect tourist demands for eating and drinking establishments. Their index is also high in counties with important interstate highway corridors (such as Kittitas, Washington, which is on the I-90 corridor as well as having tourist/recreation attractions). A similar pattern emerges for hotels and other lodging employment, another service important to tourist and recreation activity concentrations (see map 16-16).

Other important consumer-oriented services include health, social, educational, cultural, amusement, and repair services. The distribution of employment in these other consumer services is similar to the pattern exhibited by retail trade, as indicated in map 16-17, which shows the distribution of health services employment.

Business-oriented Services

Services that are primarily sold to businesses and government are referred to as the producer services. This group of services includes functions such legal, architectural and engineering, accounting, consulting, research, advertising, computer software and programming, financial, and temporary help. Figure 16-2 indicates that these services have grown very rapidly between 1987 and 1997. The geographical distribution of this group of services is much more concentrated in major urban areas than is the case with consumer-oriented services. Map 16-18 shows location quotients for producer services, and only a handful of counties have location quotients above the national average. In addition to the core counties in the Portland and Seattle metropolitan areas, we find Bonneville, Idaho, and Benton, Washington, with high indices because of the presence of U.S. Department of Energy National Laboratories engaged in research in these counties. While producer service firms sell the majority of their services within the region, there is a growing cohort of highly specialized businesses that trade their services nationally or internationally, such as Microsoft in Redmond, Washington. These highly specialized businesses have considerable locational flexibility. With advances in telecommunications, commuter air travel, and small package courier services, there is a growing cohort of producer service establishments springing up in rural locations, especially in areas with a high quality of life.

Wholesale trade serves a variety of business markets, not only supplying retailers who sell goods to household consumers, but also handling products destined for export markets, or consumed by manufacturers, governments, and service firms within the region. While the overall pattern of wholesale employment tends to mirror the aggregate distribution of population (as shown in map 16-19), there are exceptions to this generalization related to the distribution of agricultural commodities, as clearly illustrated in map 16-20. This figure shows high location quotients in many eastern Washington and southern Idaho counties with a strong agriculture sector. Fruit, vegetable, grain, and other agricultural commodity storage operations—either in fresh or processed form—are part of the channel of distribution for the Northwest's agriculture sector.

Two important service sectors have mixed consumer and business markets: transportation services, communications, and utilities; and finance,

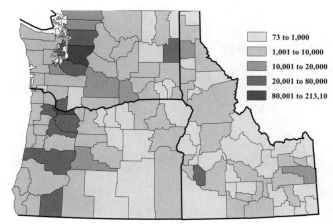

73 to 1,000
1,001 to 10,000
10,001 to 20,000
20,001 to 80,000
80,001 to 213,10

Map 16-14. Retail Employment, 1997

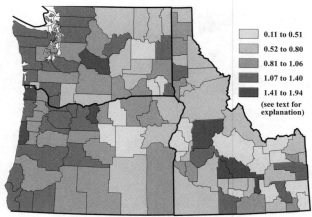

0.11 to 0.51
0.52 to 0.80
0.81 to 1.06
1.07 to 1.40
1.41 to 1.94
(see text for explanation)

Map 16-15. Eating and Drinking Employment, 1997 location quotients

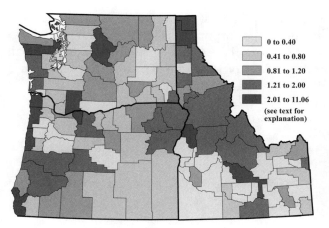

0 to 0.40
0.41 to 0.80
0.81 to 1.20
1.21 to 2.00
2.01 to 11.06
(see text for explanation)

Map 16-16. Hotel and Other Lodging Employment, 1997 location quotients

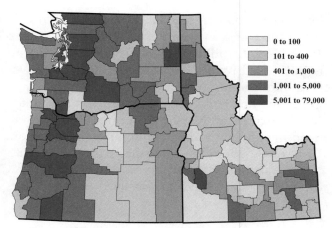

0 to 100
101 to 400
401 to 1,000
1,001 to 5,000
5,001 to 79,000

Map 16-17. Health Services Employment, 1997

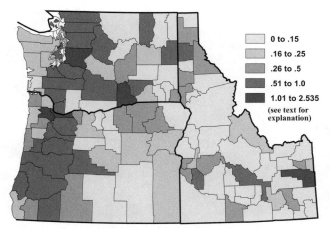

0 to .15
.16 to .25
.26 to .5
.51 to 1.0
1.01 to 2.535
(see text for explanation)

Map 16-18. Producer Services Employment, 1997 location quotients

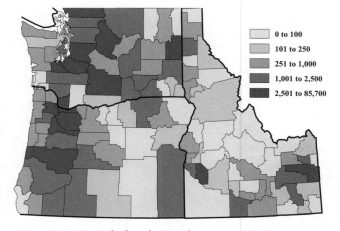

0 to 100
101 to 250
251 to 1,000
1,001 to 2,500
2,501 to 85,700

Map 16-19. Wholesale Employment, 1997

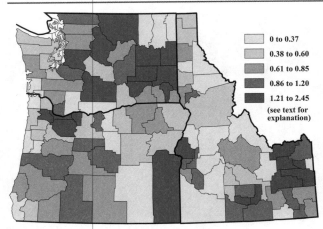

Map 16-20. Wholesale Trade Employment,
1997 location quotients

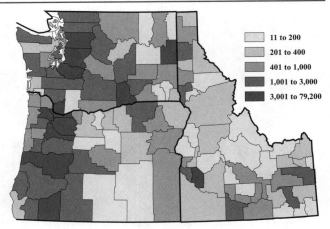

Map 16-21. Transportation Services,
Communications, and Utilities Employment, 1997

insurance, and real estate. These services are broadly distributed with population, as illustrated in map 16-21. Electrical utility employment in the Northwest is influenced by our dependence on hydropower from Columbia and Snake River dams. Lower Columbia River and Puget Sound ports play a key role in exporting Northwest grain, as well as in handling foreign trade moving through the region. Large corporations dominate the finance sector, with many branch offices distributed widely throughout the region, and with regional headquarter offices located in the largest metropolitan areas. While there are also large corporations in the insurance and real estate sectors, these two sectors also have many small independent offices selling insurance policies and residential real estate to households.

Sources

U.S. Bureau of Economic Analysis *Regional Economic Information System* (REIS)

U.S. Bureau of the Census *County Business Patterns*

Chapter 17

Outdoor Recreation Resources and Tourism

Ann L. Root

When the Lewis and Clark Expedition traveled through the Pacific Northwest in 1805 and 1806, the rugged wilderness challenged their survival skills. Expedition members hiked and horse packed through mountainous areas, ran rivers in canoes, and hunted and fished for food. As part of the Expedition's scientific studies, Lewis and Clark observed birds and other wildlife and traveled to the coast to view a whale. None of those activities were viewed as recreational by the Expedition members; however, the challenges they faced now attract millions of people to the region as recreational activities. Now during the bicentennial years for the Expedition, more tourists are expected to be attracted to the area to follow the Lewis and Clark trail and visit sites along the trail.

The various recreational opportunities in the Pacific Northwest contribute to the economies of Idaho, Oregon, and Washington. Tourism is an important generator of outside income in all three states. Tourists from outside the region and abroad spend billions of dollars in the region. Visitor expenditures have increased significantly in the last decade, 69 percent in Oregon, for example. In Washington tourism spending exceeds $10.6 billion per year and in Idaho it is the third leading industry. In addition, the variety of recreational activities in the region has attracted businesses seeking locations with a high quality of life. These businesses contributed to the economic and population boom in the region in the 1990s.

The abundance of recreational opportunities in the Northwest can largely be attributed to two factors—the diverse landscape and public policy. The geography of the Pacific Northwest has created landscapes suitable for a variety of forms of outdoor recreation. The erosional coastline along the subduction zone creates broad beaches and rugged headlands. Volcanic and other tectonic activity in the region created spectacular mountain ranges, volcanic peaks, and basalt plateaus. The abundant rainfall on the west side of the Cascade Mountains and the heavy snowfall in the Cascade and Rocky Mountains create rivers and streams that have carved valleys and gorges and provide habitat for a variety of fish species. Lush forests on the west side of the Coast

and Cascade Ranges are fed by the abundant rainfall. The rainshadow east of the Cascades creates a unique landscape of high desert plateaus and stream valleys. The expanses of forests and shrub steppe support a diversity of wildlife.

The majority of land in the Pacific Northwest is owned by the federal government. These large areas of public lands have facilitated public access for recreation. Large portions of federal lands have been developed for recreational uses with trails and campgrounds or preserved from development as wilderness areas. The state governments in Idaho, Oregon, and Washington all own sizable quantities of land, some of which is open to recreation. The federal policy of dam development in the Northwest has created vast reservoirs that provide boating and fishing opportunities. Oregon's policy of publicly owned beaches provides public access to all ocean beach areas in the state.

In addition, the Native American and exploration history of the region has resulted in several cultural and historic sites that attract visitors. The Northwest is home to many Native American tribes and several Indian reservations. Many tribes maintain visitor and cultural centers that attract tourists. The most developed of these sites are Kah-Nee-Tah Lodge and Resort at the Warm Springs Indian Reservation, Oregon; the Cultural Center on the Yakama Indian Reservation, Washington; and the Nez Perce National Historic Park, Idaho. Numerous important sites along the Lewis and Clark Trail are located in Idaho, Washington, and Oregon, including the trail's end on the Washington coast and winter headquarters at Fort Clatsop, Oregon. The Oregon Trail brought settlers to the region, and its tracks can still be seen today, allowing people to follow the trail. Visitor centers devoted to Oregon Trail history are located in Baker City, The Dalles, and Oregon City, Oregon.

Current Issues in Pacific Northwest Recreation

The increase in recreational visitors to the Northwest has not occurred without controversy or without impacts upon the recreational resources. In the 1970s and 1980s a common conflict was between preservation of forest resources for recreational uses or development for economic uses. That controversy has eased somewhat in recent years, but other controversial issues associated with public lands recreation have become prominent. These controversies are the result of increased use of resources that once seemed limitless, but are now increasingly limited by high demand.

As a result of federal budget cutbacks and changed legislation, federal agencies including the National Park Service and Forest Service have started charging access and user fees for areas that were previously free or had only nominal fees. At National Parks such as Mount Rainier and Crater Lake, entry fees have increased from $2 per vehicle to $10. In most Northwest National Forests, the only fees traditionally were nominal fees at some developed campgrounds. Now campground fees have increased, and most forests require a $5 day pass or $30 annual pass to use National Forest facilities. To a local population used to free access to a variety of recreational opportunities, these fees have generated considerable opposition and some limited protest movements.

Another controversy on recreational areas in the Pacific Northwest is the conflict between motorized and non-motorized recreational uses of public lands. This controversy centers upon snowmobile, jet ski, motorcycle, off-road-vehicle, and motorboat uses of public lands and waters. Non-motorized recreationists are demanding that motorized use be restricted, while motorized recreationists are demanding that their access be increased. In addition, on many trails in the Northwest there is controversy between hikers and mountain bikers. In an effort to satisfy all users, federal land managers have placed restrictions on areas that were previously open access.

In some areas of the Pacific Northwest, recreational areas have become so popular that land managers have had to restrict access. Wilderness areas such as Alpine Lakes in Washington require permits that must be obtained months in advance. Rafting rivers such as Oregon's Rogue River and Idaho's Salmon River require permits that must be obtained years in advance.

Major Recreational Areas in the Pacific Northwest

National Park Service Lands

The National Park Service manages a variety of lands in the Pacific Northwest to protect their scenic or historic resources (see map 17-1). There are a variety of units in the National Park System with different management mandates. National Parks are generally large land areas with scenic or cultural attractions. National Historic Sites protect areas of historic or cultural significance. National Monuments can protect either natural or cultural resources, and National Recreation Areas are generally located at human modified landscapes such as reservoirs behind dams.

National Park System units are usually well-publicized and consequently often serve as destinations for outside visitors. The eighteen National Park Service units in the Pacific Northwest attracted over 8.5 million visitors in 2000. The most visited park unit is Olympic National Park, Washington, with over three million visitors annually. Olympic is the nineteenth most visited park unit in the park system. The Northwest has one of the least visited park units in the country in Hagerman Fossil Beds, Idaho, which ranked 321 out of 344 units in 2000.

Parks Emphasizing Natural Features

Crater Lake National Park, Oregon. This park protects the area around the collapsed caldera of Mount Mazama which erupted approximately sven thousand years ago. The caldera contains a deep, sapphire blue lake 6 miles in width that is the deepest lake in the United States. Visitors drive the Rim Road that encircles the lake and some take a boat tour of the lake. There are numerous hiking trails in the park, which is a popular destination in the winter for cross-country skiers, many of whom stay at the newly remodeled lodge.

Mount Rainier National Park, Washington. This park also protects a volcanic feature in the Cascade Mountains. Mount Rainier is the highest of the chain of Cascade volcanoes, at 14,410 feet. The park surrounding the mountain encompasses areas of old-growth forests, mountain valleys, and canyons. Trails throughout the park, including the Wonderland Trail that circles the mountain, annually attract thousands of hikers and backpackers. Climbing the mountain is a popular activity, and over five thousand people successfully climb Mount Rainier each year, many

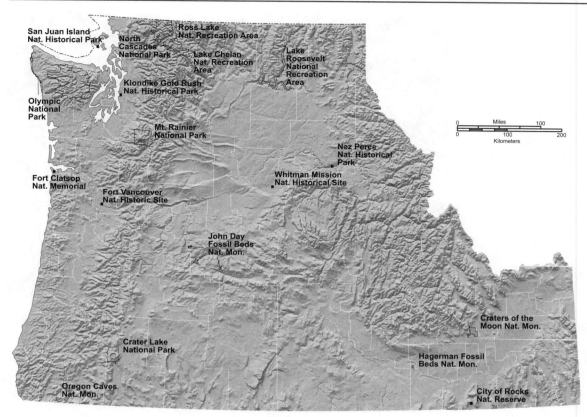

Map 17-1. National Park Service Recreation Resources

conducted by a guide service based in the park. Mount Rainier Park, a short drive from the Seattle metropolitan area, is a popular weekend destination for city dwellers. As a result weekend traffic jams and overflowing parking lots are a common occurrence.

North Cascades National Park, Washington. This national park is accessible only by hiking, horseback, or boat. Its two sections are separated from roads by Ross Lake and Lake Chelan National Recreation Areas. The national park protects the isolated alpine areas, while the Recreation Areas allow more developed recreation. North Cascades National Park, at over 500,000 acres, contains the largest concentration of glaciated peaks in the contiguous forty-eight states. The park's limited accessibility makes it one of the least-visited park units in the national system.

Olympic National Park, Washington. The diverse landscape of this 901,216-acre park ranges from the rugged Pacific coast to Blue Glacier on Mount Olympus. The west side of the Park receives over 200 inches of precipitation, the highest in the forty-eight contiguous states. That precipitation has resulted in lowland temperate rainforests, magnificent old-

growth forests along river valleys, and stable alpine icefields. Hurricane Ridge offers one of the few ski lifts in the National Park System. .

City of Rocks National Reserve, Idaho. The unique rock formations in this reserve were a landmark for travelers on the California Trail, who carved their names on the rocks. The reserve features historic interpretation, hiking trails, and bird watching, and is popular in the winter for ice climbing.

Craters of the Moon National Monument, Idaho. This area encompasses a 618-square mile lava flow that formed between fifteen thousand and two thousand years ago. The volcanic landscape includes cinder cones, lava flows, and lava caves. The monument was expanded in 2000 and is now co-managed by the Bureau of Land Management.

Hagerman Fossil Beds National Monument, Idaho. This least-visited park unit in the Northwest overlooks the Snake River. It protects the largest concentration of Hagerman Horse fossils in North America, and other fossils from the Pliocene Epoch. The Oregon Trail crosses the southern portion of the monument. There is a self-guided auto tour, and trails traverse the area.

The Oregon Coast Range provides many opportunities for hiking. (Photo by Philip L. Jackson)

John Day Fossil Beds National Monument, Oregon. This area consists of three units located in north central Oregon. As a scenic attraction it is a series of gentle "painted" hills rising from grasslands. The colors in the hills are exposed, and eroding layers of rock contain plant and animal fossils spanning forty million of the sixty-five million-year Cenozoic Era. The fossils are the subject of extensive research that has revealed much about the vegetative history of the Northwest.

Oregon Caves National Monument, Oregon. This small park unit in southern Oregon protects a system of caves and underground passages in dissolved marble. The Park Service conducts tours of the caverns. On the surface, three trails take visitors through the park's 465 acres that include an old-growth forest area.

Historical Parks

Fort Clatsop National Memorial, Oregon. This site marks the approximate spot where the Lewis and Clark Expedition spent the winter of 1805-1806. A visitor's center and a replica of the log fort constructed by the Expedition provide a glimpse into the life of the Expedition members.

Fort Vancouver National Historic Site, Washington. The Hudson's Bay Company established its western headquarters at Fort Vancouver on the Columbia River in 1825. The Fort was the center of fur-trade activity until 1846. The U.S. Military took over the Fort in 1848 and it remained an active post until 1949. Historic buildings from both the Hudson's Bay and U.S. Army occupation have been reconstructed after

extensive archaeological surveys. The Fort houses over 1.5 million artifacts, from both periods.

Klondike Gold Rush National Historic Park, Washington. This park, located in downtown Seattle, commemorates the city's role as the major embarkation point for the Alaskan gold fields in the 1880s. The park has a corresponding unit in Skagway, Alaska. The Seattle unit consists of an interpretive center, and conducts walking tours of the historic Pioneer Square area.

Nez Perce National Historic Park, Idaho. This park contains thirty-eight sites located mostly in Idaho, but also in Oregon, Wyoming, and Montana. The sites, dedicated to interpretation of the culture of the Nez Perce people, commemorate the Indian War of 1877. The main visitor center is located in Spalding, Idaho.

San Juan Island National Historic Park, Washington. The San Juan Islands, disputed territory between the United States and Great Britain, were jointly occupied by the two sides from 1859 to 1872. The park preserves the encampments of both sides of the dispute, and commemorates the peaceful resolution which awarded the islands to the United States.

Whitman Mission National Historic Site, Washington. The mission was established along the Walla Walla River in 1836 by Marcus and Narcissa Whitman. The Presbyterian mission, intended to convert the Indians, became a way-point for settlers traveling the Oregon Trail. In 1847 the Whitmans were killed by Indians, after an outbreak of measles among the tribe. The site preserves the mission foundation and the gravesite of the Whitmans.

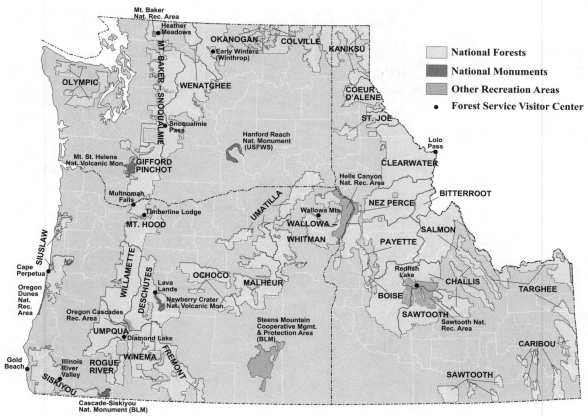

Map 17-2. U.S. Forest Service Lands and Other Recreation Areas

National Recreation Areas

Lake Roosevelt National Recreation Area, Washington. Named for Franklin D. Roosevelt, the 100,059-acre recreation area follows the shoreline of the 130-mile-long reservoir created by construction of Grand Coulee Dam on the Columbia River. The recreation area provides campgrounds and boating access.

Lake Chelan National Recreation Area, Washington. This area is part of the North Cascades National Park complex. The area is accessible only by plane, boats up Lake Chelan, or hiking. The area protects the north end of glacially carved Lake Chelan and the Stehekin River Valley. It adjoins the south unit of North Cascades National Park.

Ross Lake National Recreation Area, Washington. Ross Lake is a reservoir created by Seattle City Light's Ross Dam on the Skagit River. The recreation area surrounds the reservoir and adjoins the north and south units of North Cascades National Park. This is the only portion of the North Cascades National Park Complex that is accessible by road.

National Forests

Extensive areas of the Pacific Northwest are managed as National Forests. There are twelve National Forests in Idaho, thirteen in Oregon, and six in Washington, totaling nearly forty-six million acres (see map 17-2). These vast areas offer a broad range of recreational opportunities. The Forest Service has provided campgrounds and trails throughout the forests. Logging roads have opened vast areas to recreational users. The forests are popular in winter for cross-country skiing and snowmobiling. Unlike the National Parks, National Forests are open to hunting, and are popular hunting areas. Many downhill ski areas are located on National Forest land.

The Forest Service manages two National Monuments devoted to the volcanic history of the region, Hell's Canyon National Recreation Area, and The Oregon Dunes National Recreation Area along the Oregon Coast.

Hell's Canyon National Recreation Area. This recreation area is centered on Hell's Canyon of the Snake River between Idaho and Oregon. Hell's Canyon, at 7,800 feet deep, is the deepest gorge in North America. The river is popular for river rafting and jet boat trips.

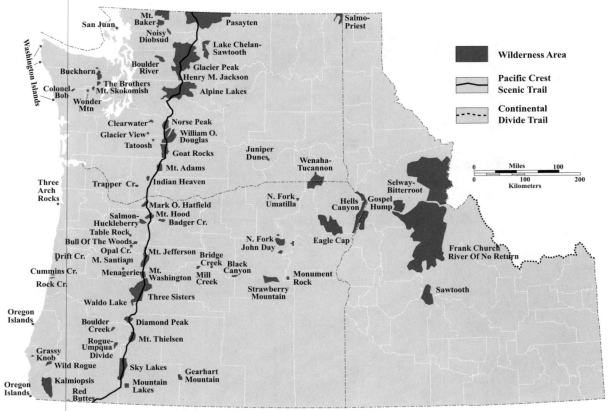

Map 17-3. Wilderness Areas and Scenic Trails

The surrounding wilderness areas attract both backpackers and horsepackers.

Mount St. Helen's National Volcanic Monument, Washington. The area around Mount St. Helens devastated by the May 18, 1980 eruption is preserved for scientific research and interpretation. Visitor centers are located at Coldwater Ridge and Johnston Ridge Observatory on the west side of the mountain and near Spirit Lake on the mountain's east side.

Newberry Crater National Volcanic Monument, Oregon. The monument is centered on Newberry Crater, a volcanic caldera. Two lakes are nestled in the caldera. Flows of basalt, obsidian, and pumice have erupted from the caldera as recently as 1,900 years ago. The visitor center is located at nearby Lava Lands at the base of a cinder cone.

Oregon Dunes National Recreation Area, Oregon. The Forest Service manages the northwest's only National Seashore, over 30 miles of shifting sand dunes on the central Oregon coast. The Recreation Area features lakes, beaches, several campgrounds, and riding areas for off-road vehicles.

Wilderness Areas

The Pacific Northwest has a high concentration of wilderness areas (see map 17-3). Large tracts of the National Parks are reserved as wilderness. The majority of wilderness areas are located on National Forest lands. These lands are protected by the 1964 Wilderness Act as areas "untrammeled by man." Permanent human structures and motorized activities are prohibited. Wilderness areas are popular for primitive recreation, including backpacking, horse and llama packing, mountain climbing, fishing, and hunting. In places popular rafting rivers flow through wilderness areas, including the Rogue and Salmon rivers. Most wilderness areas are located along the crest of the Cascade Mountains. Smaller wilderness areas have been established along the coastal areas and in Central Oregon. Several wilderness areas protect areas of old-growth forest. The Frank Church-River of No Return and adjacent Selway-Bitterroot Wilderness Areas in Idaho mark the largest undeveloped area in the lower forty-eight states.

The Bureau of Land Management (BLM) manages numerous wilderness areas in the rest of the West, but only a few areas in the Northwest—Hell's Canyon in Oregon and Idaho, Juniper Dunes in

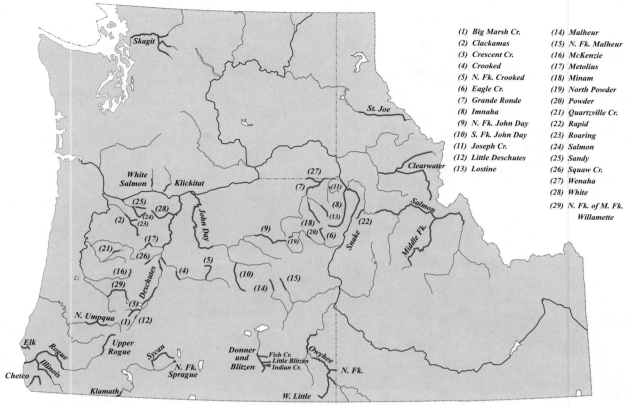

Map 17-4. Wild and Scenic Rivers (river sections highlighted in color)

(1) Big Marsh Cr.
(2) Clackamas
(3) Crescent Cr.
(4) Crooked
(5) N. Fk. Crooked
(6) Eagle Cr.
(7) Grande Ronde
(8) Imnaha
(9) N. Fk. John Day
(10) S. Fk. John Day
(11) Joseph Cr.
(12) Little Deschutes
(13) Lostine
(14) Malheur
(15) N. Fk. Malheur
(16) McKenzie
(17) Metolius
(18) Minam
(19) North Powder
(20) Powder
(21) Quartzville Cr.
(22) Rapid
(23) Roaring
(24) Salmon
(25) Sandy
(26) Squaw Cr.
(27) Wenaha
(28) White
(29) N. Fk. of M. Fk. Willamette

Wild and Scenic Rivers

The federal Wild and Scenic River System was created by Congress in 1968. The purpose of river designations is to protect rivers from development and to balance the nation's policy of dam construction. Wild and scenic rivers provide recreational activities and attract people to fish, boat, and hike along adjacent trails. Three of the eight rivers originally designated were in the Pacific Northwest—the Rogue River in Oregon, and the Middle Fork Clearwater and Middle Fork Salmon rivers in Idaho. Many of the nation's wild and scenic rivers are concentrated in the Northwest (see map 17-4). The system protects segments of forty-seven rivers in Oregon, five rivers in Idaho, and three in Washington. The Snake River along the Idaho-Oregon border is also designated. Most of the Oregon rivers were added to the system with legislation in 1988. Some rivers have been

Washington, and Table Rock and Wild Rogue in Oregon. In addition, the BLM manages the newly designated wilderness areas in the Steens Mountain area of Oregon and a small segment of the Frank Church-River of No Return Wilderness in Idaho. The U.S. Fish and Wildlife Services manages wilderness areas off the Oregon coast.

added as part of other legislation. The Klickitat and White Salmon rivers in Washington were added to the system as part of the Columbia Gorge National Scenic Area legislation and Wildhorse Creek, Little Wildhorse Creek, and Kiger Creek in Oregon were protected as part of the legislation establishing the Steens Mountain Cooperative Management and Protection Area.

The last free-flowing stretch of the Columbia River in the United States is being considered for Wild and Scenic River designation. The 51-mile Hanford Reach was protected as a National Monument by presidential proclamation in 2000.

National Scenic Trails

In 1968 Congress established a National Scenic Trails System. Portions of two of those trails are located in the Pacific Northwest. The Pacific Crest Trail follows the crest of the Cascade Mountains in Washington and Oregon; the entire trail extends from the Canadian border to Mexico. The Continental Divide Trail follows the Continental Divide along the border of Idaho and Montana. Both trails attract horse and backpackers intent on completing the entire route or traveling on a portion of the longer trail.

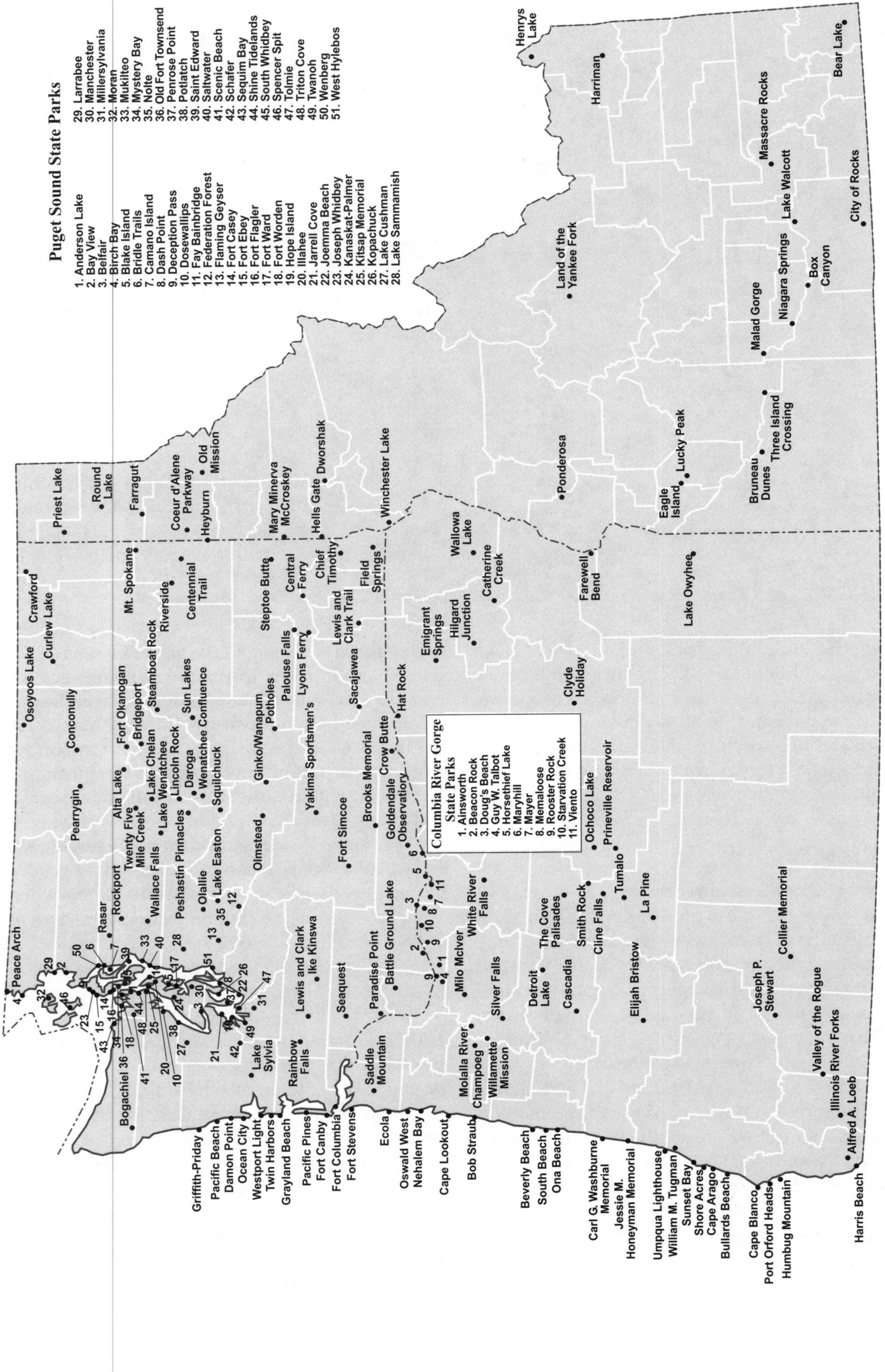
Puget Sound State Parks
1. Anderson Lake
2. Bay View
3. Belfair
4. Birch Bay
5. Blake Island
6. Bridle Trails
7. Camano Island
8. Dash Point
9. Deception Pass
10. Dosewallips
11. Fay Bainbridge
12. Federation Forest
13. Flaming Geyser
14. Fort Casey
15. Fort Ebey
16. Fort Flagler
17. Fort Ward
18. Fort Worden
19. Hope Island
20. Illahee
21. Jarrell Cove
22. Joemma Beach
23. Joseph Whidbey
24. Kanaskat-Palmer
25. Kitsap Memorial
26. Kopachuck
27. Lake Cushman
28. Lake Sammamish
29. Larrabee
30. Manchester
31. Millersylvania
32. Moran
33. Mukilteo
34. Mystery Bay
35. Nolte
36. Old Fort Townsend
37. Penrose Point
38. Potlatch
39. Saint Edward
40. Saltwater
41. Scenic Beach
42. Schafer
43. Sequim Bay
44. Shine Tidelands
45. South Whidbey
46. Spencer Spit
47. Tolmie
48. Triton Cove
49. Twanoh
50. Wenberg
51. West Hylebos
Columbia River Gorge State Parks
1. Ainsworth
2. Beacon Rock
3. Doug's Beach
4. Guy W. Talbot
5. Horsethief Lake
6. Maryhill
7. Mayer
8. Memaloose
9. Rooster Rock
10. Starvation Creek
11. Viento
Peace Arch
Rasar
Rockport
Pearrygin
Conconully
Osoyoos Lake
Curlew Lake
Crawford
Alta Lake
Twenty Five Mile Creek
Fort Okanogan
Bridgeport
Lake Chelan
Lake Wenatchee
Wallace Falls
Steamboat Rock
Mt. Spokane
Riverside
Centennial Trail
Sun Lakes
Wenatchee Confluence
Lincoln Rock
Daroga
Peshastin Pinnacles
Squilchuck
Olallie
Lake Easton
Ginko/Wanapum
Potholes
Olmstead
Steptoe Butte
Palouse Falls
Lyons Ferry
Central Ferry
Chief Timothy
Lewis and Clark Trail
Field Springs
Yakima Sportsmen's
Sacajawea
Fort Simcoe
Brooks Memorial
Crow Butte
Goldendale Observatory
Hat Rock
Bogachiel
Lake Sylvia
Rainbow Falls
Lewis and Clark
Ike Kinswa
Seaquest
Paradise Point
Battle Ground Lake
Saddle Mountain
Griffith-Priday
Pacific Beach
Damon Point
Ocean City
Westport Light
Twin Harbors
Grayland Beach
Pacific Pines
Fort Canby
Fort Columbia
Fort Stevens
Ecola
Oswald West
Nehalem Bay
Cape Lookout
Bob Straub
Beverly Beach
South Beach
Ona Beach
Carl G. Washburne Memorial
Jessie M. Honeyman Memorial
Umpqua Lighthouse
William M. Tugman
Sunset Bay
Shore Acres
Cape Arago
Bullards Beach
Cape Blanco
Port Orford Heads
Humbug Mountain
Harris Beach
Alfred A. Loeb
Illinois River Forks
Valley of the Rogue
Joseph P. Stewart
Collier Memorial
Molalla River
Champoeg
Willamette Mission
Milo McIver
Silver Falls
White River Falls
Detroit Lake
Cascadia
The Cove Palisades
Smith Rock
Cline Falls
Tumalo
La Pine
Elijah Bristow
Ochoco Lake
Prineville Reservoir
Clyde Holiday
Emigrant Springs
Hilgard Junction
Catherine Creek
Wallowa Lake
Farewell Bend
Lake Owyhee
Priest Lake
Round Lake
Farragut
Coeur d'Alene Parkway
Heyburn
Old Mission
Mary Minerva McCroskey
Hells Gate
Dworshak
Winchester Lake
Ponderosa
Eagle Island
Lucky Peak
Bruneau Dunes
Three Island Crossing
Land of the Yankee Fork
Malad Gorge
Niagara Springs
Box Canyon
Massacre Rocks
Lake Walcott
City of Rocks
Harriman
Henrys Lake
Bear Lake

Map 17-5. State Parks

Bureau of Land Management Lands

Bureau of Land Management lands also provide recreational areas in the Northwest. In addition to the wilderness areas it manages, the BLM provides campgrounds in some areas, and its lands are often used for primitive camping and hunting. Presidential designations of National Monuments and legislation protecting the Steens Mountain area in Oregon have recently added to the BLM's recreational lands.

Craters of the Moon National Monument. This Idaho monument, expanded in 2000 to include BLM lands, will be jointly managed by the Park Service and BLM.

Cascade-Siskyou National Monument. This monument is located near the California border in southern Oregon. It was created to protect the unique ecological values of the area, especially the unique plant life. The Siskyou Mountains were not heavily glaciated during the Ice Ages, and served as a refuge for many plant species that disappeared from other parts of the Northwest.

Steens Mountain Cooperative Management and Protection Area. This designation settles a long dispute over whether the Steens Mountain area in southeast Oregon should be designated as a National Park or wilderness area. The legislation is a compromise that allows some existing land uses to continue and protects other areas. Within the 500,000-acre area there are 175,000 acres of wilderness, three new Wild and Scenic rivers and additions to the Donner und Blitzen River Scenic River, and a Redband Trout Reserve. The legislation established an advisory council to guide management of the area.

State Parks

The three states of the Pacific Northwest have well-developed state park systems, especially in Oregon and Washington (see map 17-5). Some of these parks are just roadside areas, but many provide camping, hiking, boating, and other recreational opportunities. Many of Oregon's state parks provide access to Pacific coastal beaches. Oregon's 230 state park and recreation areas had over thirty-six million visitors in 1999. In Washington over forty-six million visitors participated in activities at its 125 units, and Idaho's twenty-seven parks attracted over 2.5 million people in 2000.

Other Recreation Activities

The most popular recreation activities for residents of the Pacific Northwest include walking, bird watching, wildlife viewing, sight-seeing, visiting beaches, camping, boating, and hiking. Camping, hiking, backpacking, mountain climbing, and rock climbing are more popular in the Northwest than in other regions of the country; the presence of public lands and the topography create more opportunities for residents of the Northwest to participate in these activities. Smith Rock State Park, a unique geologic feature of welded volcanic ash, is considered one of the best rock climbing areas in the world, with over one thousand climbing routes.

The Cascades and Rocky Mountains, along with smaller mountain ranges in the Northwest, provide abundant snowfall and opportunities for winter sports. Downhill and cross-country skiing and snowmobiling are popular, as are snowshoeing and snow camping. Ski areas are scattered throughout the Cascades and Rocky Mountain areas. These ski resorts provide skiing opportunities for local residents and attract large numbers of out-of-state visitors annually.

The abundant water bodies in the region provide opportunities for a variety of water sports. These include motor boating, jet-skiing, sailing, wind-surfing, canoeing, kayaking and sea kayaking. Water sports take place on the ocean and bays, natural lakes, reservoirs, and rivers. The Puget Sound in Washington is one of the best pleasure-boating areas in the United States with numerous marinas and boat launching areas. The Columbia River Gorge with its steady easterly winds attracts windsurfers from around the world to the Hood River area.

Bird watching is one of the fastest-growing recreational activities in the United States and in the Pacific Northwest. The Northwest, located along the Pacific Flyway, provides good opportunities for sighting resident, migrating, and vagrant birds. Malheur National Wildlife Refuge in southeastern Oregon is a desert oasis along the Donner und Blitzen River that attracts a wide variety of birds, including vagrants from other parts of the country. Birders rate Malheur as one of the top birding locations in North America. The Klamath Basin Refuges in southern Oregon are another important North American birding area. Klamath Falls, Oregon, hosts an annual eagle festival in February. Other birding festivals in the region are the Shorebird Migration at Gray's Harbor, Washington, and the Sandhill Crane Festival in Othello, Washington.

Chapter Eighteen
Hunting and Fishing
Gordon E. Matzke

The Pacific Northwest has wild land and water resources in sufficient supply to support substantial populations of many fish and game species. Since much of the wild land is in public ownership, even non-landowners have access to considerable hunting and fishing opportunities.

A primary management tool used by states to regulate harvest and raise revenues for fish and game work is the sale of licenses which authorize an individual to attempt to harvest specified species. The trend in sales of licenses in the three state areas shows participation rates in fishing and hunting dropping in Oregon and Washington while rising only slightly in Idaho. Although participation rates are generally declining in the United States, about

half of the people in the Pacific Northwest still pursue an interest in fishing. As a percentage of the population, there are fewer hunters, but they are proportionally more common in Idaho (see map 18-1).

The reasons for the slowly declining interest in fishing and hunting in the Pacific Northwest are subject to substantial speculation. In some cases resource management decisions, including endangered species protections that decrease fishing opportunities in many waters, intervene to complicate and discourage participation. More importantly, a smaller proportion of residents have been reared in rural areas where hunting and fishing norms are strongest. There is also a higher proportion of female-headed housholds, which produce fewer hunting recruits than households headed by males. The drop in the numbers of license holders is causing revenue difficulties for the state agencies which use the income to support much of the game management budget.

The likelihood that an individual will participate in hunting or fishing varies according to a combination of factors, including previous experience, the abundance of game, and the accessibility of recreation sites. Participation rates decline with increased urbanization of the population. In the context of the Pacific Northwest, this means that Idaho residents are most likely to hunt or fish, while people from Washington are least likely to participate in these sports. The statewide averages mask substantial variation in participation between groups within the general population. For example, studies have shown about 95 percent of hunters and 68 percent of fishers are males. In the United States as a whole, whites are twice as likely to hunt or fish than nonwhites, and the dominance of the urban residence pattern for Blacks in the Pacific Northwest suggests they would have even lower participation rates in this part of the country.

Hunting

The abundance of fish and game available for harvest varies greatly from place to place, and over time in any one place. The variation in waterfowl harvest is an

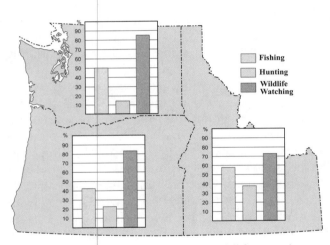

Map 18-1. Fishing, Hunting, and Wildlife Watching, 1996 (percent of state residents 16 years and older participating)

Table 18-1. Holders of Paid Hunting and Fishing Licenses, 1990 and 2000		
	1990	2000
Hunting Licenses		
Idaho	241,475	249,188
Oregon	347,819	310,739
Washington	268,653	214,,969
Fishing Licenses		
Idaho	417,684	439,606
Oregon	751,945	666,050
Washington	965,825	709,067

322222

2222222222222222

excellent illustration. The size of the annual migration fluctuates with changing conditions on the northern breeding grounds, the hunting pressure en route, and the quality of the wintering habitats. The distribution of the harvest within the Pacific Northwest is strongly associated with traditional migratory flight lines, resting and feeding areas, and the attractiveness of refuge areas (see map 18-2). Although every county shares in the waterfowl harvest, higher than average numbers are harvested in the counties along the Columbia, Snake, and Willamette rivers and in the Puget Sound area. The largest harvests occur in two counties with especially large wetland habitats: Washington's Grant County (the Potholes Reservoir) and Oregon's Klamath County (the Klamath Marsh).

Wildlife management in the Pacific Northwest has achieved some notable successes in assisting the recovery of game populations which were devastated by the early part of the twentieth century. All three states have large populations of deer and elk which owe their existence to extensive restoration efforts such as restocking, protection, and controlled harvests. These efforts continue in an attempt to

Six subspecies of Canada geese winter in the Willamette Valley.. (Photo by Philip L. Jackson)

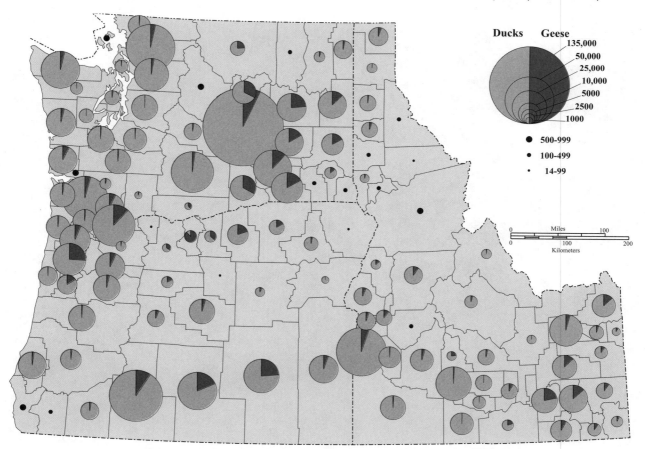

Map 18-2. Distribution of Wildfowl Harvest. Circle size is proportional to the number of waterfowl harvested in each county.

restore several other big game species. The mountain goat—which had disappeared from most of Idaho and Washington and was extinct in Oregon—now has at least a small wild population in each state, and all three states have active programs aimed at restoring the mountain sheep to portions of its former range. Now populations are secure enough to allow some tightly controlled harvesting of rams in all three states.

The success of restoration operations is nowhere more obvious than in the level and pattern of deer and elk harvest (see map 18-3). Nearly every suitable piece of habitat produces harvestable surpluses of deer, while management efforts are still needed to expand the range of elk in only a few locations, most notably in western Oregon. In many places, the former problems of low to nonexistent populations have been replaced by problems of big game abundance. Hence, timber interests complain of seedling damage caused by game animals, and ranchers complain of the competition for forage when game descends onto the limited winter range of the interior valleys. Harvest management attempts to balance the desire of hunters for more deer and

elk against the preference of ranching and timber interests for lower populations.

The spatial pattern of big game harvest exhibits several characteristics, including the scarcity of deer and total absence of elk in the driest regions, heavy elk harvests in northeastern Oregon and in a few locations in the Oregon Coast Range, and a widespread large-scale deer harvest with excepionally heavy takes in most areas of Oregon, northeastern Washington, and the accessible fringes of the Idaho mountains. These patterns are the result of a combination of management policy, habitat quality, accessibility, and population size.

Fishing

Sportfishing is a major recreational activity in all three states. Fishing opportunities are as varied as anywhere in the world, with both cold and warm freshwater fisheries as well as the Pacific Ocean. In addition, nine species of anadromous fish move back and forth between fresh and salt water throughout the still accessible portions of the Columbia River drainage and most of the coastal streams.

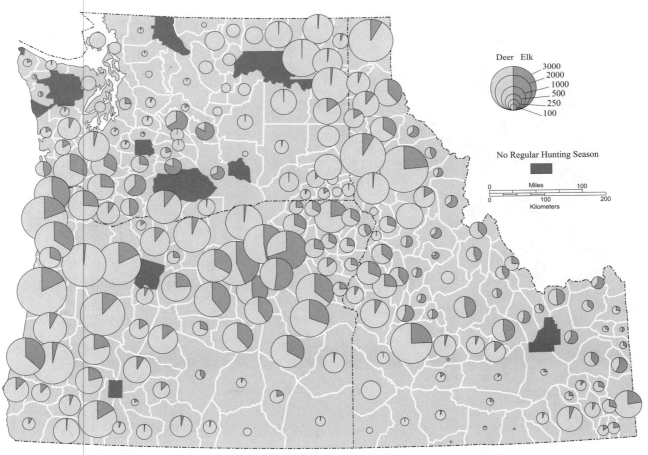

Map 18-3. Deer and Elk Harvest by Management Unit. Average harvest for 1999 and 2000 seasons

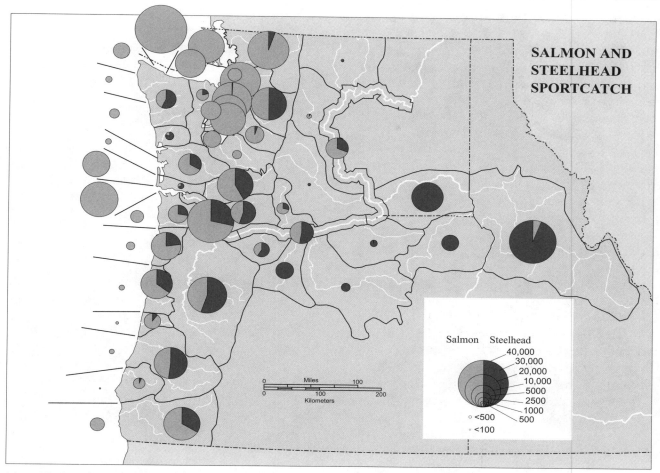

Map 18-4. Salmon and Steelhead Sportcatch. Average catch 1997 and 1998 seasons

The anadromous fishery, including both salmon and steelhead, shows an interesting geographic pattern. Sportfishers compete for salmon against a heavy commercial fishing effort, especially in the ocean, and with Indian treaty fishing rights on certain rivers, particularly in Washington. The near absence of saltwater steelhead catch is due to the species' ocean movements and elusive behavior. In fact, the only steelhead caught in the ocean are accidental landings by fishers seeking other species. Since salmon flesh is in its best condition during the saltwater part of the life cycle, salmon fishers concentrate on the saltwater harvest, and most are taken by hook and line methods before they enter fresh water.

The total anadromous fish catch declines dramatically with distance from the sea. The decline is so great that there is no salmon season in Idaho, and only a few thousand steelhead are taken (see map 18-4). This decrease reflects the combined influence of heavy oceanward fishing pressure, the dominance of downstream hatchery production in the fish

White sturgeon are abundant in the Lower Columbia River. (Photo by Philip L. Jackson)

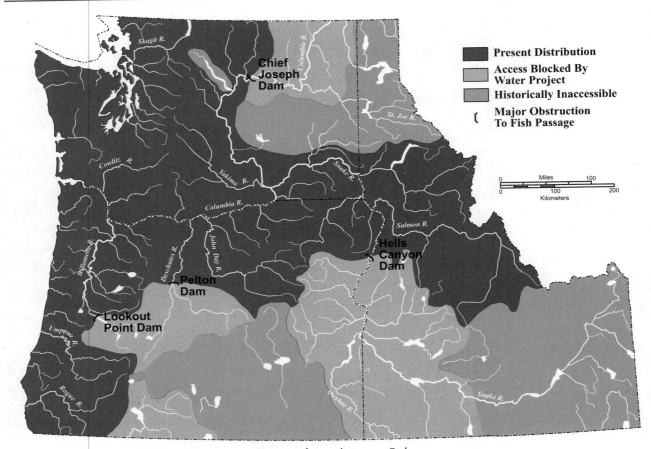

Map 18-5. General Present and Past Distribution of Anadromous Fish

reproduction picture, the destruction of river habitat, and the difficulties of passage (in both directions) through dams and associated impoundments (see map 18-5). The decrease in wild Columbia Watershed anadromous fish populations was sufficiently alarming that restrictions aimed at protecting some of Idaho's endangered anadromous fish stocks were first instituted in 1992. Dealing with the maintenance and improvement of endangered anadromous fish stocks will involve much more than limitations on sportfishing. Commercial and Indian fishers, hatchery managers, livestock owners, irrigators, power producers, timber harvesters, dam operators, and a variety of industrial water users will likely have to adjust to the needs of the fish. Without successful recovery efforts, upstream fishing for wild Columbia River anadromous fish will be relegated to a footnote in the history of sportfishing.

Contributors

William B. Beyers, Department of Geography, University of Washington

J. Douglas Brodie, Forest Resources Department (emeritus), Oregon State University

Robert E. Frenkel, Department of Geosciences (emeritus), Oregon State University

Philip L. Jackson, Department of Geosciences, Oregon State University

James W. Good, Extension Specialist - Coastal Resources, Oregon State University

Julia A. Jones, Department of Geosciences, Oregon State University

Steven R. Kale, Oregon Department of Transportation

A. Jon Kimerling (cartographer), Department of Geosciences, Oregon State University

Robert Kuhlken, Department of Geography and Land Studies, Central Washington University

Gordon E. Matzke, Department of Geosciences, Oregon State University

Keith W. Muckleston, Department of Geosciences (emeritus), Oregon State University

Ann L. Root, Adolfson Associates, Inc.

Charles L. Rosenfeld, Department of Geosciences, Oregon State University

Alex Sifford, Sifford Energy Associates

Robert D. Thompson, Jr., Ethnic Studies Department, Oregon State University

Peter Wampler, Department of Geosciences, Oregon State University and Oregon Department of Geology and Mineral Industries

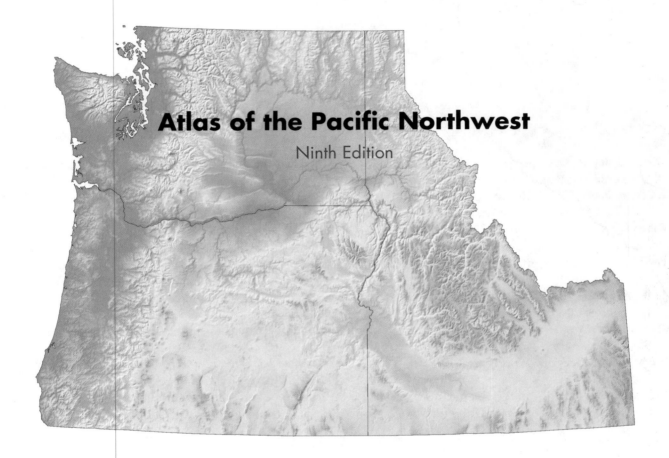

Atlas of the Pacific Northwest
Ninth Edition